DEATH FOLLOWS ™

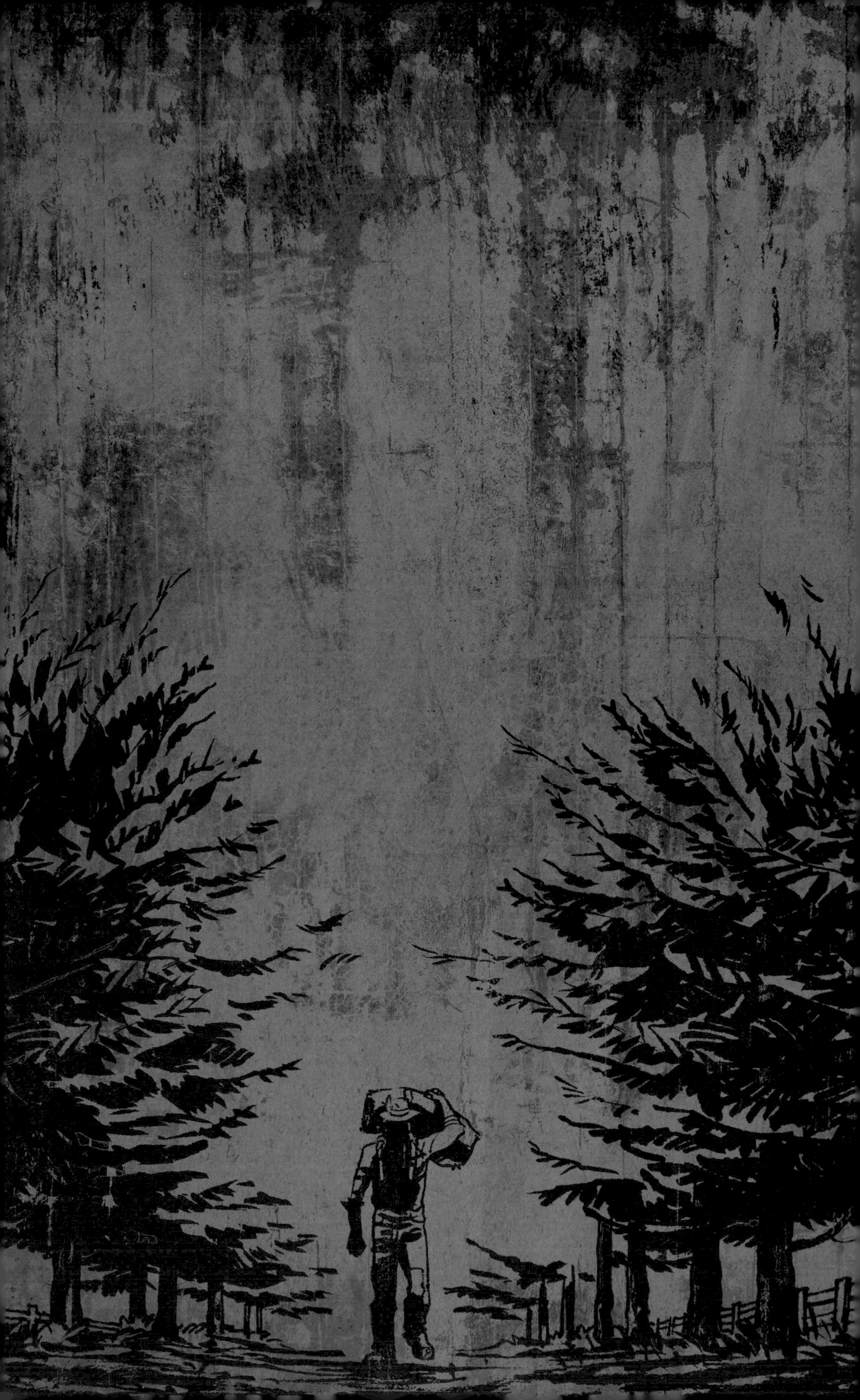

DEATH FOLLOWS ™

STORY BY **CULLEN BUNN**

ART BY **A. C. ZAMUDIO**

COLORS BY **CARLOS NICOLAS ZAMUDIO**

LETTERS BY **A. C. ZAMUDIO** AND **CARLOS NICOLAS ZAMUDIO**

COVER ART BY **SIMON BISLEY**

CHAPTER BREAKS BY **A. C. ZAMUDIO** AND **CARLOS NICOLAS ZAMUDIO**

DARK HORSE BOOKS

President & Publisher MIKE RICHARDSON
Editor DANIEL CHABON
Assistant Editor CARDNER CLARK
Designer SARAH TERRY
Digital Art Technician RYAN JORGENSEN

DEATH FOLLOWS

This volume collects issues #1–#4 of the Monkeybrain digital comics series The Remains.

Names: Bunn, Cullen, author. | Zamudio, A. C., illustrator. | Zamudio, Carlos
  Nicolas, illustrator. | Bisley, Simon, illustrator.
Title: Death follows / story by Cullen Bunn ; art by A. C. Zamudio ; colors
  by Carlos Nicolas Zamudio ; letters by A. C. Zamudio and Carlos Nicolas
  Zamudio ; cover art by Simon Bisley ; chapter breaks by A. C. Zamudio and
  Carlos Nicolas Zamudio.
Description: First edition. | Milwaukie, OR : Dark Horse Books, 2016.
Identifiers: LCCN 2015046663 | ISBN 9781616559519 (paperback)
Subjects: LCSH: Graphic novels. | Comic books, strips, etc. | BISAC: COMICS &
  GRAPHIC NOVELS / Horror.
Classification: LCC PN6727.B845 D44 2016 | DDC 741.5/973--dc23
LC record available at http://lccn.loc.gov/2015046663

Published by Dark Horse Books
A division of Dark Horse Comics, Inc.
10956 SE Main Street | Milwaukie, OR 97222 | DarkHorse.com

To find a comics shop in your area, call the Comic Shop Locator Service toll-free at 1-888-266-4226.
International Licensing: (503) 905-2377

First edition: May 2016
ISBN 978-1-61655-951-9

10 9 8 7 6 5 4 3 2 1
Printed in China

Neil Hankerson Executive Vice President | Tom Weddle Chief Financial Officer | Randy Stradley Vice President of
Publishing | Michael Martens Vice President of Book Trade Sales | Matt Parkinson Vice President of Marketing | David
Scroggy Vice President of Product Development | Dale LaFountain Vice President of Information Technology | Cara
Niece Vice President of Production and Scheduling | Nick McWhorter Vice President of Media Licensing | Ken Lizzi
General Counsel | Dave Marshall Editor in Chief | Davey Estrada Editorial Director | Scott Allie Executive Senior Editor
Chris Warner Senior Books Editor | Cary Grazzini Director of Print and Development | Lia Ribacchi Art Director | Mark
Bernardi Director of Digital Publishing | Michael Gombos Director of International Publishing and Licensing

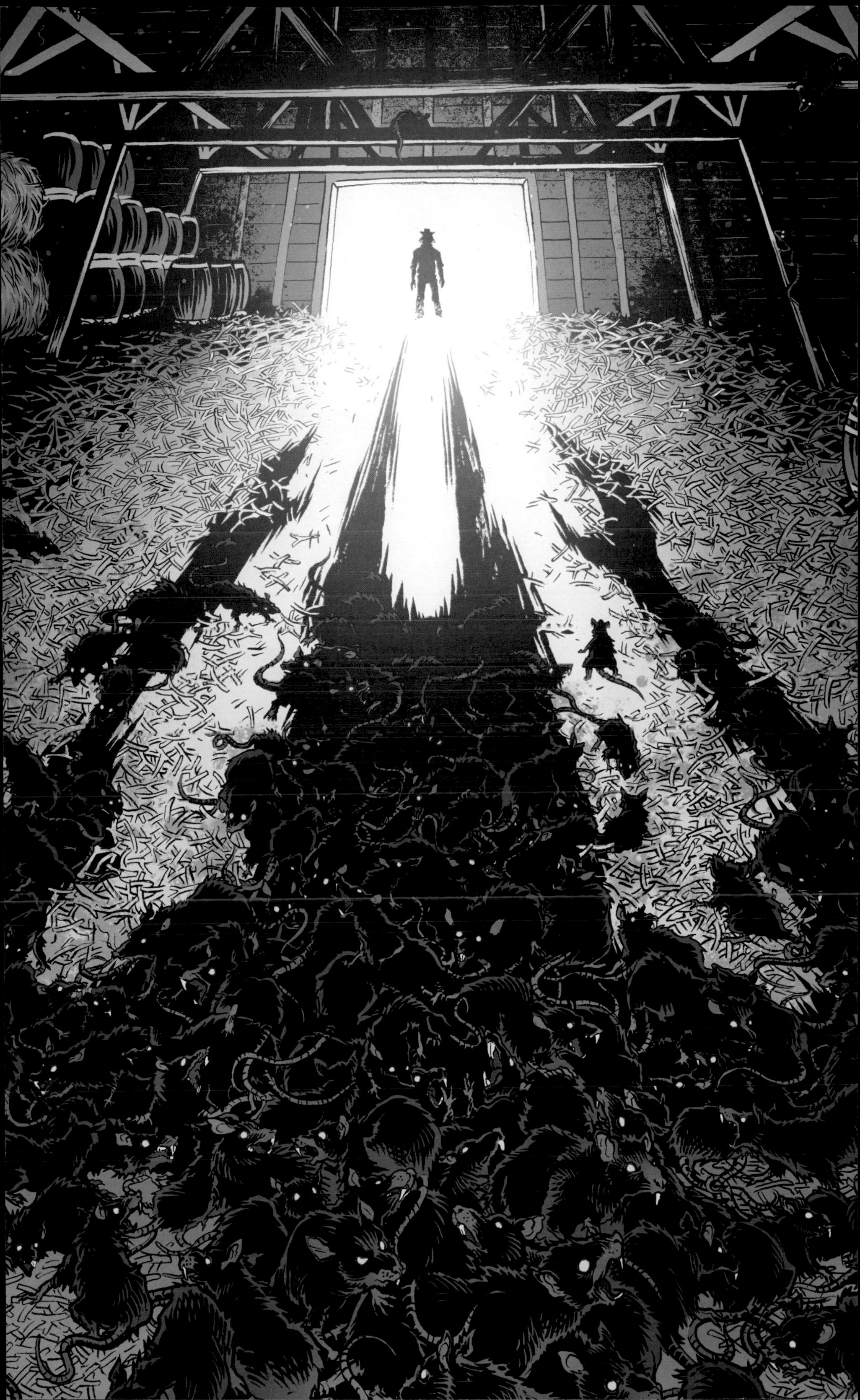

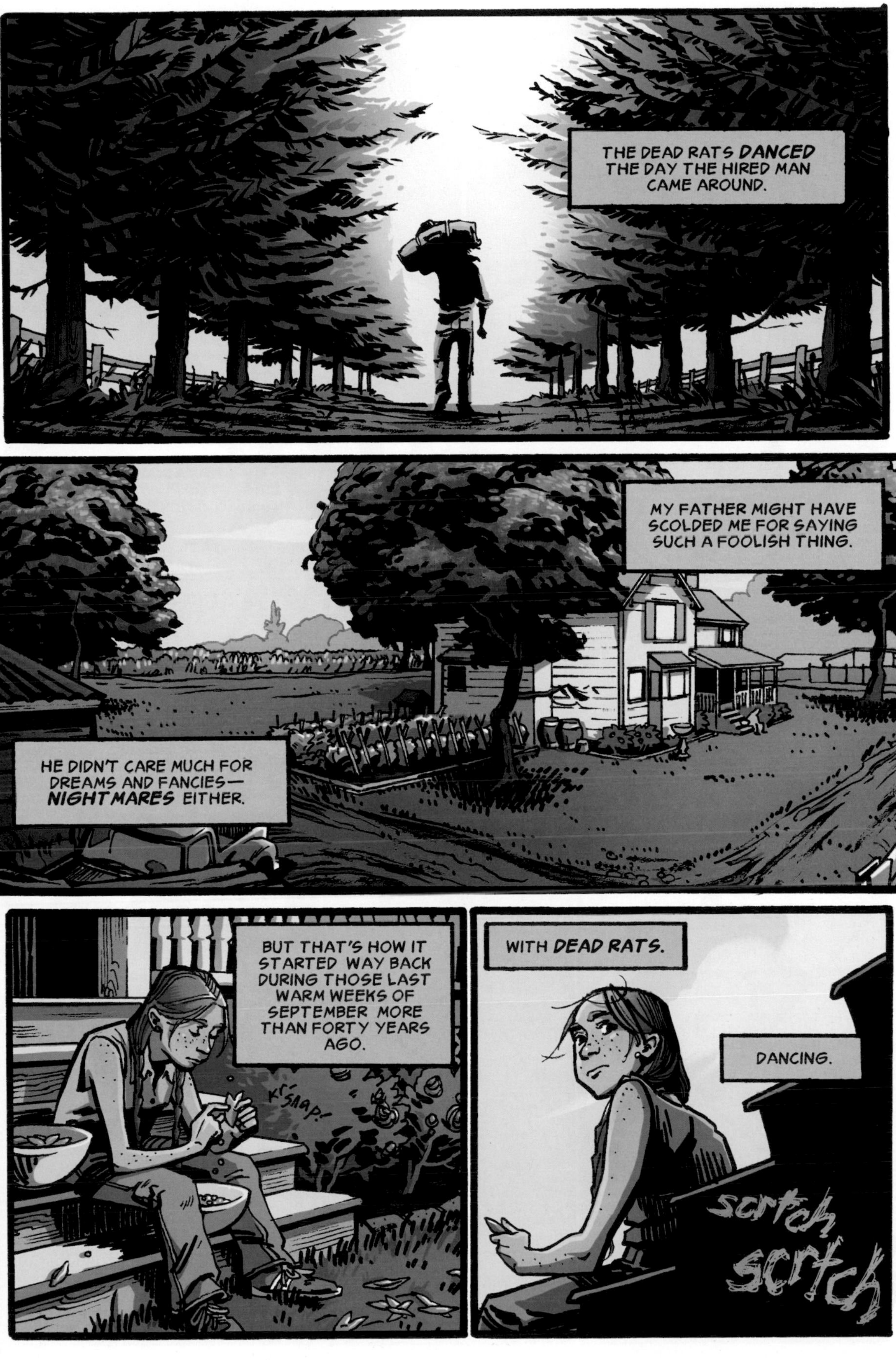
THE DEAD RATS DANCED THE DAY THE HIRED MAN CAME AROUND.
MY FATHER MIGHT HAVE SCOLDED ME FOR SAYING SUCH A FOOLISH THING.
HE DIDN'T CARE MUCH FOR DREAMS AND FANCIES— NIGHTMARES EITHER.
BUT THAT'S HOW IT STARTED WAY BACK DURING THOSE LAST WARM WEEKS OF SEPTEMBER MORE THAN FORTY YEARS AGO.
KR-SNAP!
WITH DEAD RATS.
DANCING.
SCRTCH SCRTCH

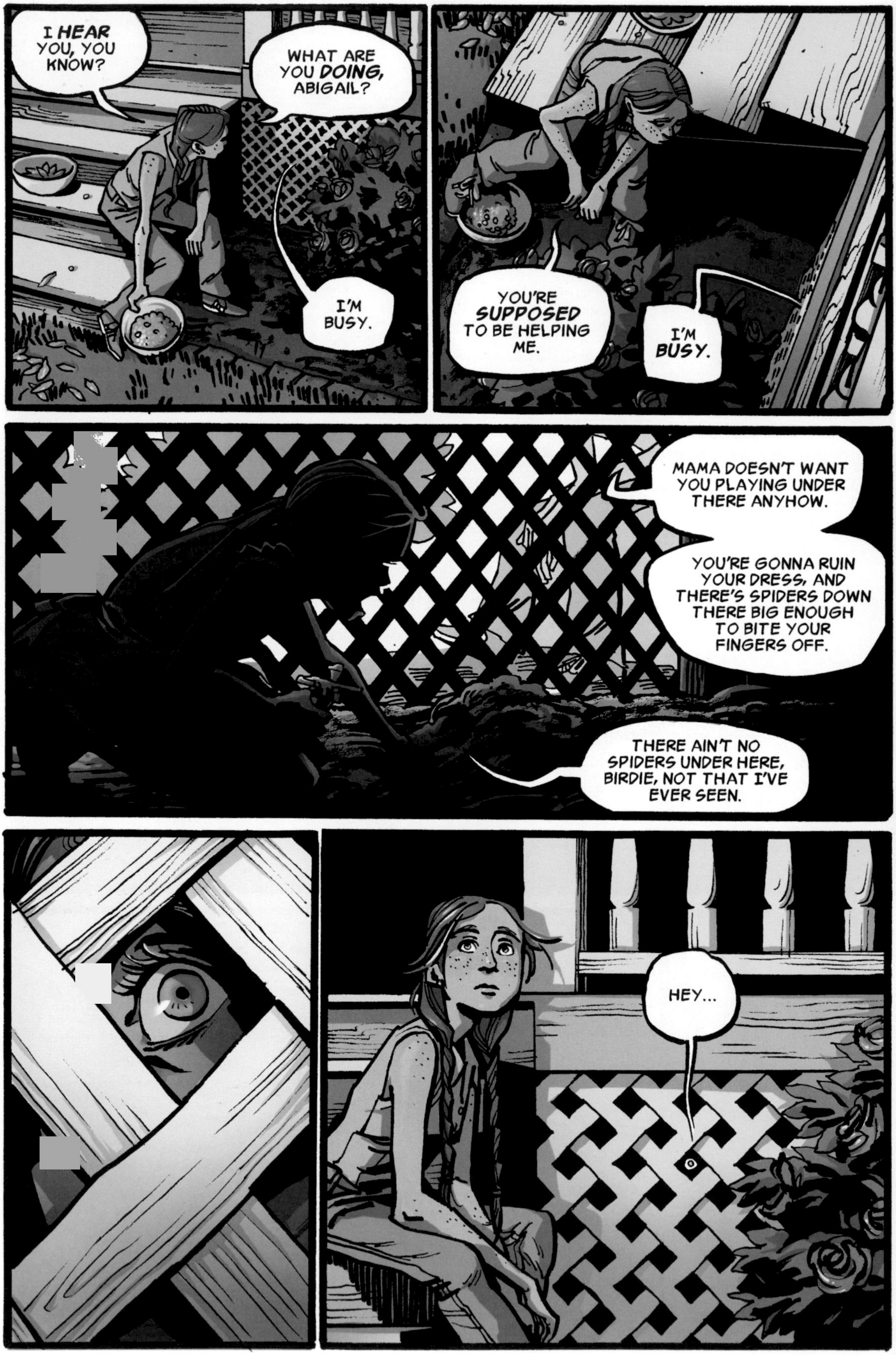
I HEAR YOU, YOU KNOW?
WHAT ARE YOU DOING, ABIGAIL?
I'M BUSY.
YOU'RE SUPPOSED TO BE HELPING ME.
I'M BUSY.
MAMA DOESN'T WANT YOU PLAYING UNDER THERE ANYHOW.
YOU'RE GONNA RUIN YOUR DRESS, AND THERE'S SPIDERS DOWN THERE BIG ENOUGH TO BITE YOUR FINGERS OFF.
THERE AIN'T NO SPIDERS UNDER HERE, BIRDIE, NOT THAT I'VE EVER SEEN.
HEY...

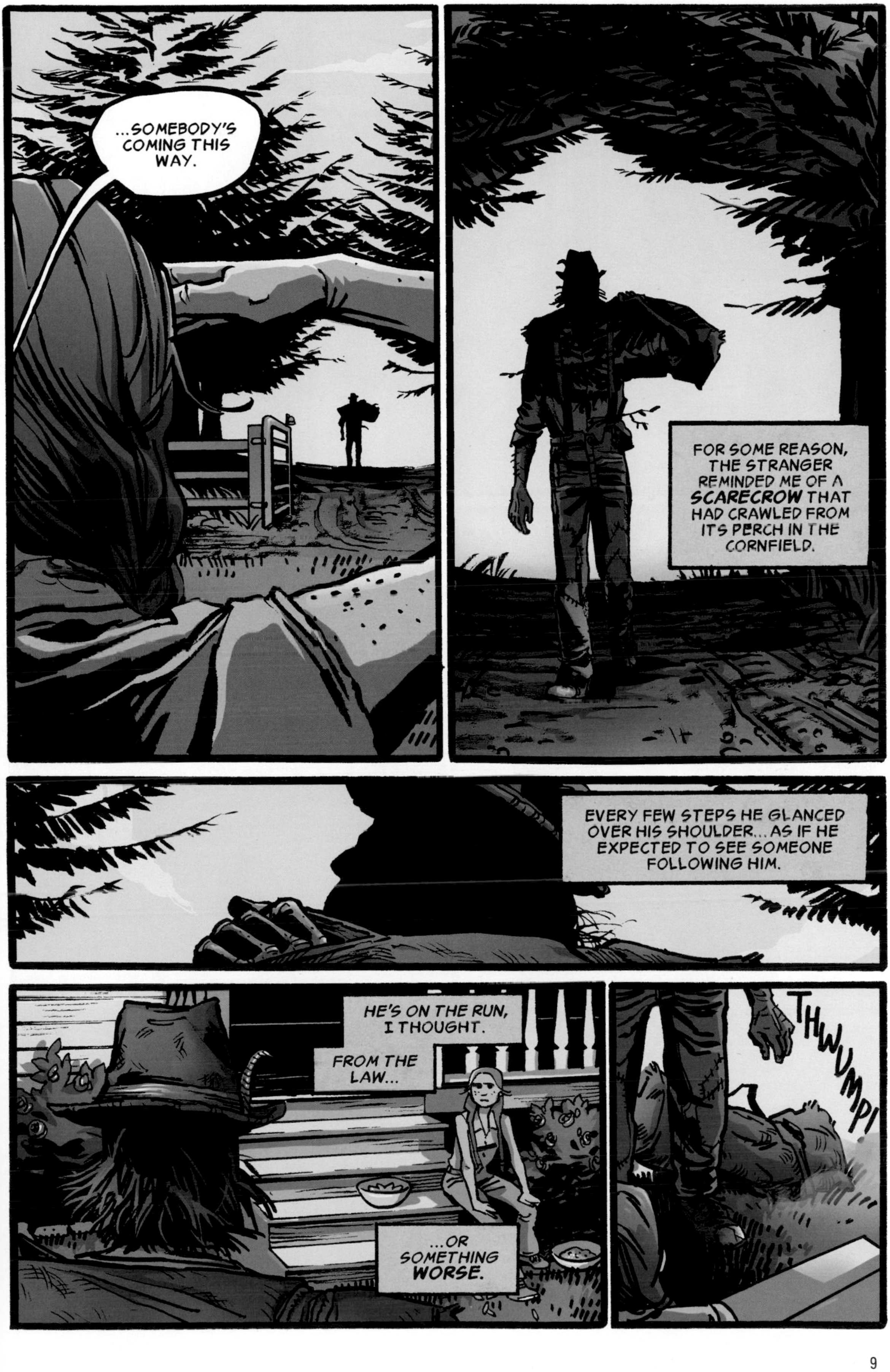
...SOMEBODY'S COMING THIS WAY.
FOR SOME REASON, THE STRANGER REMINDED ME OF A SCARECROW THAT HAD CRAWLED FROM ITS PERCH IN THE CORNFIELD.
EVERY FEW STEPS HE GLANCED OVER HIS SHOULDER... AS IF HE EXPECTED TO SEE SOMEONE FOLLOWING HIM.
HE'S ON THE RUN, I THOUGHT.
FROM THE LAW...
...OR SOMETHING WORSE.
THWUMP!

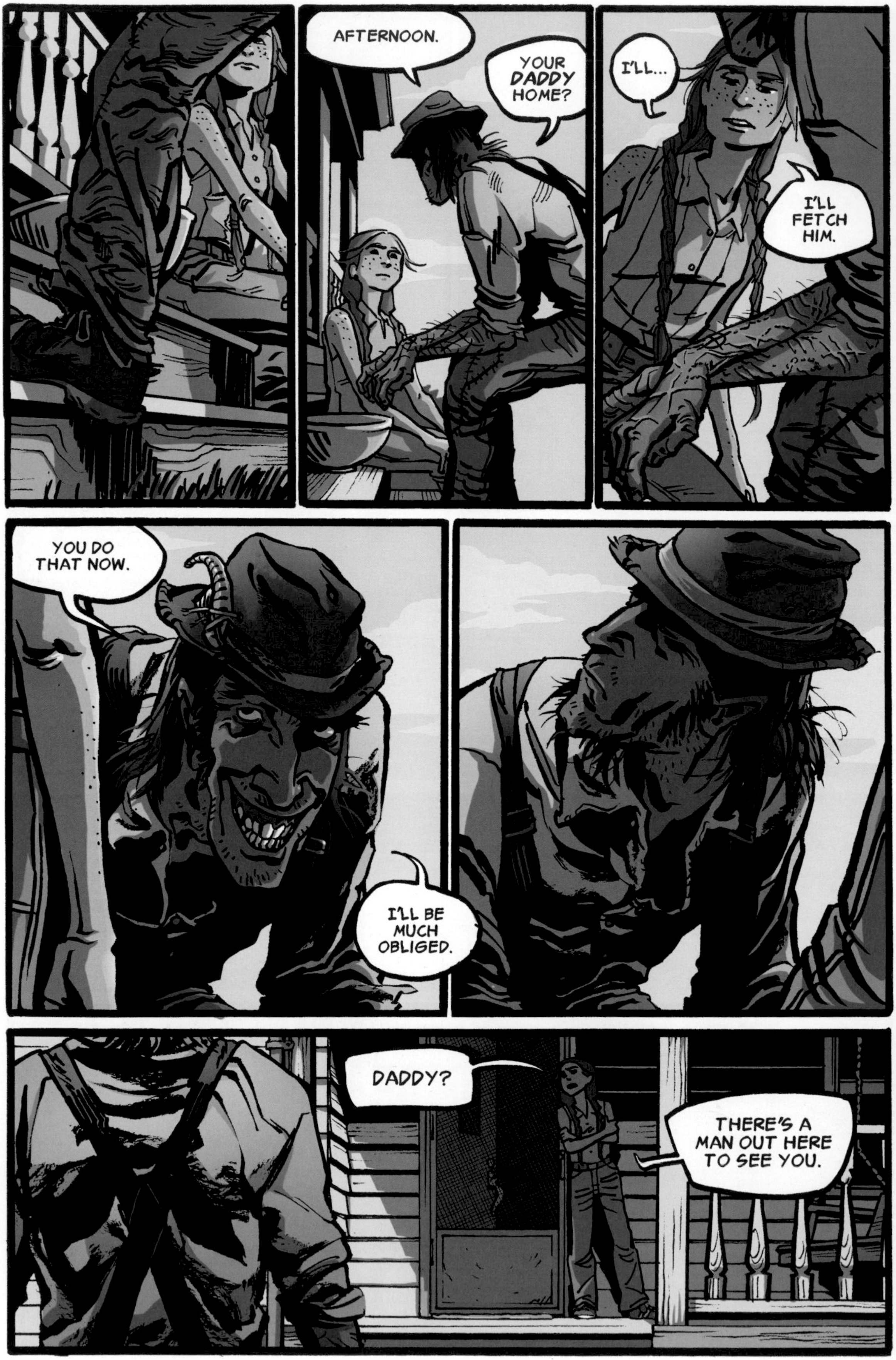
AFTERNOON.
YOUR DADDY HOME?
I'LL...
I'LL FETCH HIM.
YOU DO THAT NOW.
I'LL BE MUCH OBLIGED.
DADDY?
THERE'S A MAN OUT HERE TO SEE YOU.

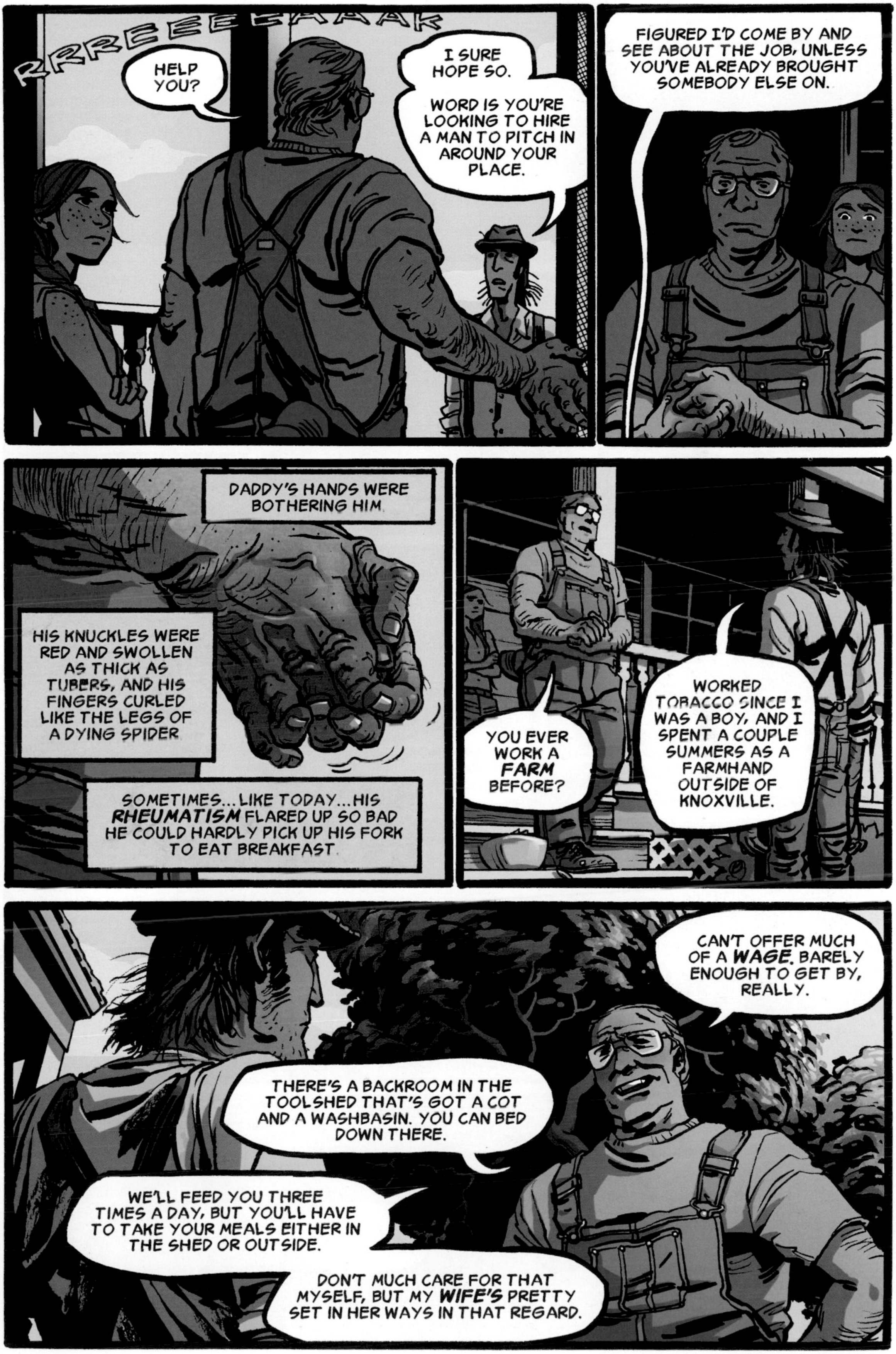
RRREEEEAAAK
HELP YOU?
I SURE HOPE SO.
WORD IS YOU'RE LOOKING TO HIRE A MAN TO PITCH IN AROUND YOUR PLACE.
FIGURED I'D COME BY AND SEE ABOUT THE JOB, UNLESS YOU'VE ALREADY BROUGHT SOMEBODY ELSE ON.
DADDY'S HANDS WERE BOTHERING HIM.
HIS KNUCKLES WERE RED AND SWOLLEN AS THICK AS TUBERS, AND HIS FINGERS CURLED LIKE THE LEGS OF A DYING SPIDER.
SOMETIMES... LIKE TODAY... HIS RHEUMATISM FLARED UP SO BAD HE COULD HARDLY PICK UP HIS FORK TO EAT BREAKFAST.
YOU EVER WORK A FARM BEFORE?
WORKED TOBACCO SINCE I WAS A BOY, AND I SPENT A COUPLE SUMMERS AS A FARMHAND OUTSIDE OF KNOXVILLE.
CAN'T OFFER MUCH OF A WAGE, BARELY ENOUGH TO GET BY, REALLY.
THERE'S A BACKROOM IN THE TOOLSHED THAT'S GOT A COT AND A WASHBASIN. YOU CAN BED DOWN THERE.
WE'LL FEED YOU THREE TIMES A DAY, BUT YOU'LL HAVE TO TAKE YOUR MEALS EITHER IN THE SHED OR OUTSIDE.
DON'T MUCH CARE FOR THAT MYSELF, BUT MY WIFE'S PRETTY SET IN HER WAYS IN THAT REGARD.

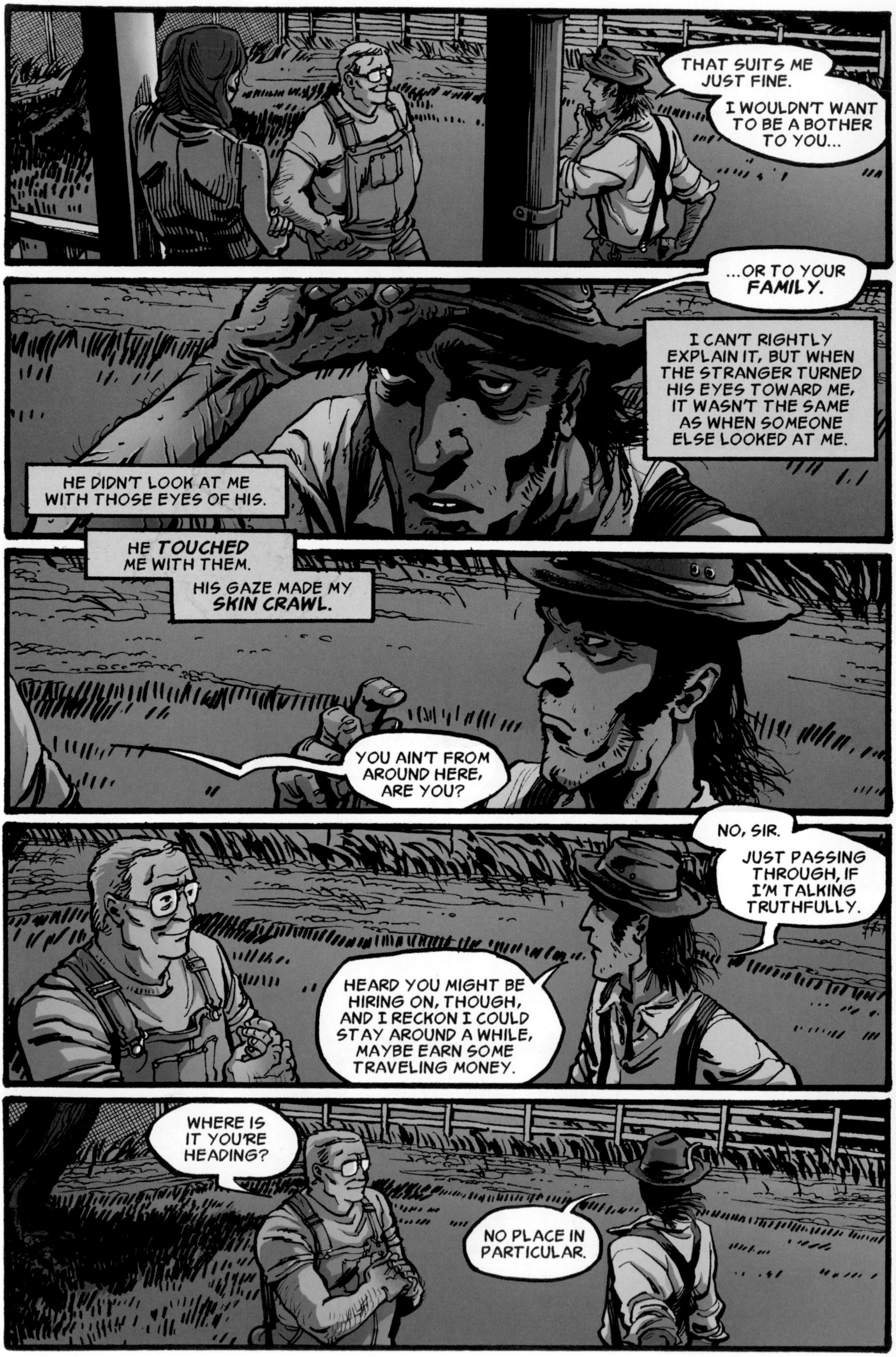
THAT SUITS ME JUST FINE.
I WOULDN'T WANT TO BE A BOTHER TO YOU...
...OR TO YOUR FAMILY.
I CAN'T RIGHTLY EXPLAIN IT, BUT WHEN THE STRANGER TURNED HIS EYES TOWARD ME, IT WASN'T THE SAME AS WHEN SOMEONE ELSE LOOKED AT ME.
HE DIDN'T LOOK AT ME WITH THOSE EYES OF HIS.
HE TOUCHED ME WITH THEM.
HIS GAZE MADE MY SKIN CRAWL.
YOU AIN'T FROM AROUND HERE, ARE YOU?
NO, SIR.
JUST PASSING THROUGH, IF I'M TALKING TRUTHFULLY.
HEARD YOU MIGHT BE HIRING ON, THOUGH, AND I RECKON I COULD STAY AROUND A WHILE, MAYBE EARN SOME TRAVELING MONEY.
WHERE IS IT YOU'RE HEADING?
NO PLACE IN PARTICULAR.

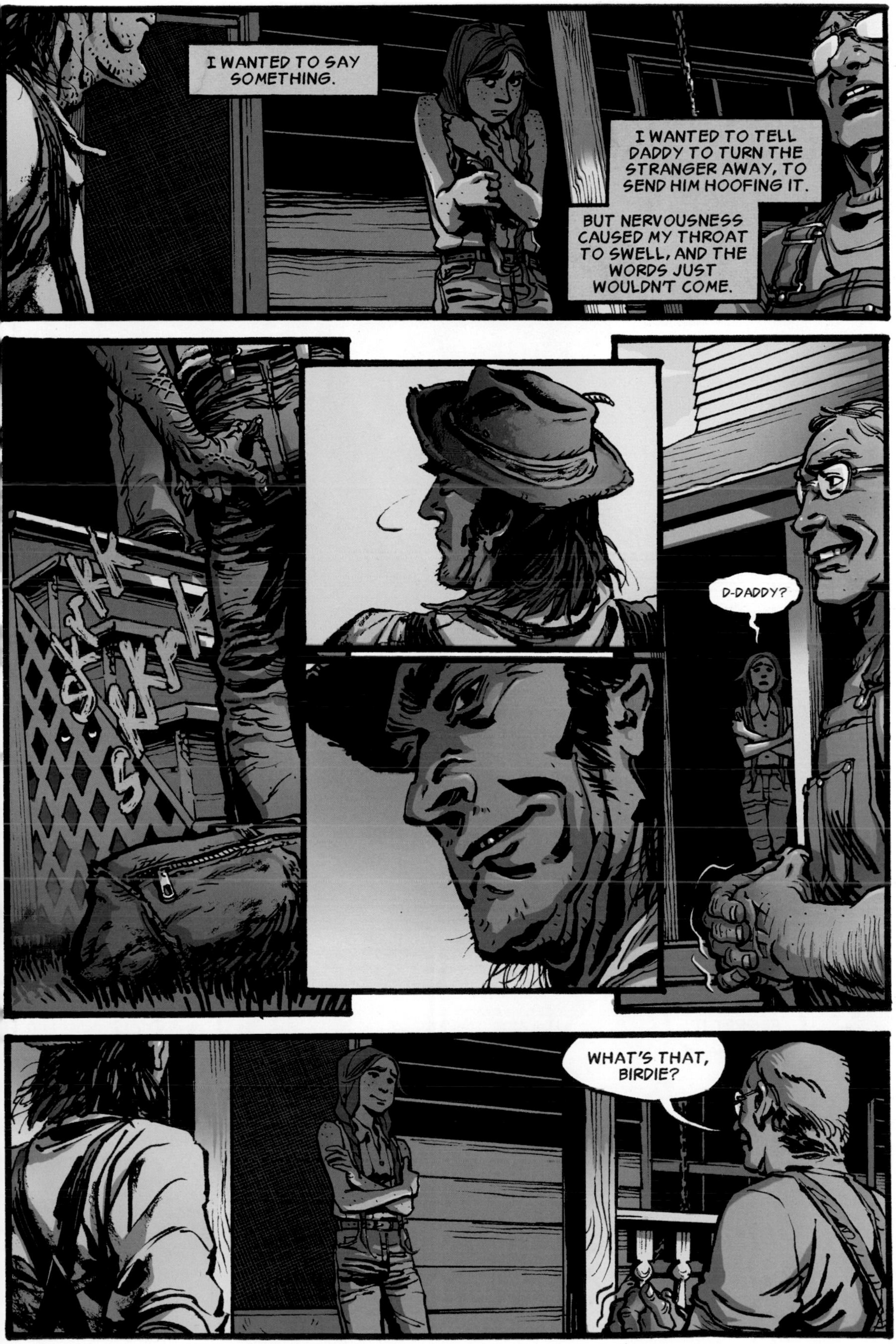
I WANTED TO SAY SOMETHING.
I WANTED TO TELL DADDY TO TURN THE STRANGER AWAY, TO SEND HIM HOOFING IT.
BUT NERVOUSNESS CAUSED MY THROAT TO SWELL, AND THE WORDS JUST WOULDN'T COME.
D-DADDY?
WHAT'S THAT, BIRDIE?

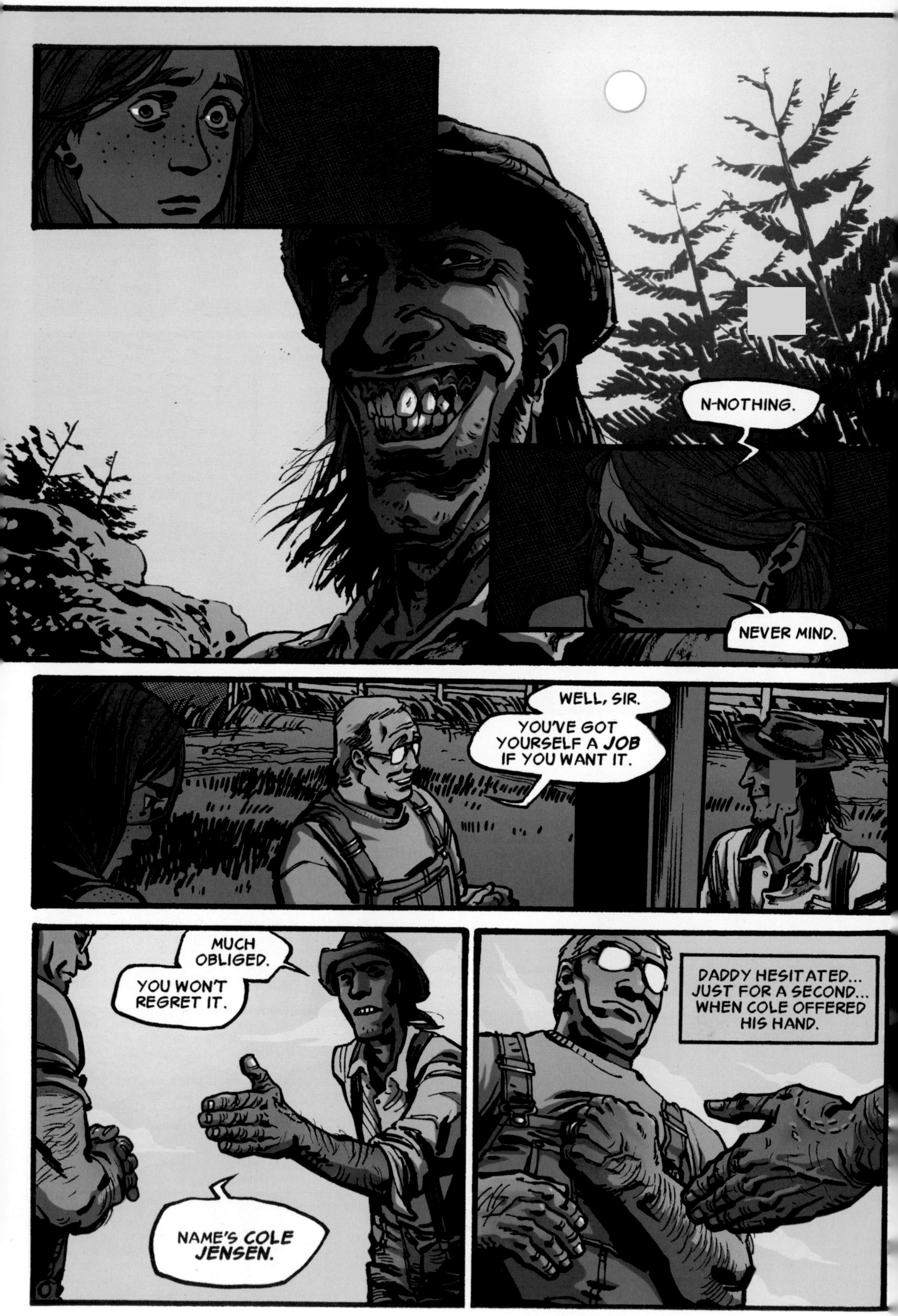
N-NOTHING.
NEVER MIND.
WELL, SIR.
YOU'VE GOT YOURSELF A JOB IF YOU WANT IT.
MUCH OBLIGED.
YOU WON'T REGRET IT.
NAME'S COLE JENSEN.
DADDY HESITATED... JUST FOR A SECOND... WHEN COLE OFFERED HIS HAND.

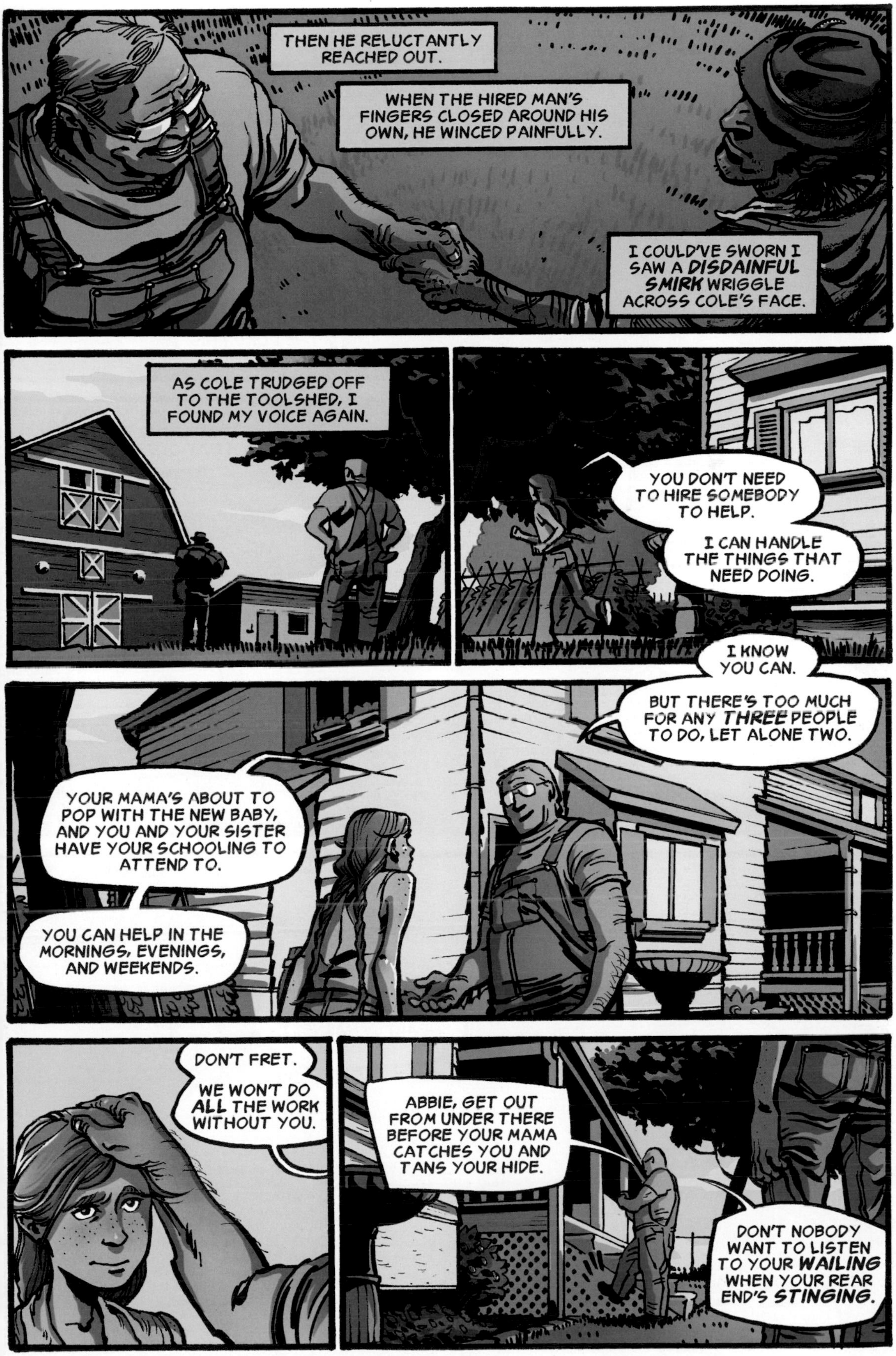
THEN HE RELUCTANTLY REACHED OUT.
WHEN THE HIRED MAN'S FINGERS CLOSED AROUND HIS OWN, HE WINCED PAINFULLY.
I COULD'VE SWORN I SAW A DISDAINFUL SMIRK WRIGGLE ACROSS COLE'S FACE.
AS COLE TRUDGED OFF TO THE TOOLSHED, I FOUND MY VOICE AGAIN.
YOU DON'T NEED TO HIRE SOMEBODY TO HELP.
I CAN HANDLE THE THINGS THAT NEED DOING.
I KNOW YOU CAN.
BUT THERE'S TOO MUCH FOR ANY THREE PEOPLE TO DO, LET ALONE TWO.
YOUR MAMA'S ABOUT TO POP WITH THE NEW BABY, AND YOU AND YOUR SISTER HAVE YOUR SCHOOLING TO ATTEND TO.
YOU CAN HELP IN THE MORNINGS, EVENINGS, AND WEEKENDS.
DON'T FRET.
WE WON'T DO ALL THE WORK WITHOUT YOU.
ABBIE, GET OUT FROM UNDER THERE BEFORE YOUR MAMA CATCHES YOU AND TANS YOUR HIDE.
DON'T NOBODY WANT TO LISTEN TO YOUR WAILING WHEN YOUR REAR END'S STINGING.

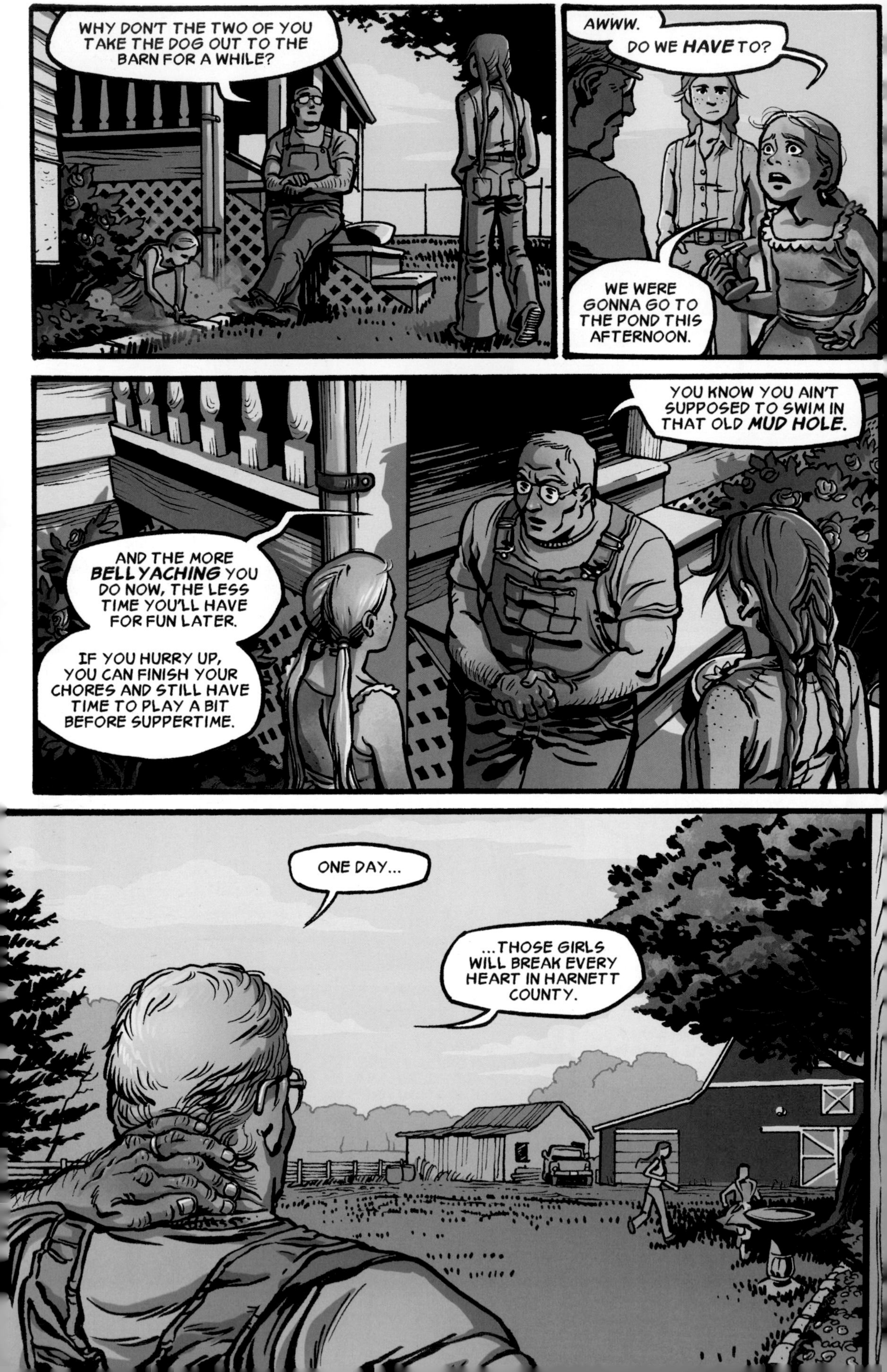
WHY DON'T THE TWO OF YOU TAKE THE DOG OUT TO THE BARN FOR A WHILE?
AWWW.
DO WE HAVE TO?
WE WERE GONNA GO TO THE POND THIS AFTERNOON.
YOU KNOW YOU AIN'T SUPPOSED TO SWIM IN THAT OLD MUD HOLE.
AND THE MORE BELLYACHING YOU DO NOW, THE LESS TIME YOU'LL HAVE FOR FUN LATER.
IF YOU HURRY UP, YOU CAN FINISH YOUR CHORES AND STILL HAVE TIME TO PLAY A BIT BEFORE SUPPERTIME.
ONE DAY...
...THOSE GIRLS WILL BREAK EVERY HEART IN HARNETT COUNTY.

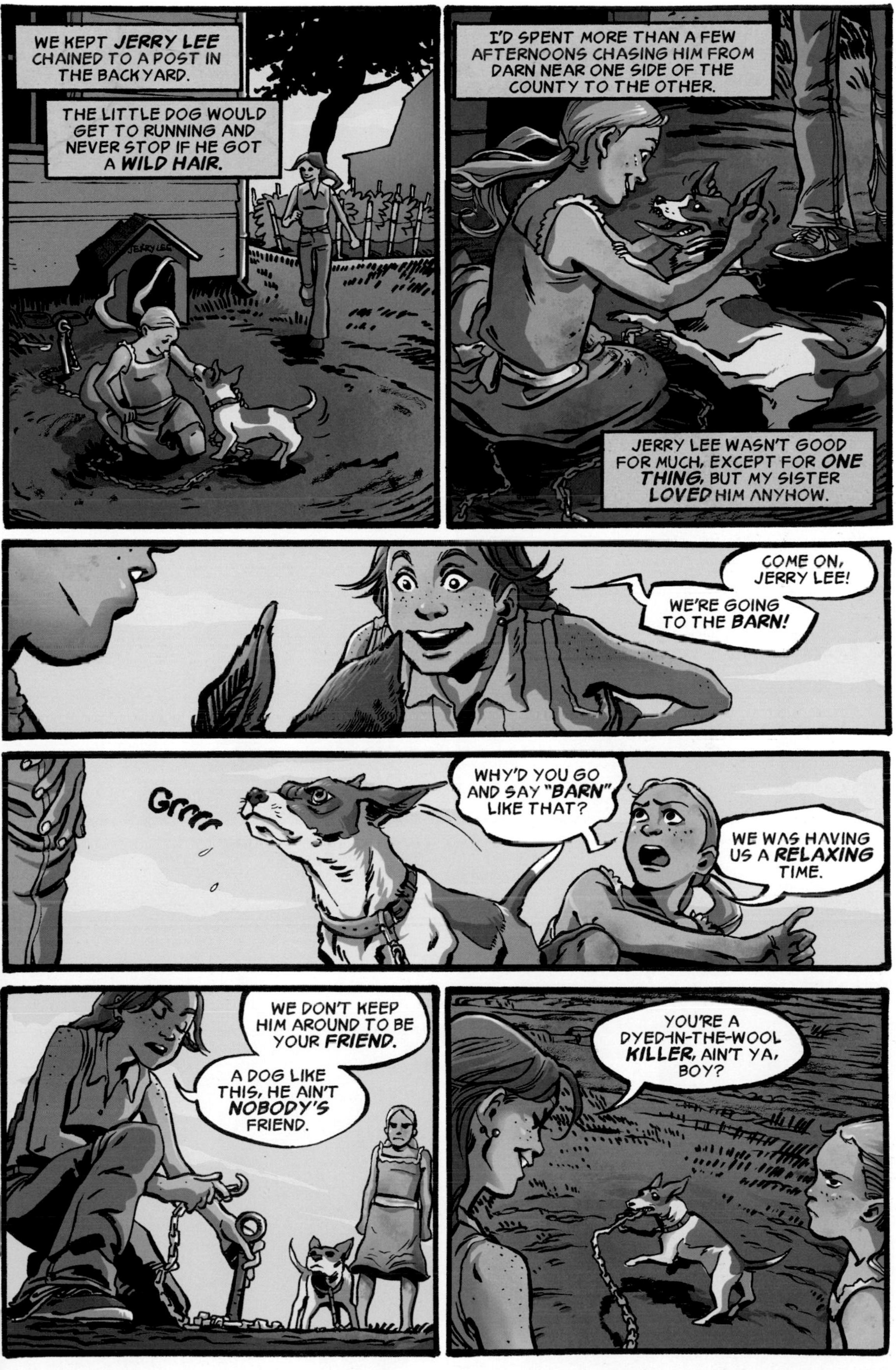
WE KEPT JERRY LEE CHAINED TO A POST IN THE BACKYARD.
THE LITTLE DOG WOULD GET TO RUNNING AND NEVER STOP IF HE GOT A WILD HAIR.
JERRY LEE
I'D SPENT MORE THAN A FEW AFTERNOONS CHASING HIM FROM DARN NEAR ONE SIDE OF THE COUNTY TO THE OTHER.
JERRY LEE WASN'T GOOD FOR MUCH, EXCEPT FOR ONE THING, BUT MY SISTER LOVED HIM ANYHOW.
COME ON, JERRY LEE!
WE'RE GOING TO THE BARN!
Grrrr
WHY'D YOU GO AND SAY "BARN" LIKE THAT?
WE WAS HAVING US A RELAXING TIME.
WE DON'T KEEP HIM AROUND TO BE YOUR FRIEND.
A DOG LIKE THIS, HE AIN'T NOBODY'S FRIEND.
YOU'RE A DYED-IN-THE-WOOL KILLER, AIN'T YA, BOY?

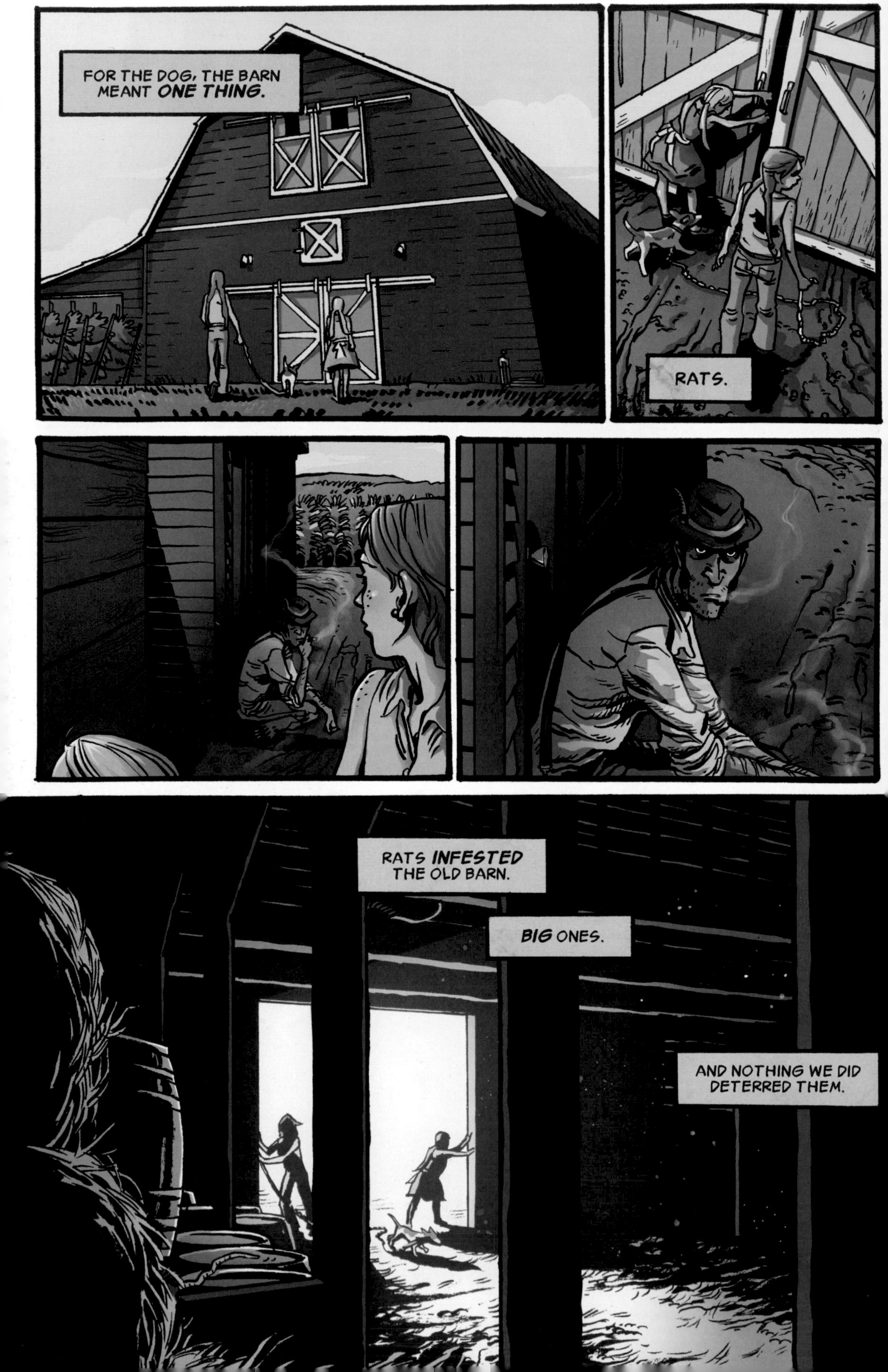
FOR THE DOG, THE BARN MEANT ONE THING.
RATS.
RATS INFESTED THE OLD BARN.
BIG ONES.
AND NOTHING WE DID DETERRED THEM.

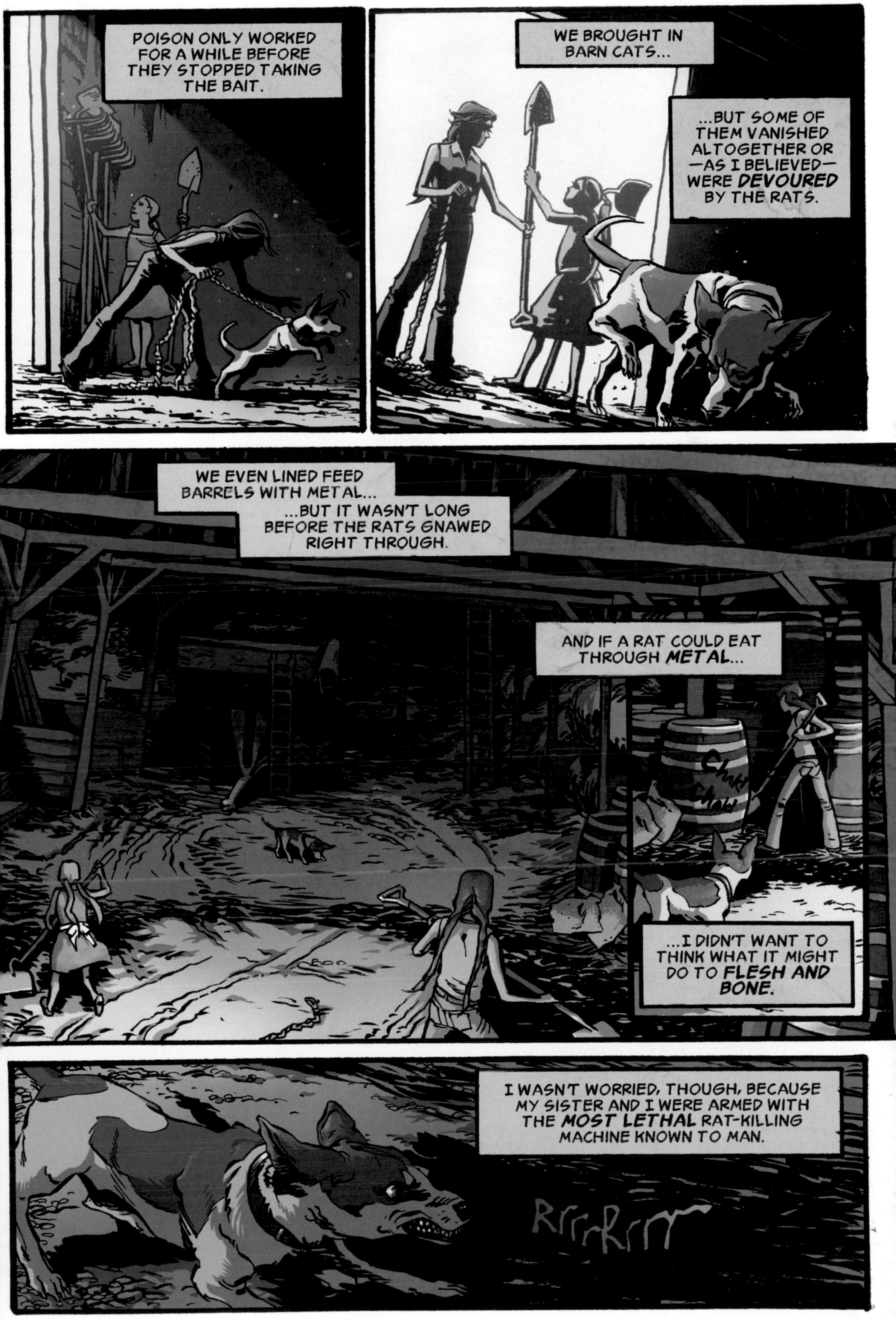
POISON ONLY WORKED FOR A WHILE BEFORE THEY STOPPED TAKING THE BAIT.
WE BROUGHT IN BARN CATS...
...BUT SOME OF THEM VANISHED ALTOGETHER OR —AS I BELIEVED— WERE DEVOURED BY THE RATS.
WE EVEN LINED FEED BARRELS WITH METAL...
...BUT IT WASN'T LONG BEFORE THE RATS GNAWED RIGHT THROUGH.
AND IF A RAT COULD EAT THROUGH METAL...
...I DIDN'T WANT TO THINK WHAT IT MIGHT DO TO FLESH AND BONE.
I WASN'T WORRIED, THOUGH, BECAUSE MY SISTER AND I WERE ARMED WITH THE MOST LETHAL RAT-KILLING MACHINE KNOWN TO MAN.
RrrrRrrr

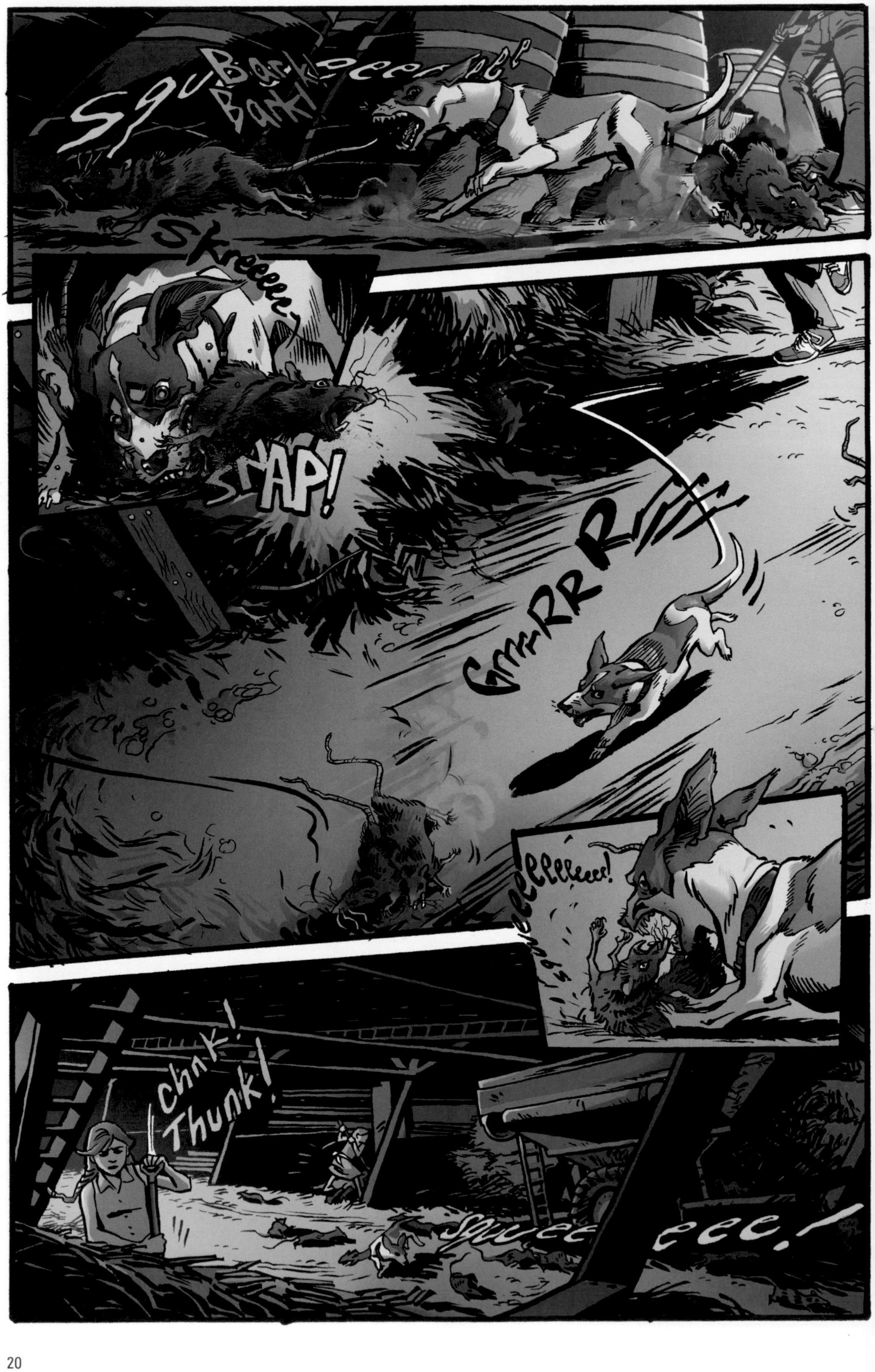
Bark!
Bark!
SNAP!
GrrrRRR
Chnk!
Thunk!

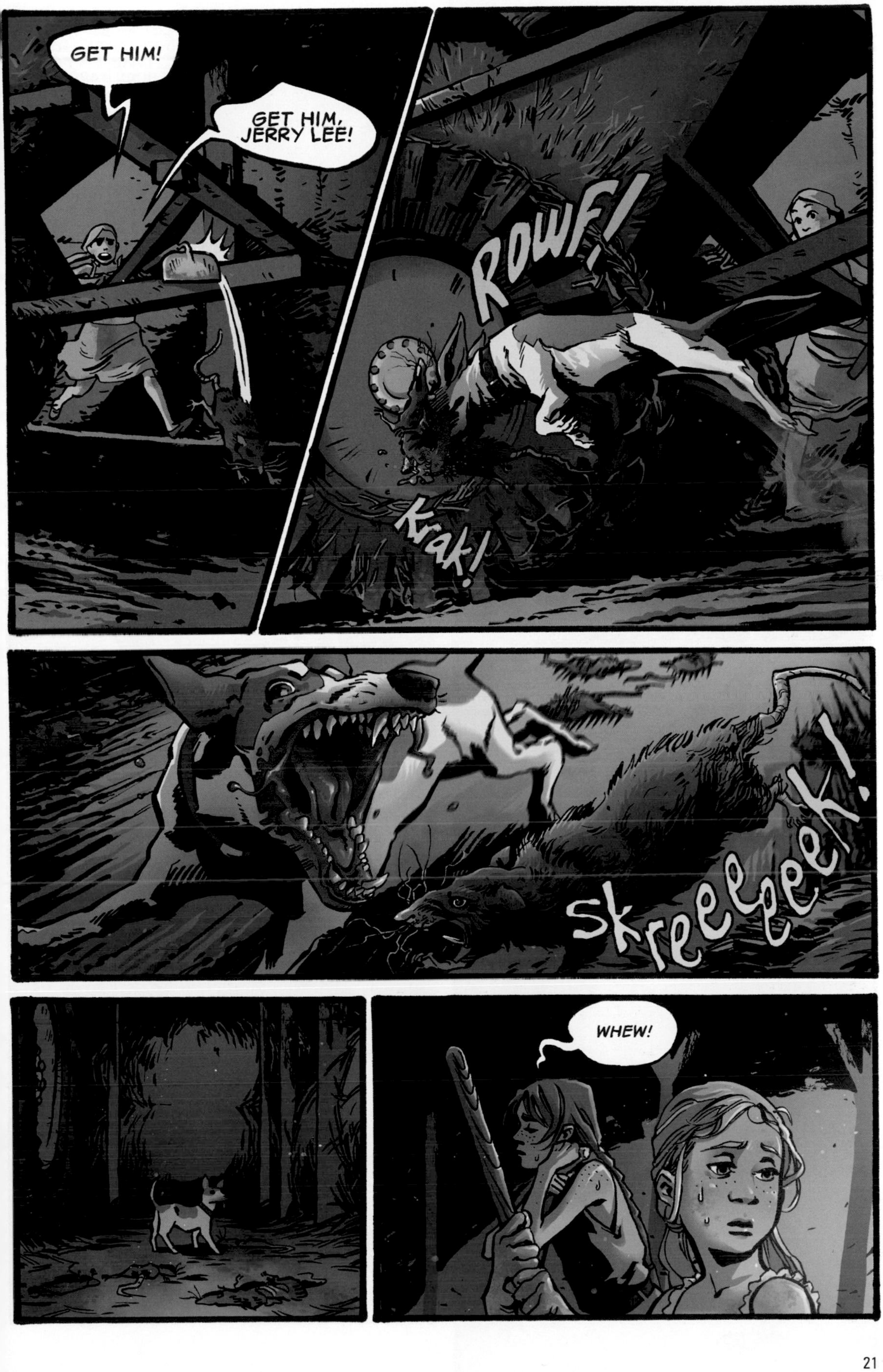
GET HIM!
GET HIM, JERRY LEE!
ROWF!
KRAK!
SKREEEEEEK!
WHEW!

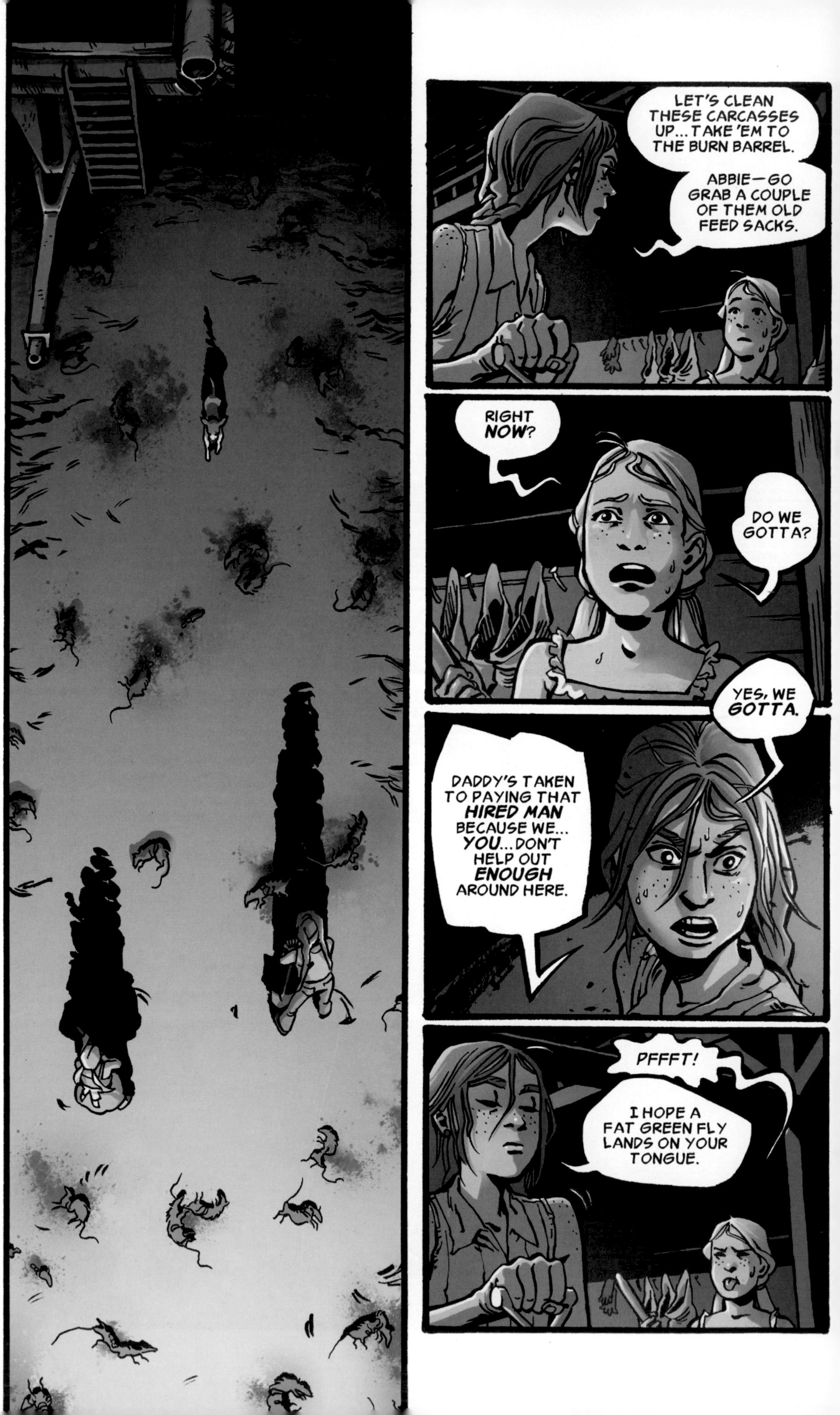
LET'S CLEAN THESE CARCASSES UP... TAKE 'EM TO THE BURN BARREL.
ABBIE—GO GRAB A COUPLE OF THEM OLD FEED SACKS.
RIGHT NOW?
DO WE GOTTA?
YES, WE GOTTA.
DADDY'S TAKEN TO PAYING THAT HIRED MAN BECAUSE WE... YOU...DON'T HELP OUT ENOUGH AROUND HERE.
PFFFT!
I HOPE A FAT GREEN FLY LANDS ON YOUR TONGUE.

snf
snf

sgguu— e.e.kk—kk—rrrk

WHA—

THAT RAT WAS **DEAD** AS A **DOORNAIL.**

I WOULD HAVE PUT MY HAND ON THE **BIBLE** AND **SWORN** IT.

Hssssss.sk

BUT IT WAS **ALIVE** AGAIN.

SssSss

Hsss

SOMEHOW.

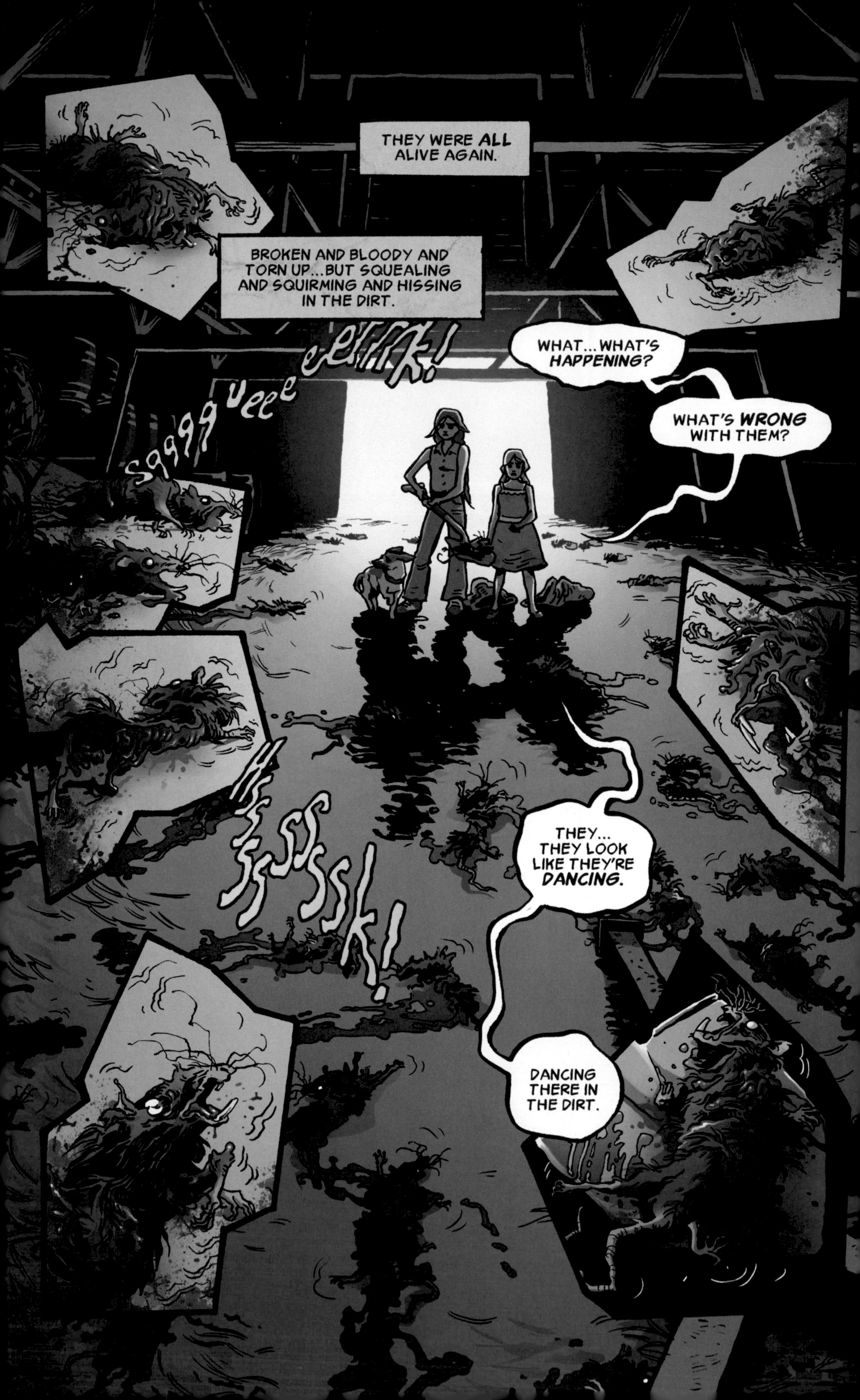
THEY WERE ALL ALIVE AGAIN.
BROKEN AND BLOODY AND TORN UP...BUT SQUEALING AND SQUIRMING AND HISSING IN THE DIRT.
SQQQQUEEEEEEEK!
WHAT...WHAT'S HAPPENING?
WHAT'S WRONG WITH THEM?
HISSSSSK!
THEY... THEY LOOK LIKE THEY'RE DANCING.
DANCING THERE IN THE DIRT.

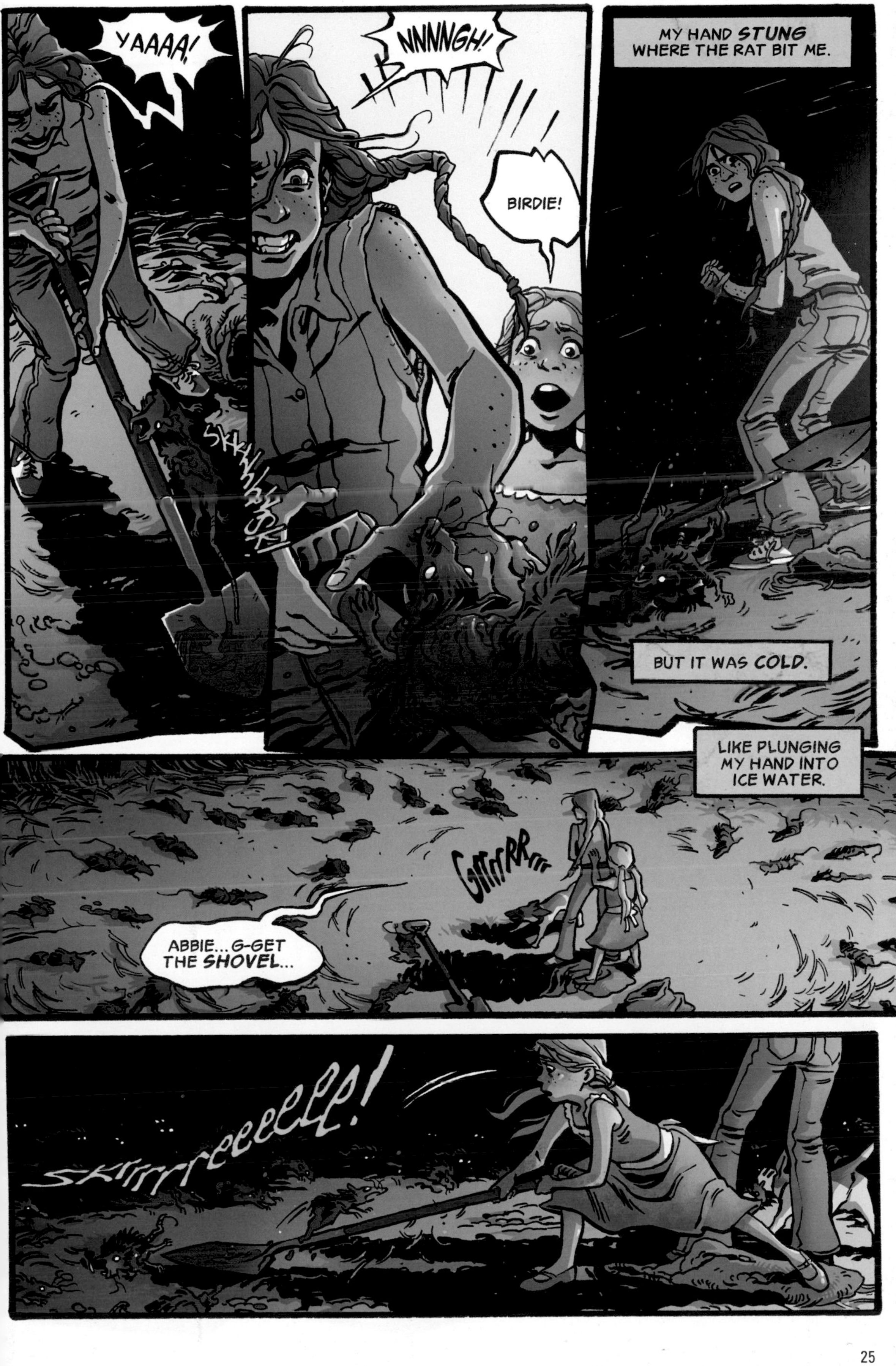
YAAAA!
NNNNGH!
SKWAWKSK!
BIRDIE!
MY HAND STUNG WHERE THE RAT BIT ME.
BUT IT WAS COLD.
LIKE PLUNGING MY HAND INTO ICE WATER.
GrrrrRRrrr
ABBIE... G-GET THE SHOVEL...
SKRRRRREEEEELLE!

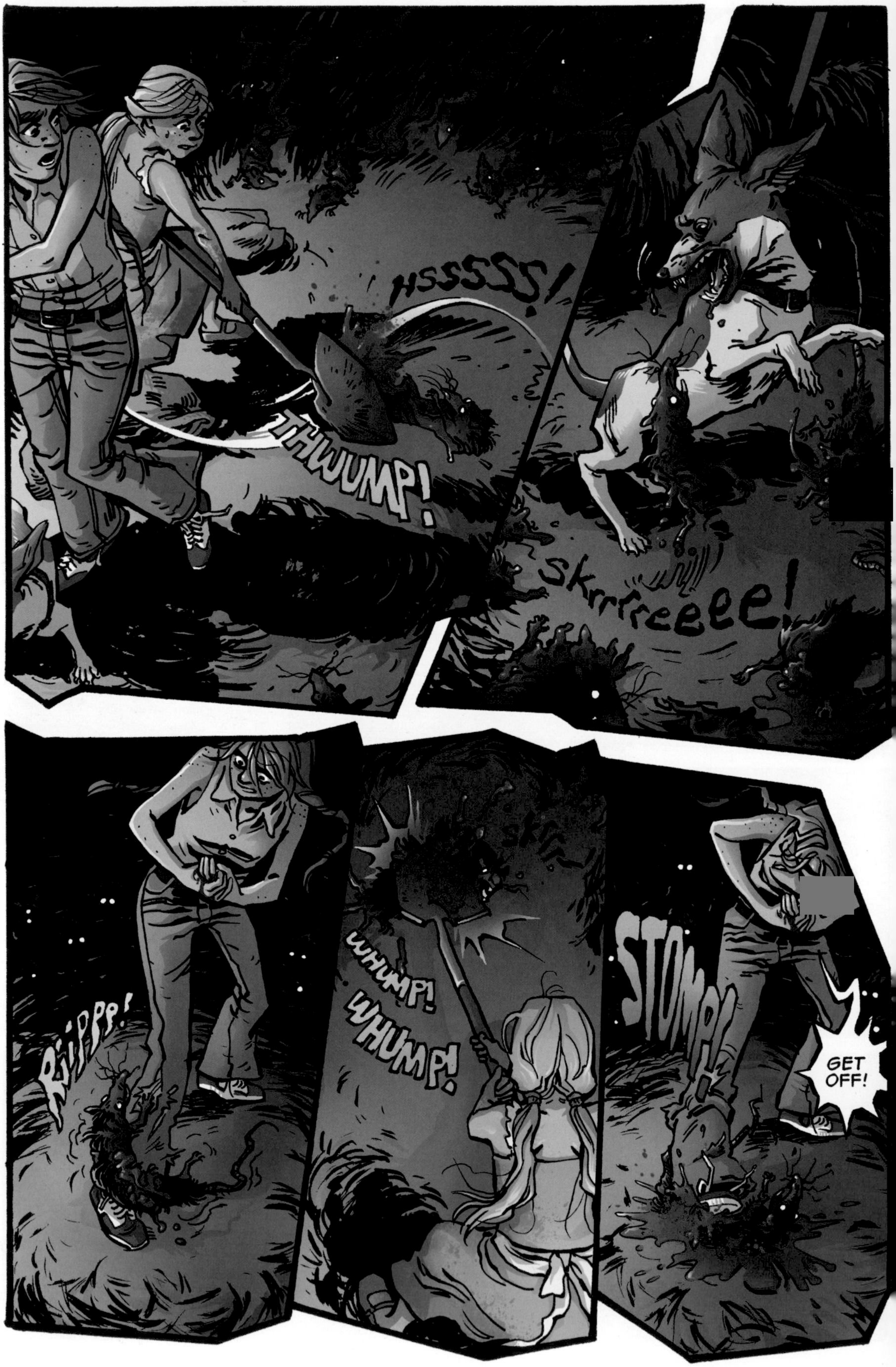
HSSSSS!
THWUMP!
Skrrrreeeee!
RIIPPP!
WHUMP!
WHUMP!
STOMP!
GET OFF!

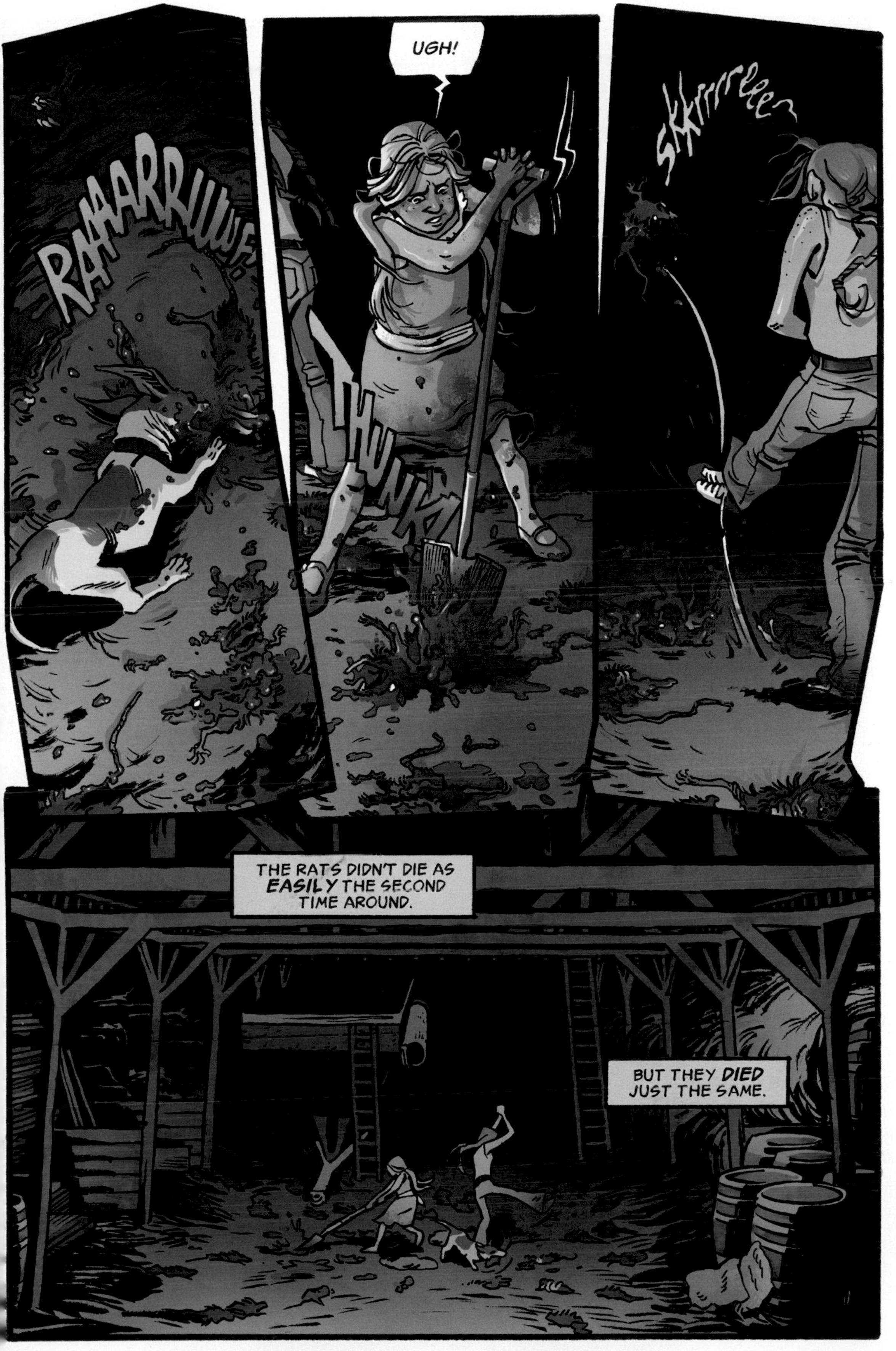
RAAARRUUUF!
UGH!
THUNK!
SKKRRRLEEE
THE RATS DIDN'T DIE AS EASILY THE SECOND TIME AROUND.
BUT THEY DIED JUST THE SAME.

UP UNTIL THAT VERY DAY, I *LOVED* THAT OLD FARM.

BUT EVERYTHING *CHANGED* WHEN THE DEAD RATS DANCED.

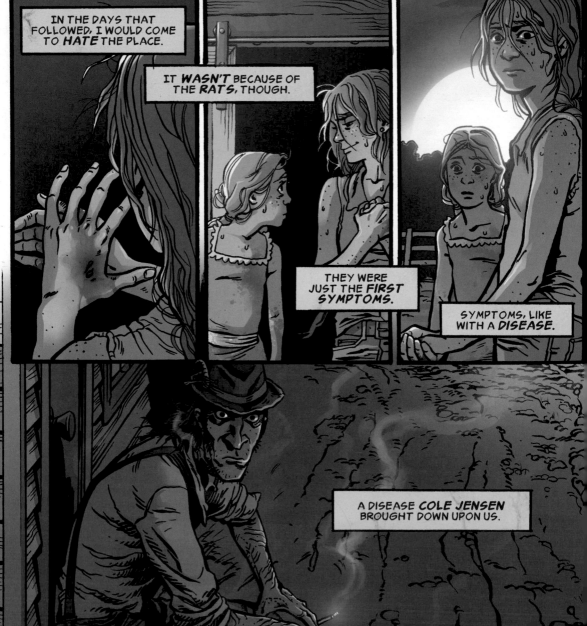

IN THE DAYS THAT FOLLOWED, I WOULD COME TO *HATE* THE PLACE.

IT *WASN'T* BECAUSE OF THE *RATS*, THOUGH.

THEY WERE JUST THE *FIRST* SYMPTOMS.

SYMPTOMS, LIKE WITH A *DISEASE*.

A DISEASE *COLE JENSEN* BROUGHT DOWN UPON US.

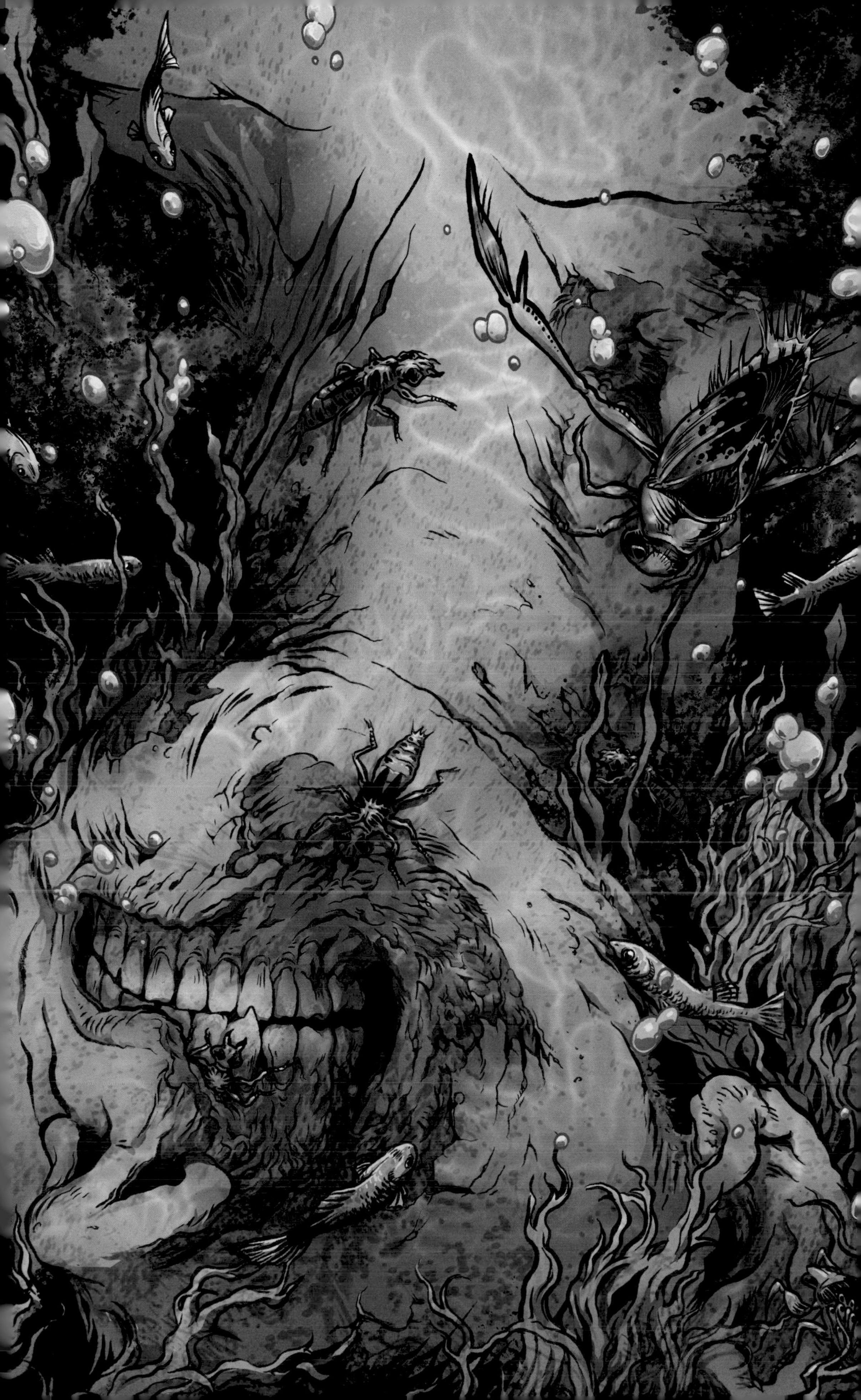

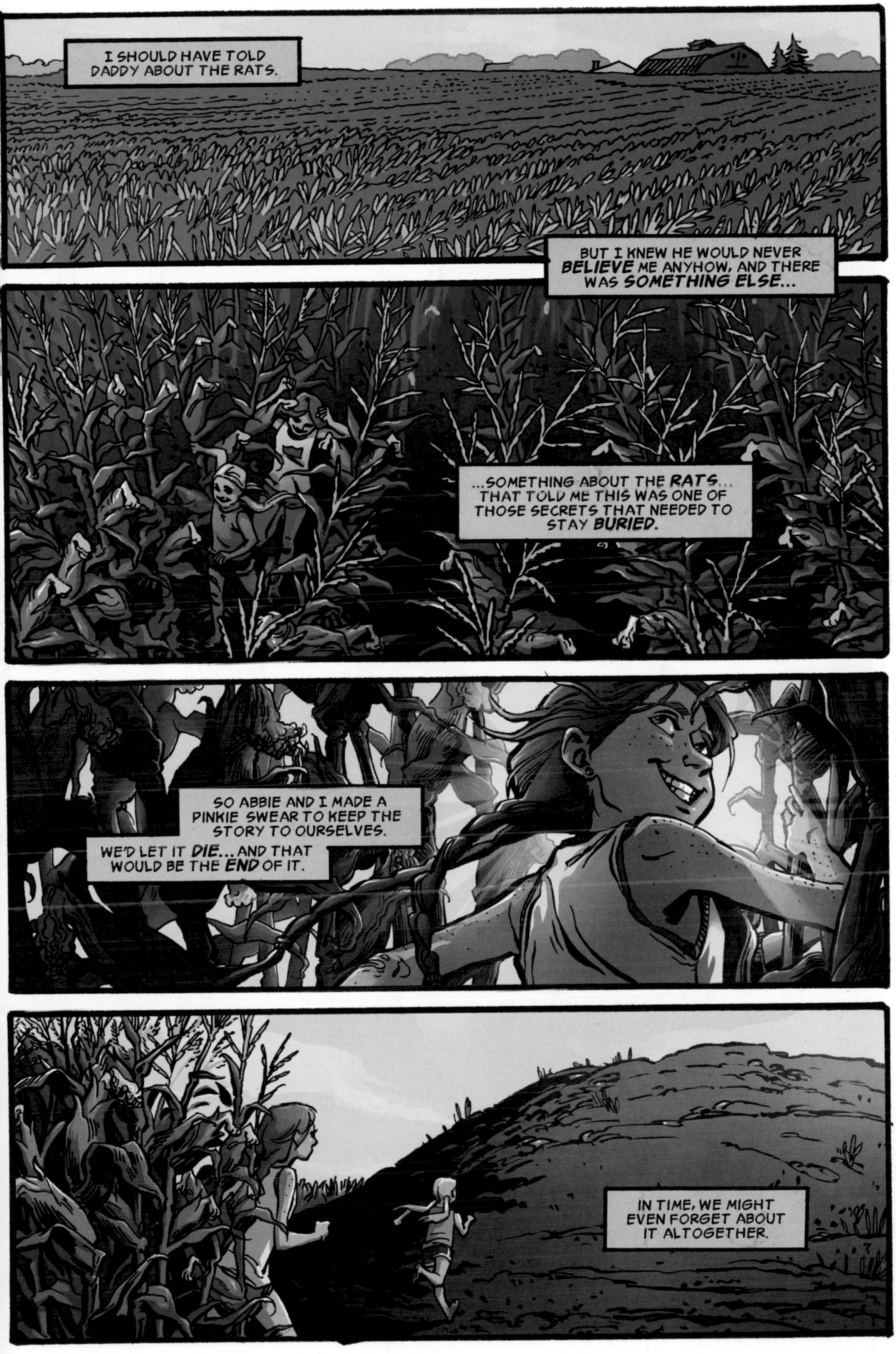
I SHOULD HAVE TOLD DADDY ABOUT THE RATS.
BUT I KNEW HE WOULD NEVER BELIEVE ME ANYHOW, AND THERE WAS SOMETHING ELSE...
...SOMETHING ABOUT THE RATS... THAT TOLD ME THIS WAS ONE OF THOSE SECRETS THAT NEEDED TO STAY BURIED.
SO ABBIE AND I MADE A PINKIE SWEAR TO KEEP THE STORY TO OURSELVES.
WE'D LET IT DIE... AND THAT WOULD BE THE END OF IT.
IN TIME, WE MIGHT EVEN FORGET ABOUT IT ALTOGETHER.

COME ON, BIRDIE!

DON'T BE SUCH A SLOWPOKE!

MY HAND STILL BURNED COLDLY WHERE THE RAT BIT ME.

BUT IF ANYONE ASKED ME ABOUT IT, I'D JUST MAKE UP A STORY ABOUT CUTTING MYSELF ON A NAIL.

AS LONG AS THE RATS STAYED DEAD, WE'D BE ALL RIGHT.

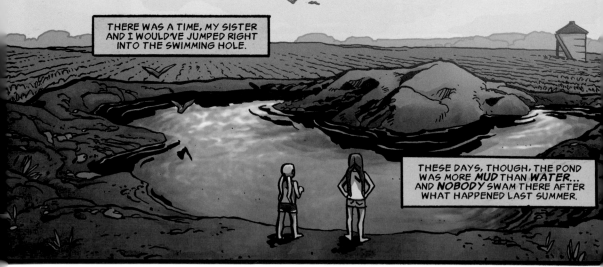

THERE WAS A TIME, MY SISTER AND I WOULD'VE JUMPED RIGHT INTO THE SWIMMING HOLE.

THESE DAYS, THOUGH, THE POND WAS MORE MUD THAN WATER... AND NOBODY SWAM THERE AFTER WHAT HAPPENED LAST SUMMER.

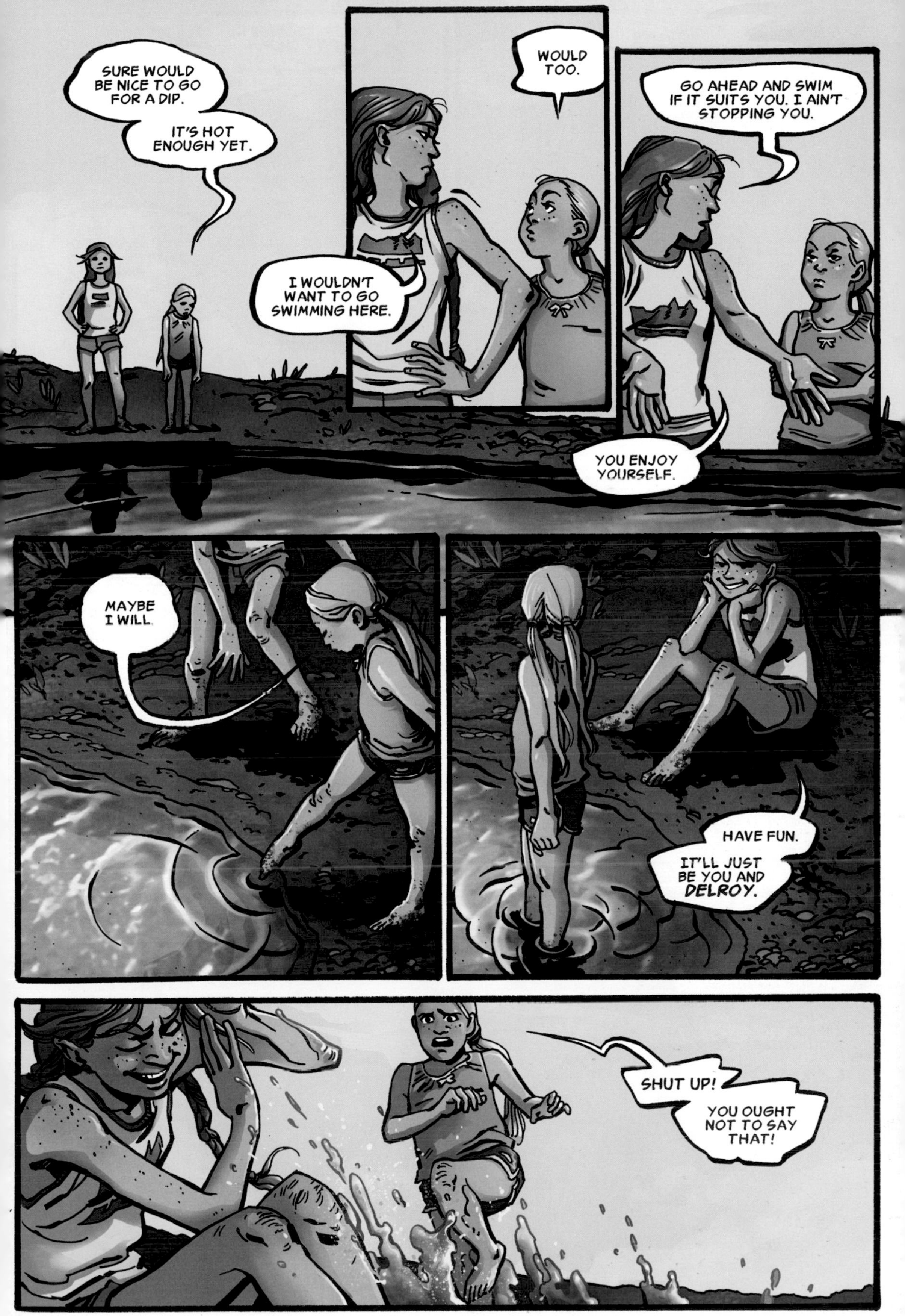
SURE WOULD BE NICE TO GO FOR A DIP.
IT'S HOT ENOUGH YET.
I WOULDN'T WANT TO GO SWIMMING HERE.
WOULD TOO.
GO AHEAD AND SWIM IF IT SUITS YOU. I AIN'T STOPPING YOU.
YOU ENJOY YOURSELF.
MAYBE I WILL.
HAVE FUN.
IT'LL JUST BE YOU AND DELROY.
SHUT UP!
YOU OUGHT NOT TO SAY THAT!

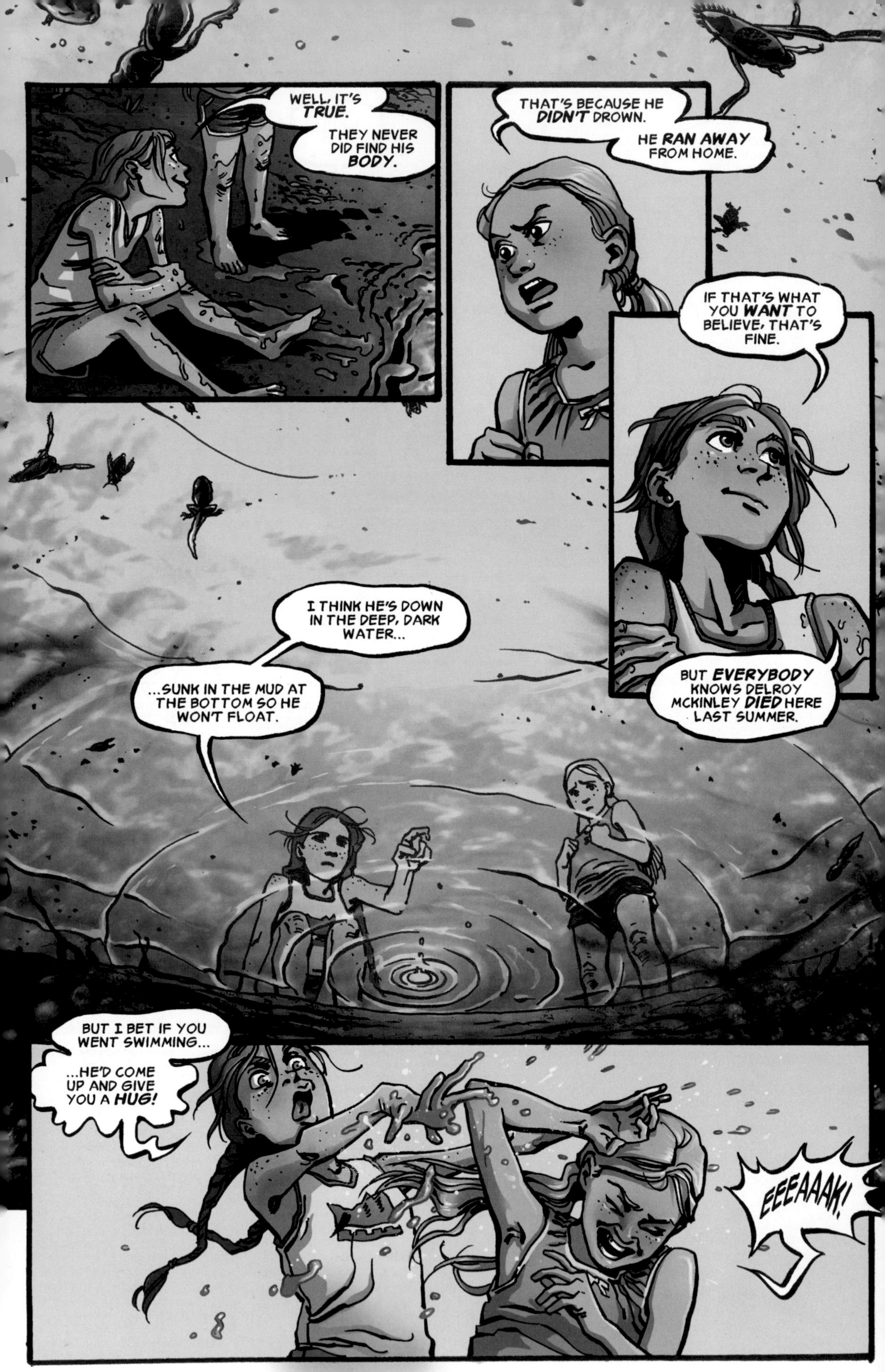
WELL, IT'S TRUE.
THEY NEVER DID FIND HIS BODY.
THAT'S BECAUSE HE DIDN'T DROWN.
HE RAN AWAY FROM HOME.
IF THAT'S WHAT YOU WANT TO BELIEVE, THAT'S FINE.
BUT EVERYBODY KNOWS DELROY MCKINLEY DIED HERE LAST SUMMER.
I THINK HE'S DOWN IN THE DEEP, DARK WATER...
...SUNK IN THE MUD AT THE BOTTOM SO HE WON'T FLOAT.
BUT I BET IF YOU WENT SWIMMING...
...HE'D COME UP AND GIVE YOU A HUG!
EEEAAAK!

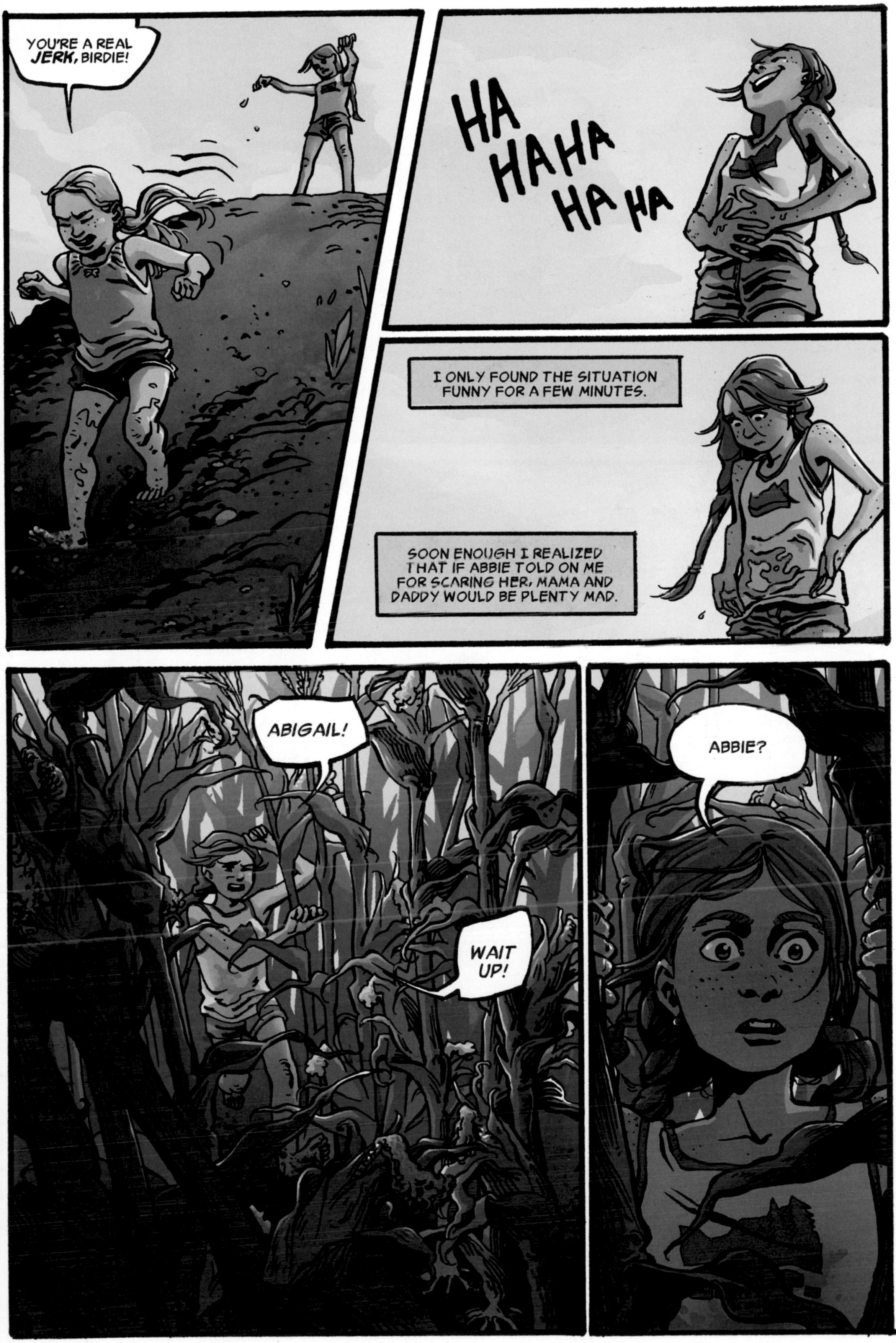
YOU'RE A REAL JERK, BIRDIE!
HA HAHA HA HA
I ONLY FOUND THE SITUATION FUNNY FOR A FEW MINUTES.
SOON ENOUGH I REALIZED THAT IF ABBIE TOLD ON ME FOR SCARING HER, MAMA AND DADDY WOULD BE PLENTY MAD.
ABIGAIL!
WAIT UP!
ABBIE?

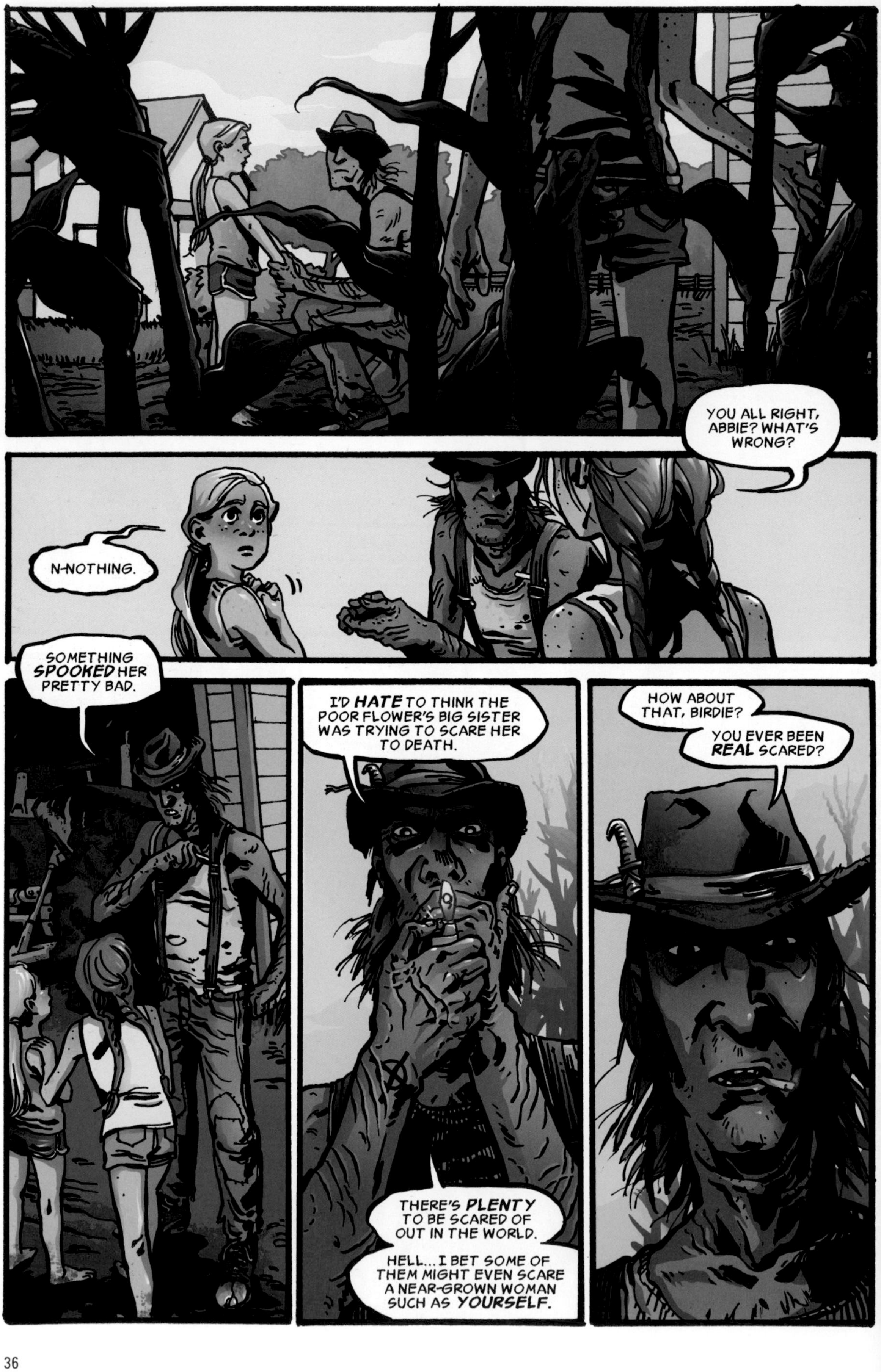
YOU ALL RIGHT, ABBIE? WHAT'S WRONG?
N-NOTHING.
SOMETHING SPOOKED HER PRETTY BAD.
I'D HATE TO THINK THE POOR FLOWER'S BIG SISTER WAS TRYING TO SCARE HER TO DEATH.
THERE'S PLENTY TO BE SCARED OF OUT IN THE WORLD.
HELL... I BET SOME OF THEM MIGHT EVEN SCARE A NEAR-GROWN WOMAN SUCH AS YOURSELF.
HOW ABOUT THAT, BIRDIE?
YOU EVER BEEN REAL SCARED?

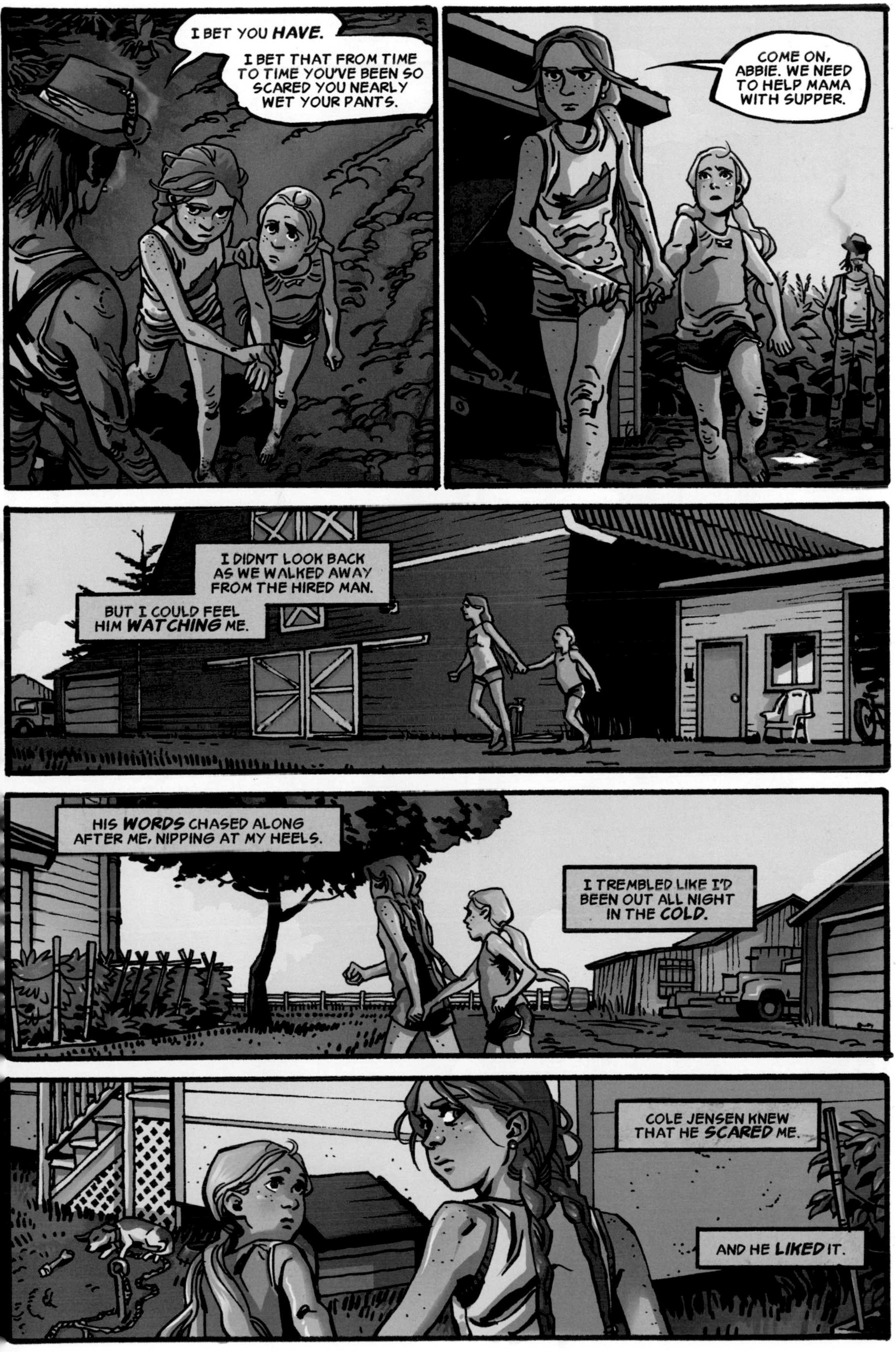
I BET YOU HAVE.
I BET THAT FROM TIME TO TIME YOU'VE BEEN SO SCARED YOU NEARLY WET YOUR PANTS.
COME ON, ABBIE. WE NEED TO HELP MAMA WITH SUPPER.
I DIDN'T LOOK BACK AS WE WALKED AWAY FROM THE HIRED MAN.
BUT I COULD FEEL HIM WATCHING ME.
HIS WORDS CHASED ALONG AFTER ME, NIPPING AT MY HEELS.
I TREMBLED LIKE I'D BEEN OUT ALL NIGHT IN THE COLD.
COLE JENSEN KNEW THAT HE SCARED ME.
AND HE LIKED IT.

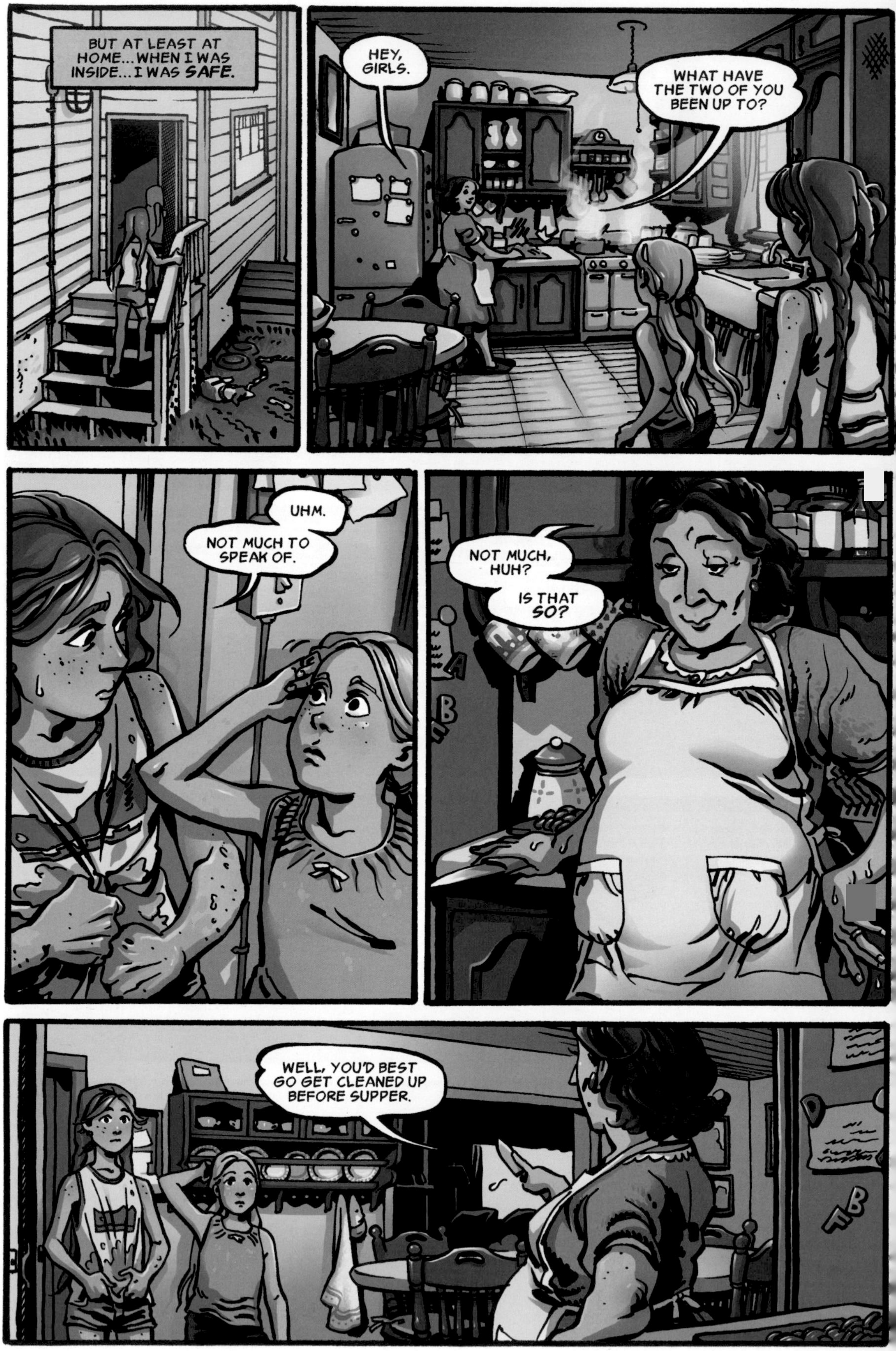
BUT AT LEAST AT HOME...WHEN I WAS INSIDE...I WAS SAFE.
HEY, GIRLS.
WHAT HAVE THE TWO OF YOU BEEN UP TO?
UHM.
NOT MUCH TO SPEAK OF.
NOT MUCH, HUH?
IS THAT SO?
WELL, YOU'D BEST GO GET CLEANED UP BEFORE SUPPER.

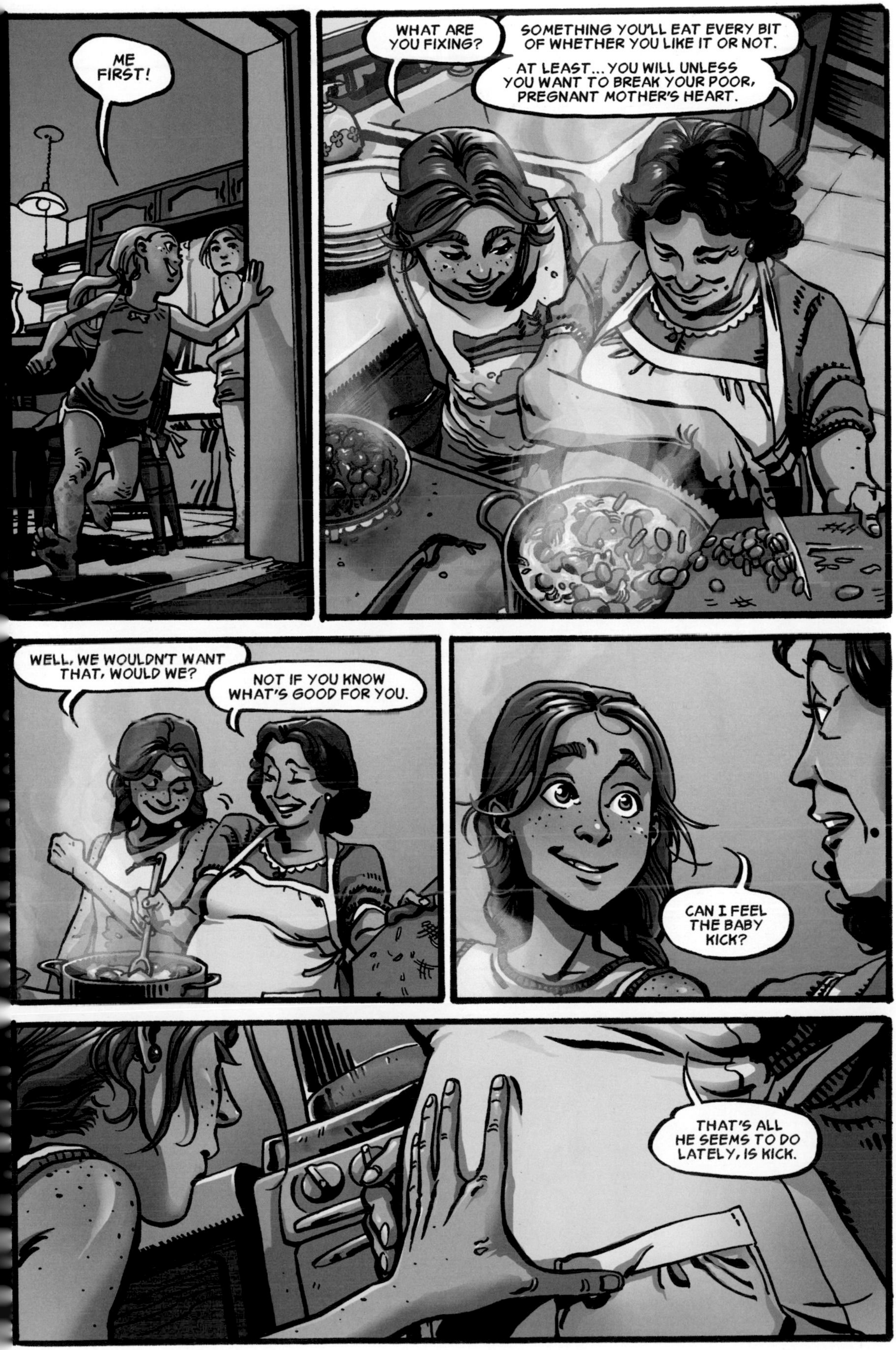
ME FIRST!
WHAT ARE YOU FIXING?
SOMETHING YOU'LL EAT EVERY BIT OF WHETHER YOU LIKE IT OR NOT.
AT LEAST... YOU WILL UNLESS YOU WANT TO BREAK YOUR POOR, PREGNANT MOTHER'S HEART.
WELL, WE WOULDN'T WANT THAT, WOULD WE?
NOT IF YOU KNOW WHAT'S GOOD FOR YOU.
CAN I FEEL THE BABY KICK?
THAT'S ALL HE SEEMS TO DO LATELY, IS KICK.

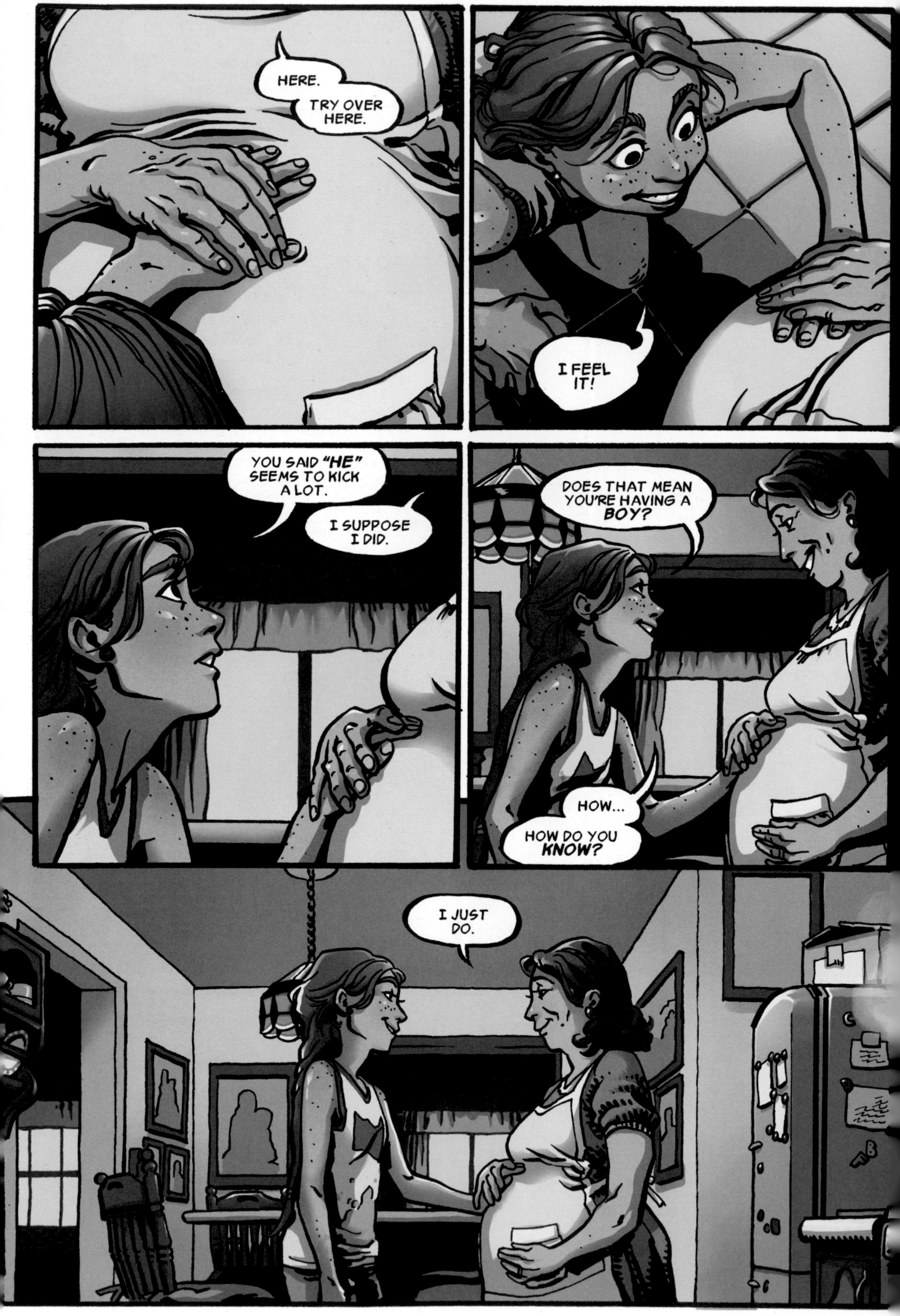
HERE.
TRY OVER HERE.
I FEEL IT!
YOU SAID "HE" SEEMS TO KICK A LOT.
I SUPPOSE I DID.
DOES THAT MEAN YOU'RE HAVING A BOY?
HOW...
HOW DO YOU KNOW?
I JUST DO.

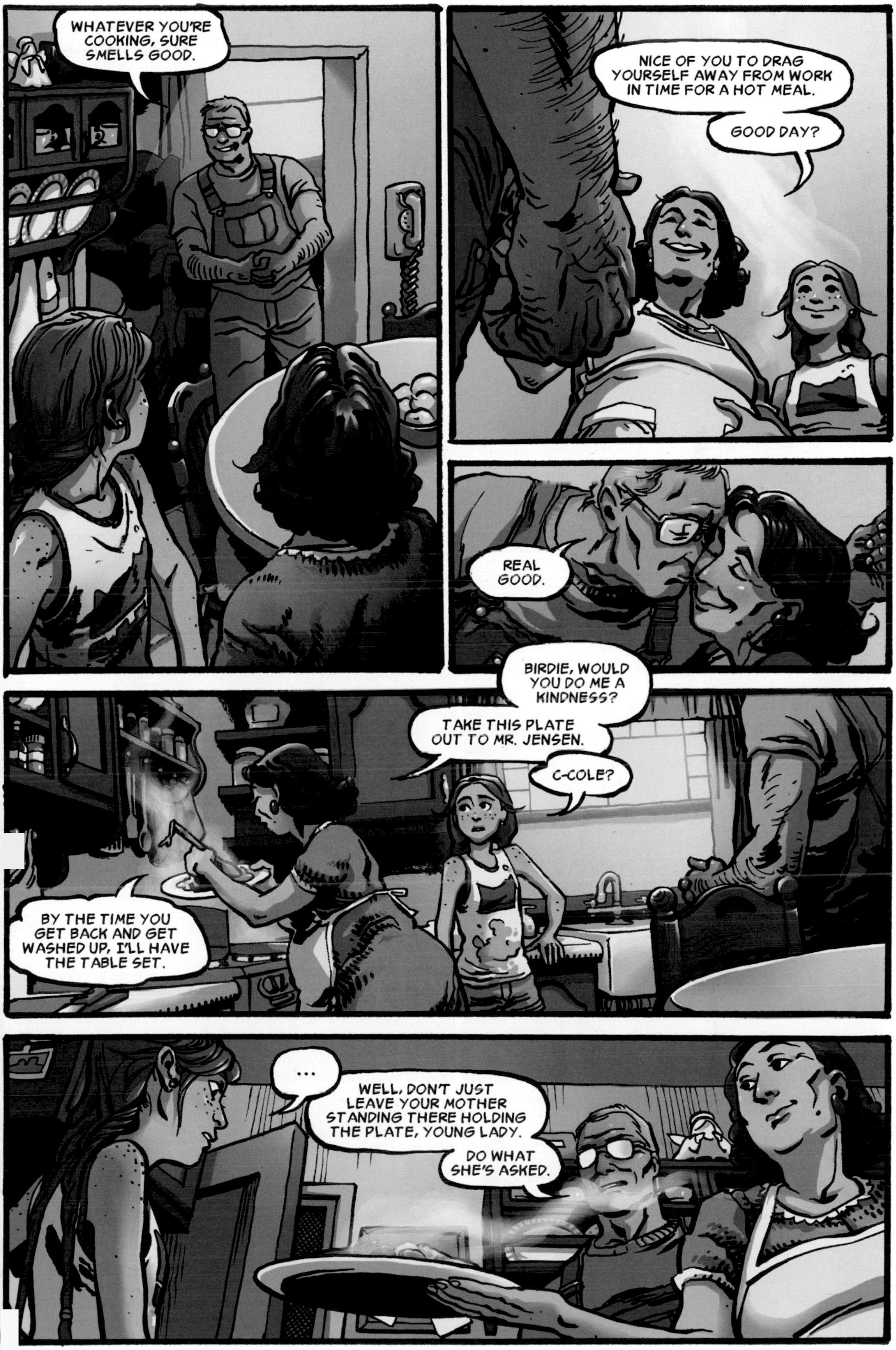
WHATEVER YOU'RE COOKING, SURE SMELLS GOOD.
NICE OF YOU TO DRAG YOURSELF AWAY FROM WORK IN TIME FOR A HOT MEAL.
GOOD DAY?
REAL GOOD.
BIRDIE, WOULD YOU DO ME A KINDNESS?
TAKE THIS PLATE OUT TO MR. JENSEN.
C-COLE?
BY THE TIME YOU GET BACK AND GET WASHED UP, I'LL HAVE THE TABLE SET.
...
WELL, DON'T JUST LEAVE YOUR MOTHER STANDING THERE HOLDING THE PLATE, YOUNG LADY.
DO WHAT SHE'S ASKED.

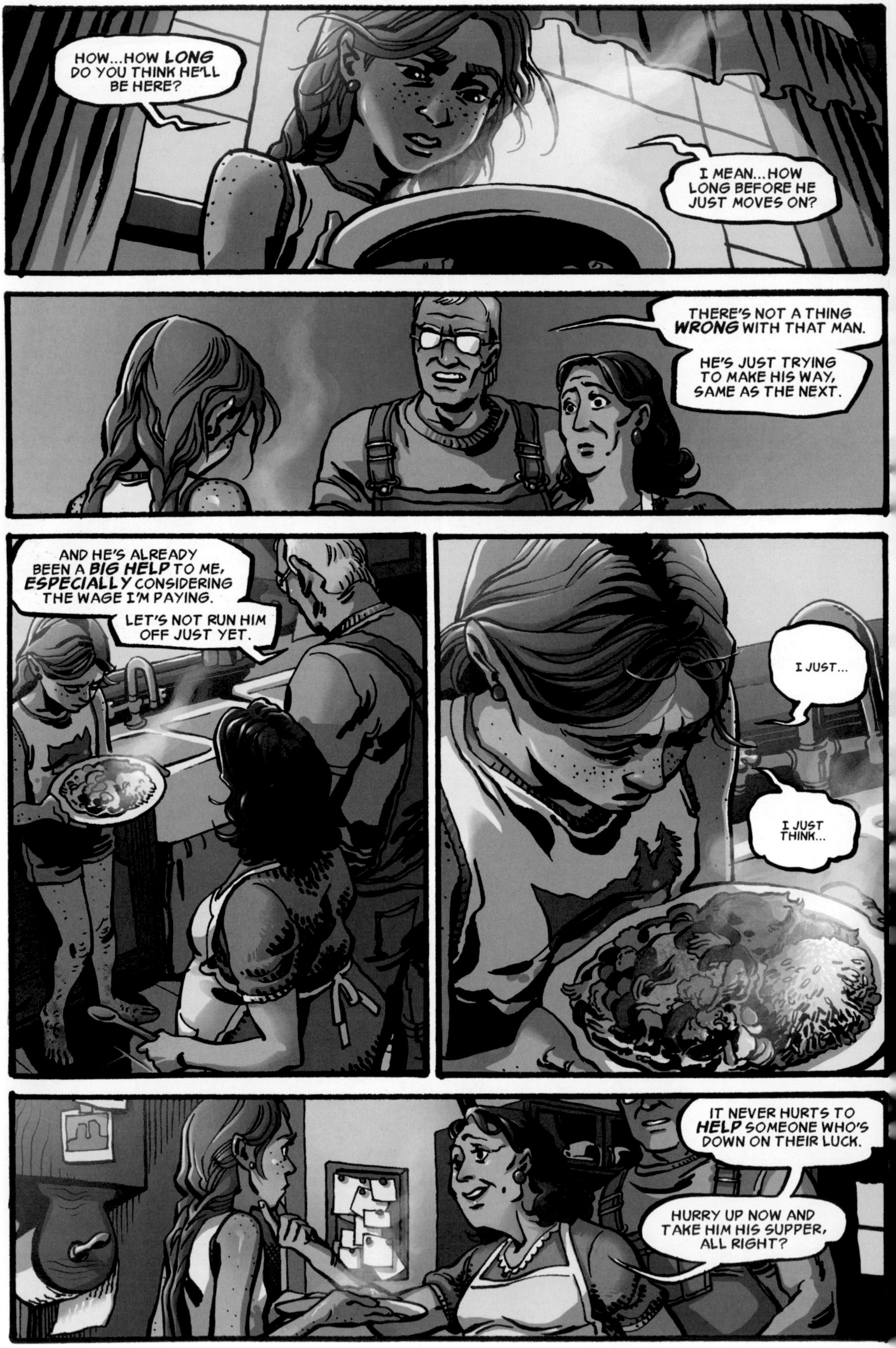
HOW...HOW **LONG** DO YOU THINK HE'LL BE HERE?
I MEAN...HOW LONG BEFORE HE JUST MOVES ON?
THERE'S NOT A THING **WRONG** WITH THAT MAN.
HE'S JUST TRYING TO MAKE HIS WAY, SAME AS THE NEXT.
AND HE'S ALREADY BEEN A **BIG HELP** TO ME, **ESPECIALLY** CONSIDERING THE WAGE I'M PAYING.
LET'S NOT RUN HIM OFF JUST YET.
I JUST...
I JUST THINK...
IT NEVER HURTS TO **HELP** SOMEONE WHO'S DOWN ON THEIR LUCK.
HURRY UP NOW AND TAKE HIM HIS SUPPER, ALL RIGHT?

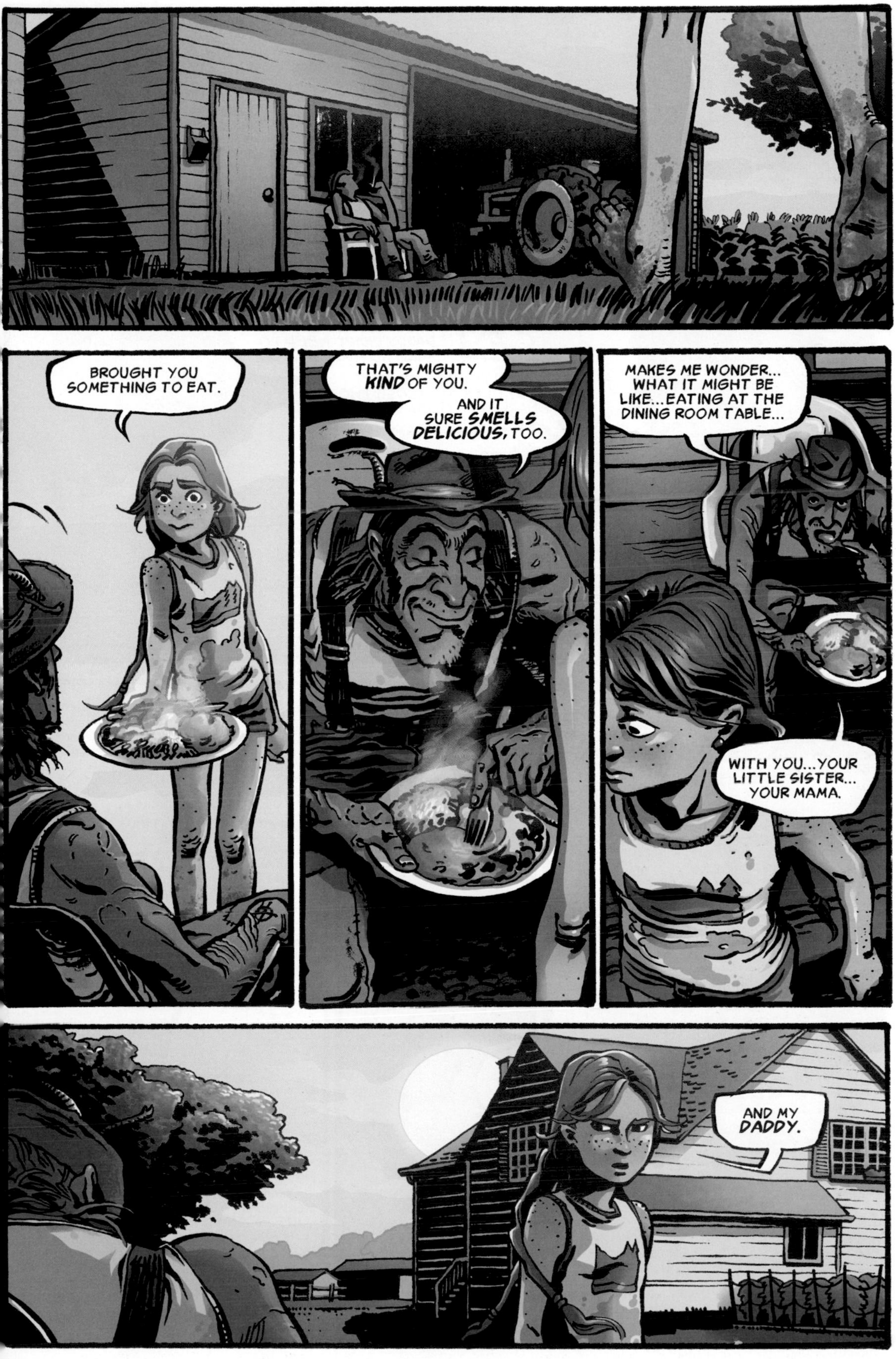
BROUGHT YOU SOMETHING TO EAT.
THAT'S MIGHTY KIND OF YOU.
AND IT SURE SMELLS DELICIOUS, TOO.
MAKES ME WONDER... WHAT IT MIGHT BE LIKE...EATING AT THE DINING ROOM TABLE...
WITH YOU...YOUR LITTLE SISTER... YOUR MAMA.
AND MY DADDY.

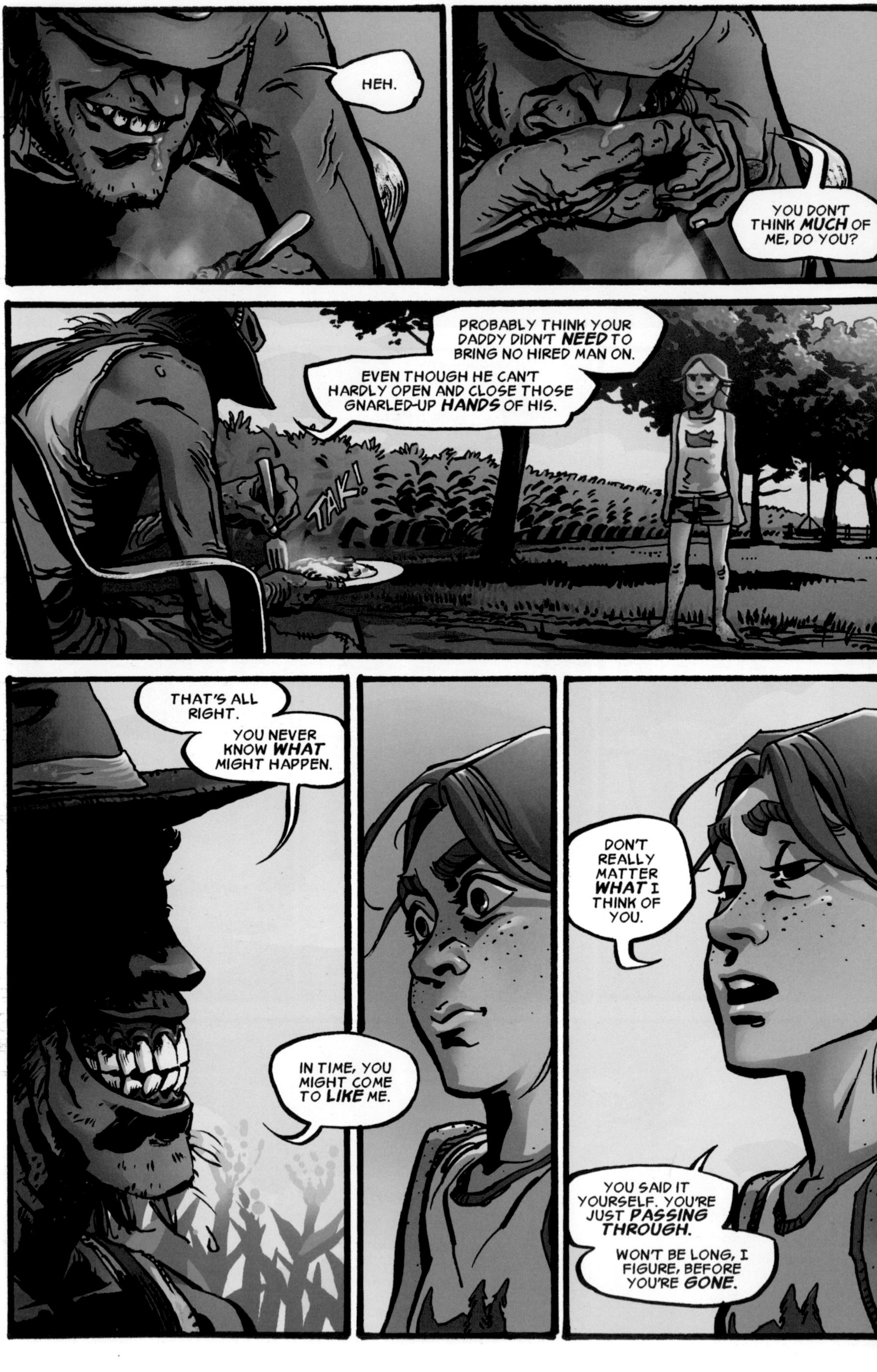
HEH.
YOU DON'T THINK MUCH OF ME, DO YOU?
PROBABLY THINK YOUR DADDY DIDN'T NEED TO BRING NO HIRED MAN ON.
EVEN THOUGH HE CAN'T HARDLY OPEN AND CLOSE THOSE GNARLED-UP HANDS OF HIS.
TAK!
THAT'S ALL RIGHT.
YOU NEVER KNOW WHAT MIGHT HAPPEN.
IN TIME, YOU MIGHT COME TO LIKE ME.
DON'T REALLY MATTER WHAT I THINK OF YOU.
YOU SAID IT YOURSELF. YOU'RE JUST PASSING THROUGH.
WON'T BE LONG, I FIGURE, BEFORE YOU'RE GONE.

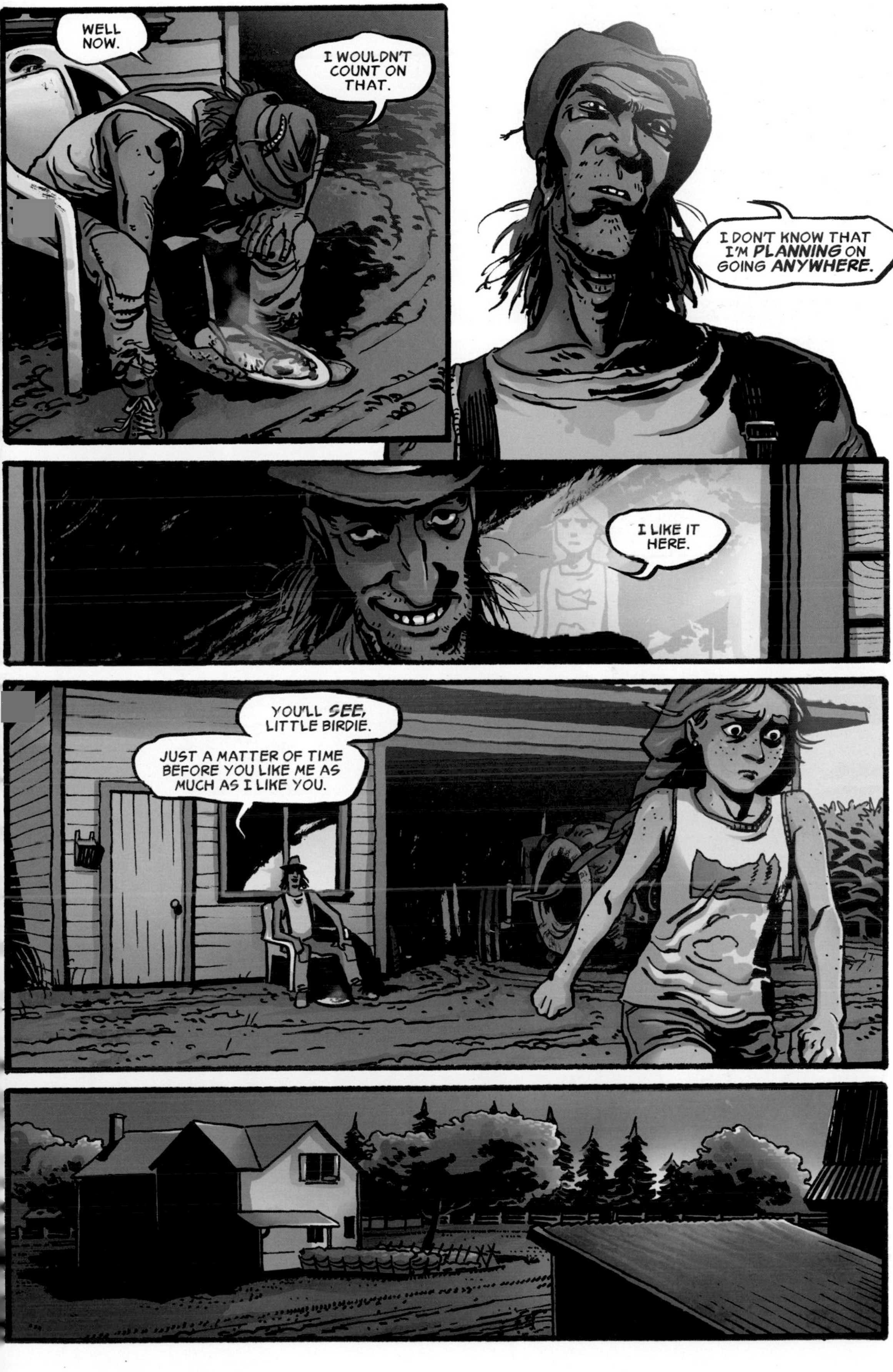
WELL NOW.
I WOULDN'T COUNT ON THAT.
I DON'T KNOW THAT I'M PLANNING ON GOING ANYWHERE.
I LIKE IT HERE.
YOU'LL SEE, LITTLE BIRDIE.
JUST A MATTER OF TIME BEFORE YOU LIKE ME AS MUCH AS I LIKE YOU.

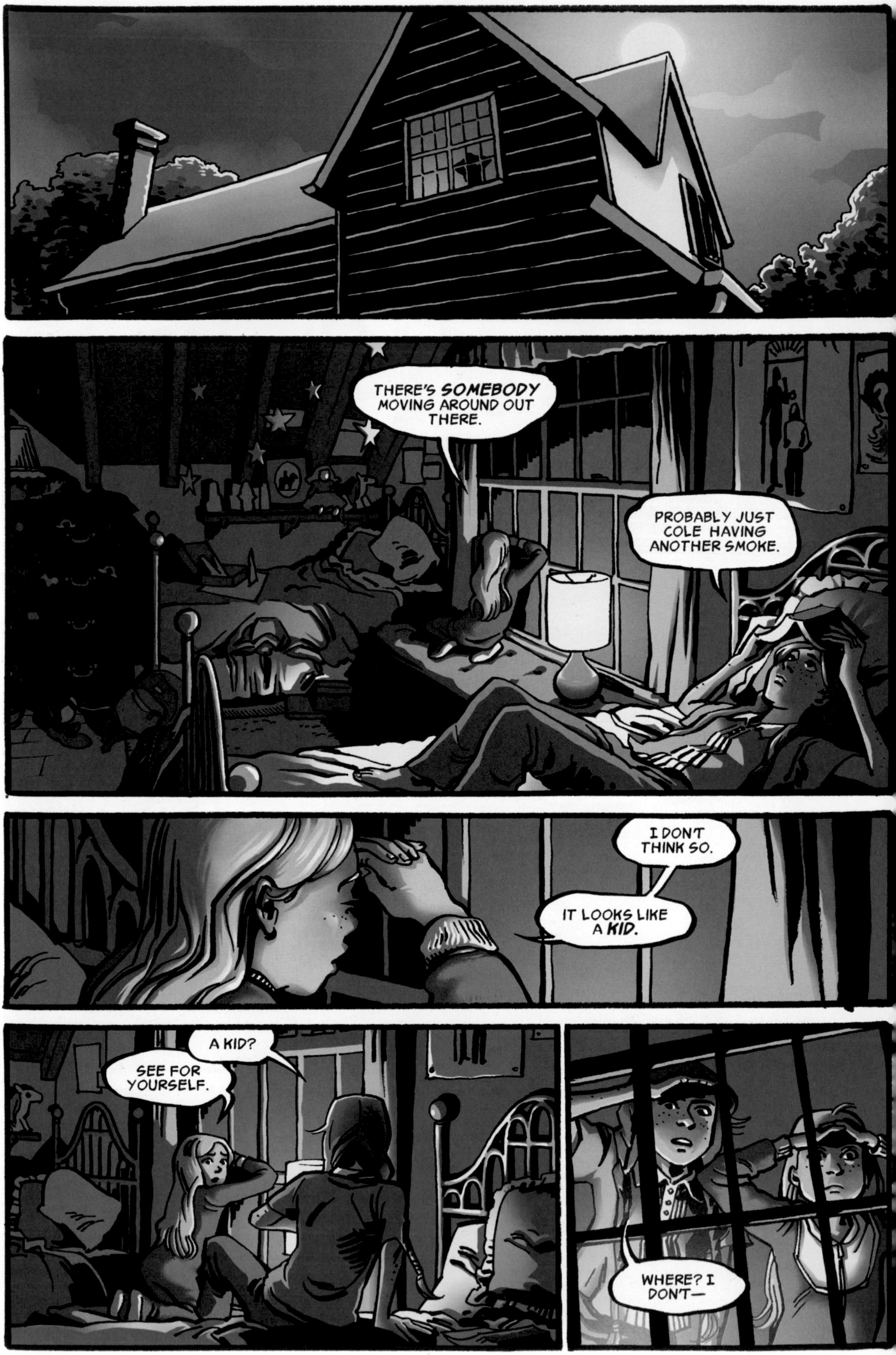
THERE'S SOMEBODY MOVING AROUND OUT THERE.
PROBABLY JUST COLE HAVING ANOTHER SMOKE.
I DON'T THINK SO.
IT LOOKS LIKE A KID.
A KID?
SEE FOR YOURSELF.
WHERE? I DON'T—

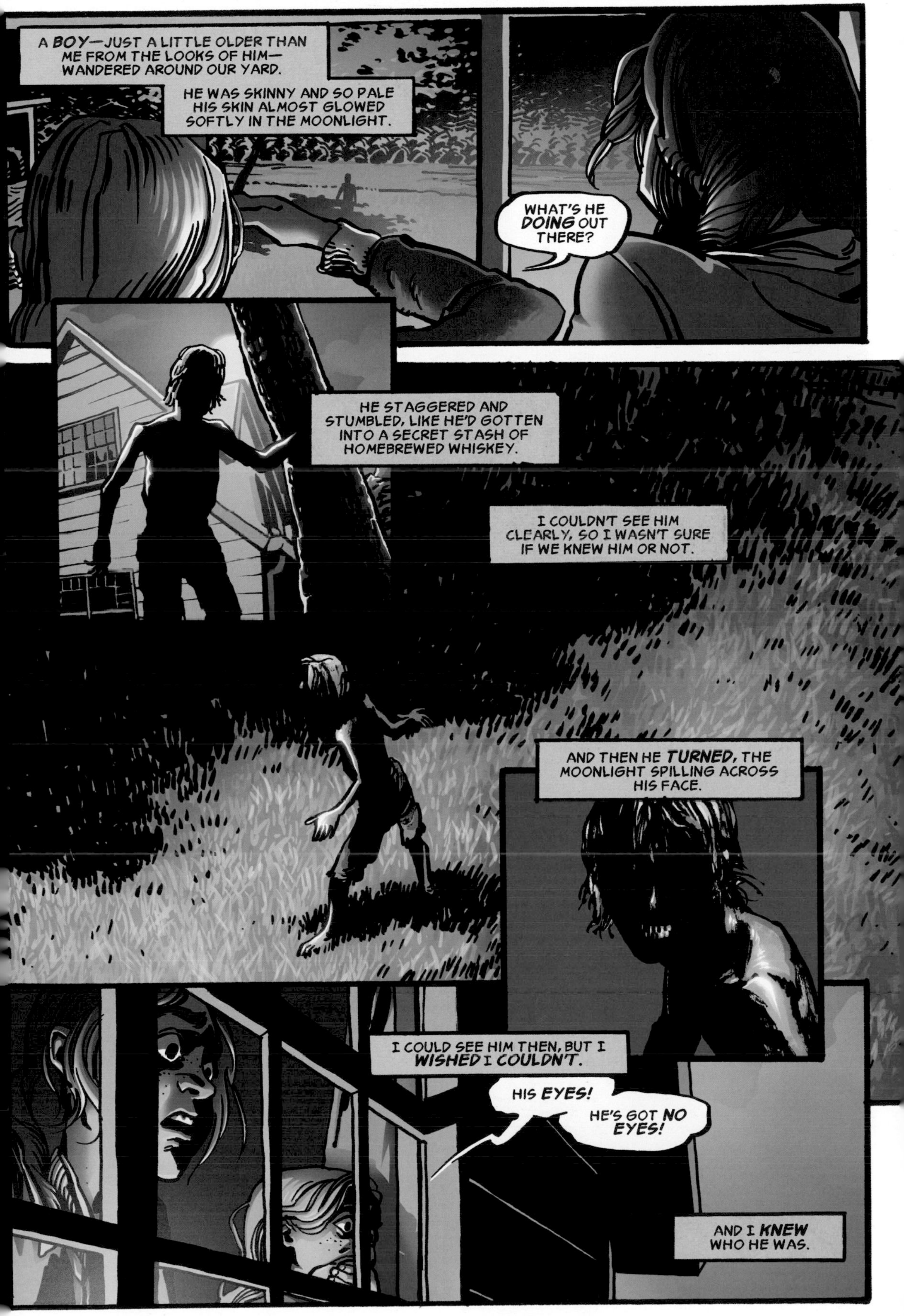
A BOY—JUST A LITTLE OLDER THAN ME FROM THE LOOKS OF HIM—WANDERED AROUND OUR YARD.
HE WAS SKINNY AND SO PALE HIS SKIN ALMOST GLOWED SOFTLY IN THE MOONLIGHT.
WHAT'S HE DOING OUT THERE?
HE STAGGERED AND STUMBLED, LIKE HE'D GOTTEN INTO A SECRET STASH OF HOMEBREWED WHISKEY.
I COULDN'T SEE HIM CLEARLY, SO I WASN'T SURE IF WE KNEW HIM OR NOT.
AND THEN HE TURNED, THE MOONLIGHT SPILLING ACROSS HIS FACE.
I COULD SEE HIM THEN, BUT I WISHED I COULDN'T.
HIS EYES!
HE'S GOT NO EYES!
AND I KNEW WHO HE WAS.

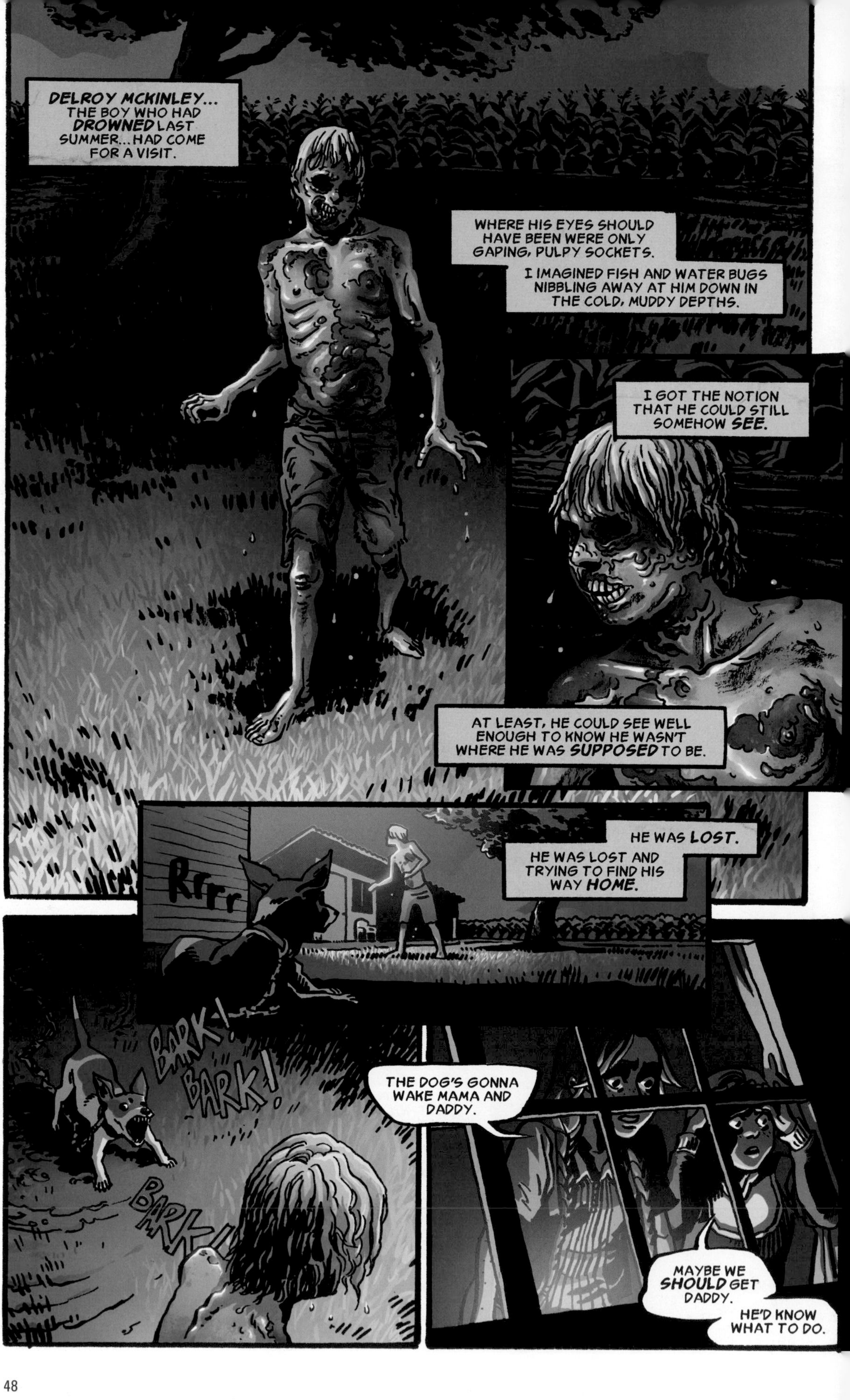
DELROY MCKINLEY... THE BOY WHO HAD DROWNED LAST SUMMER... HAD COME FOR A VISIT.
WHERE HIS EYES SHOULD HAVE BEEN WERE ONLY GAPING, PULPY SOCKETS.
I IMAGINED FISH AND WATER BUGS NIBBLING AWAY AT HIM DOWN IN THE COLD, MUDDY DEPTHS.
I GOT THE NOTION THAT HE COULD STILL SOMEHOW SEE.
AT LEAST, HE COULD SEE WELL ENOUGH TO KNOW HE WASN'T WHERE HE WAS SUPPOSED TO BE.
HE WAS LOST.
HE WAS LOST AND TRYING TO FIND HIS WAY HOME.
Rrrr
BARK! BARK!
BARK!
THE DOG'S GONNA WAKE MAMA AND DADDY.
MAYBE WE SHOULD GET DADDY.
HE'D KNOW WHAT TO DO.

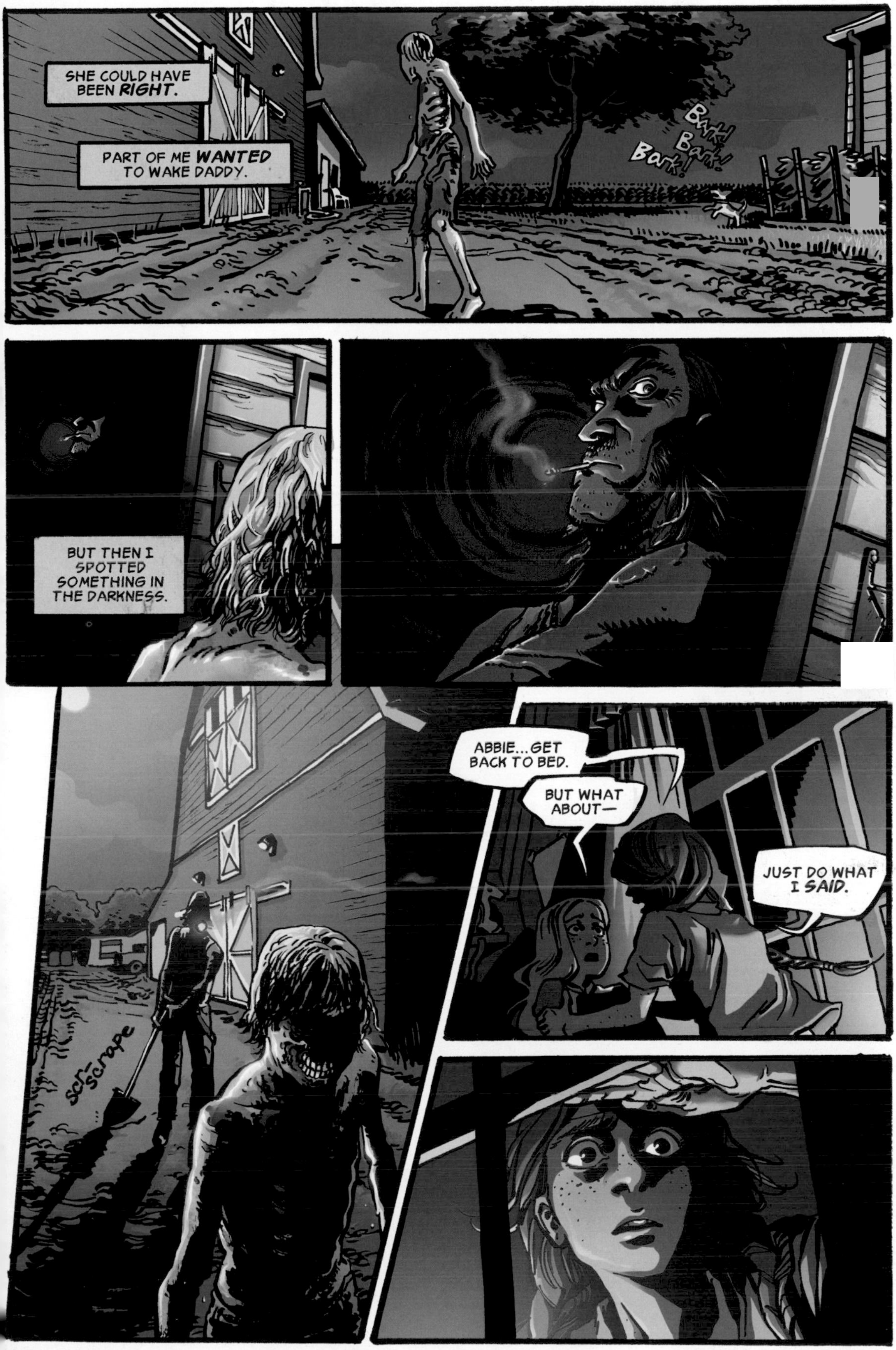
SHE COULD HAVE BEEN RIGHT.
PART OF ME WANTED TO WAKE DADDY.
Bark! Bark! Bark!
BUT THEN I SPOTTED SOMETHING IN THE DARKNESS.
scr- scrape
ABBIE...GET BACK TO BED.
BUT WHAT ABOUT—
JUST DO WHAT I SAID.

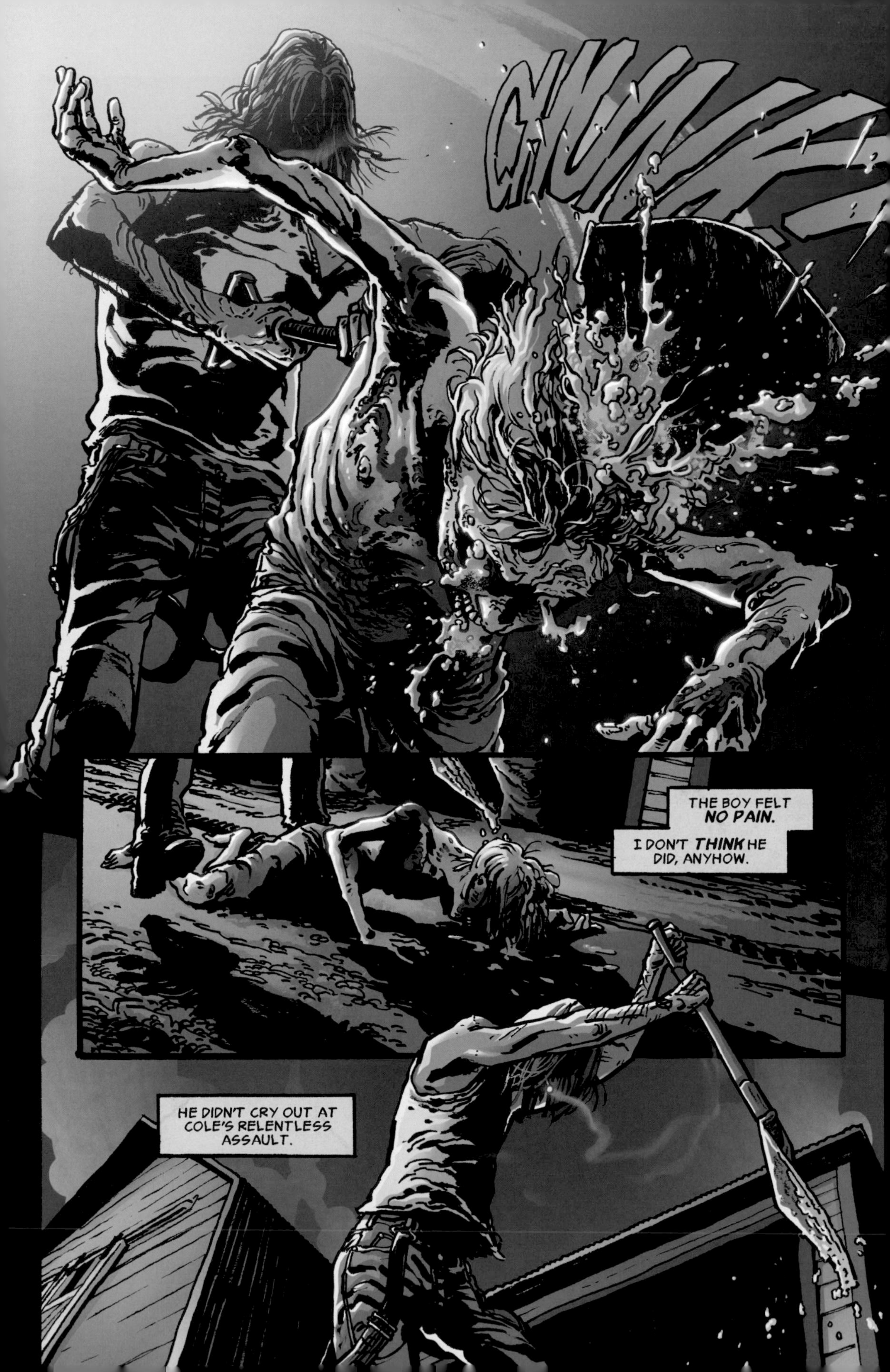
THE BOY FELT **NO PAIN.**
I DON'T ***THINK*** HE DID, ANYHOW.
HE DIDN'T CRY OUT AT COLE'S RELENTLESS ASSAULT.

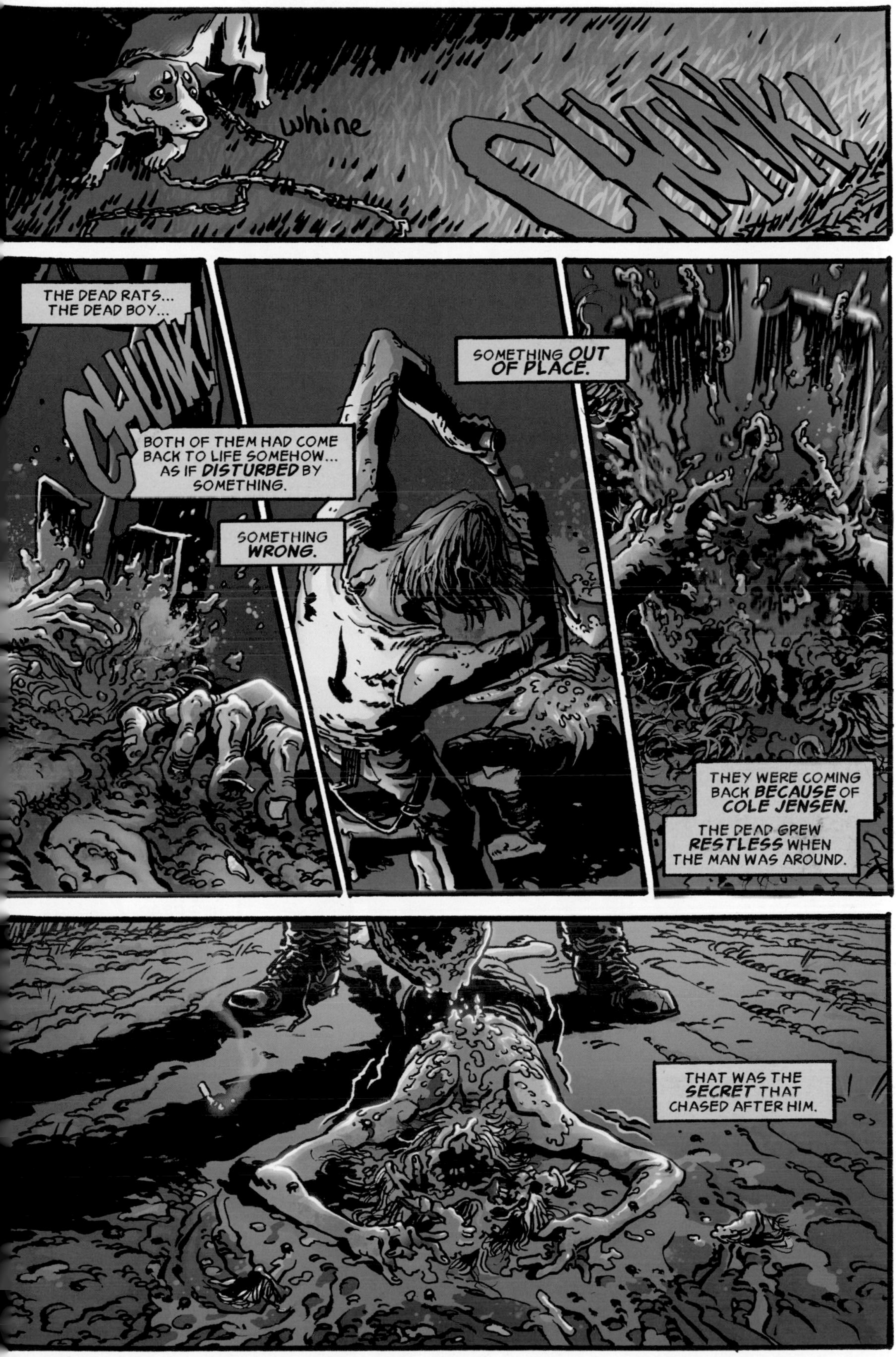
whine
CHUNK!
THE DEAD RATS... THE DEAD BOY...
CHUNK!
BOTH OF THEM HAD COME BACK TO LIFE SOMEHOW... AS IF DISTURBED BY SOMETHING.
SOMETHING WRONG.
SOMETHING OUT OF PLACE.
THEY WERE COMING BACK BECAUSE OF COLE JENSEN.
THE DEAD GREW RESTLESS WHEN THE MAN WAS AROUND.
THAT WAS THE SECRET THAT CHASED AFTER HIM.

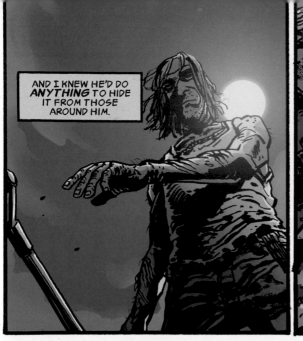

AND I KNEW HE'D DO *ANYTHING* TO HIDE IT FROM THOSE AROUND HIM.

KILLING THE BOY, THAT WAS HOW COLE KEPT THE TRUTH HIDDEN.

HE'D DO THE SAME TO ME...OR TO MY FAMILY... IF HE NEEDED TO.

WHAT IS IT? WHAT'S *HAPPENING?*

NOTHING. THE BOY.... HE'S *DEAD.*

I SHOULD HAVE SAID THE BOY WAS *GONE*—NOT DEAD—BUT THE *TRUTH* SORT OF SLIPPED OUT.

WHEN I SPOKE AGAIN, THOUGH, I FOUND THE WHEREWITHAL TO *LIE.*

WE'RE GOING TO BE *FINE.*

JUST *FINE.*

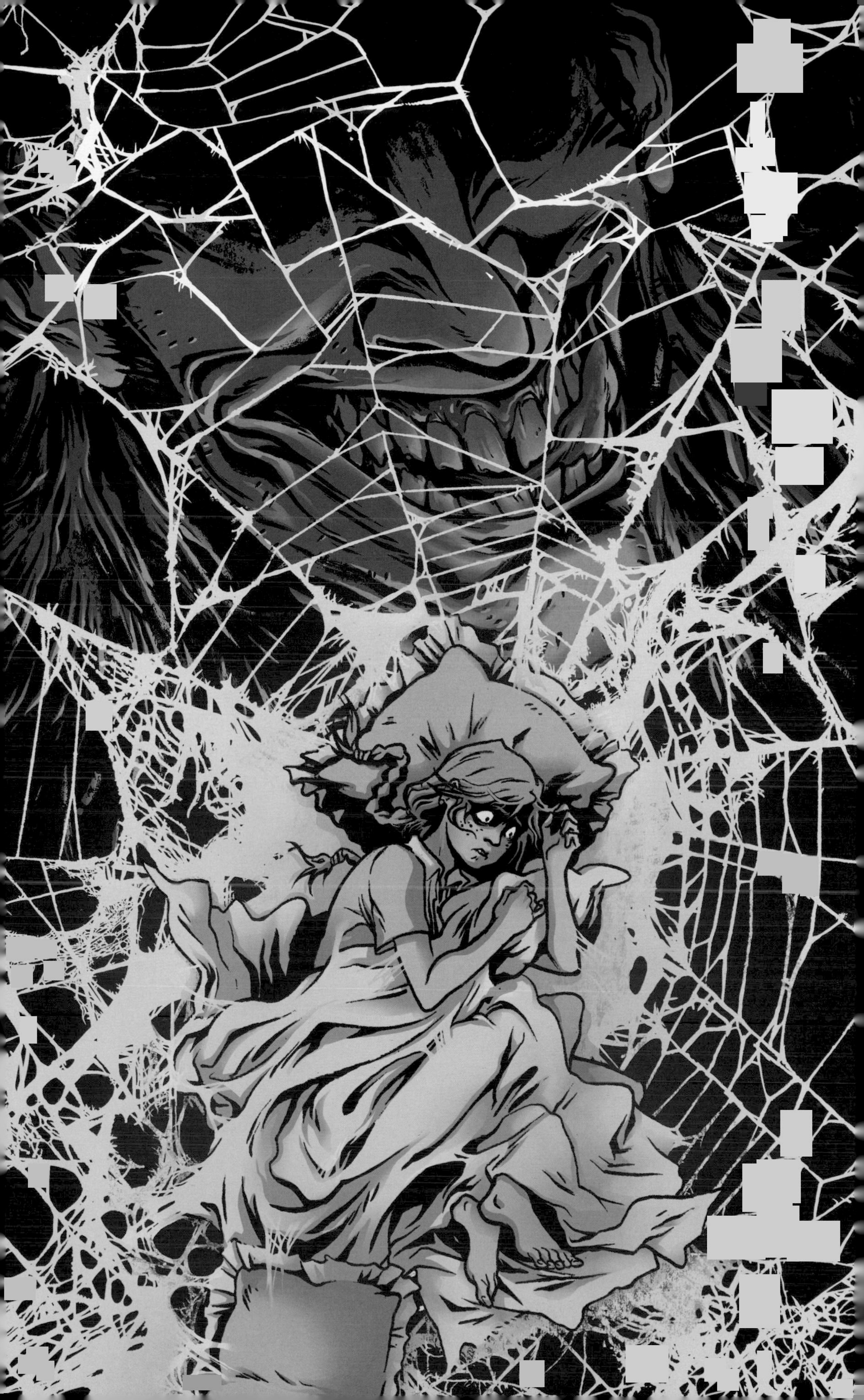

THE DAYS TURNED TO WEEKS... AND THE HIRED MAN SHOWED NO SIGNS OF LEAVING.

WORSE, I COULD TELL MY FATHER GENUINELY *LIKED* THE MAN.

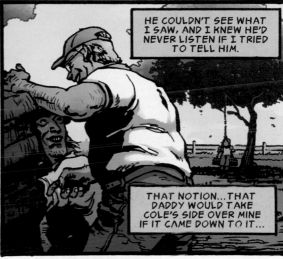

HE COULDN'T SEE WHAT I SAW, AND I KNEW HE'D NEVER LISTEN IF I TRIED TO TELL HIM.

THAT NOTION...THAT DADDY WOULD TAKE COLE'S SIDE OVER MINE IF IT CAME DOWN TO IT...

...IT *NAGGED* AT ME.

LIKE *RATS*...CHEWING AWAY AT MY INSIDES.

G'g'— WUNK!

YEEEEAAAAARRRGHH!

GRRRAAA!

SGLLK!

NNGGEEEAAAAHH!

I SILENTLY WISHED FOR THE TRACTOR'S ENGINE TO SPRING TO LIFE...

...TO CLAMP DOWN ON COLE AND YANK HIM INTO THE ENGINE TO BE MULCHED AMONG THE GEARS.

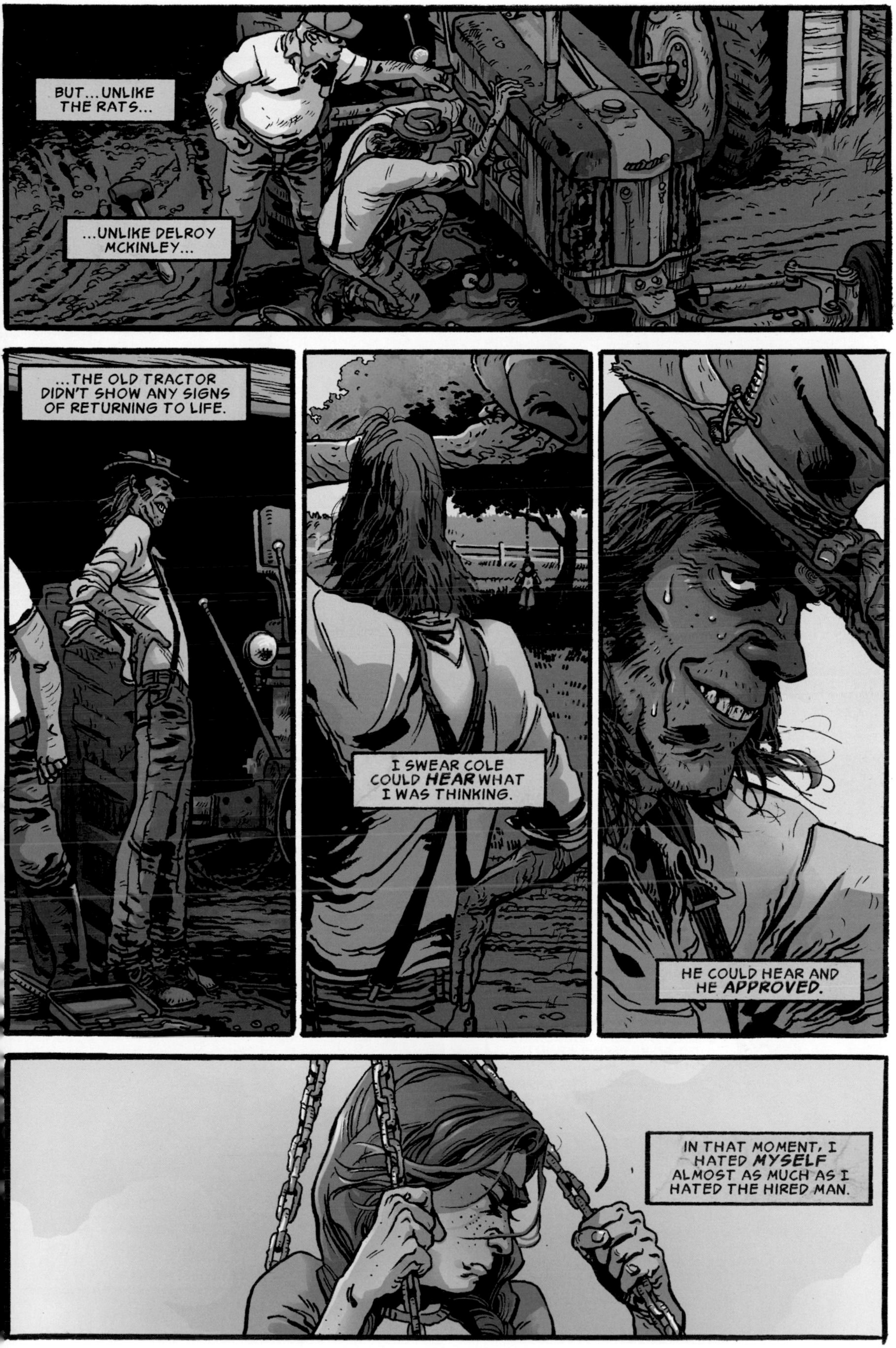
BUT...UNLIKE THE RATS...
...UNLIKE DELROY MCKINLEY...
...THE OLD TRACTOR DIDN'T SHOW ANY SIGNS OF RETURNING TO LIFE.
I SWEAR COLE COULD HEAR WHAT I WAS THINKING.
HE COULD HEAR AND HE APPROVED.
IN THAT MOMENT, I HATED MYSELF ALMOST AS MUCH AS I HATED THE HIRED MAN.

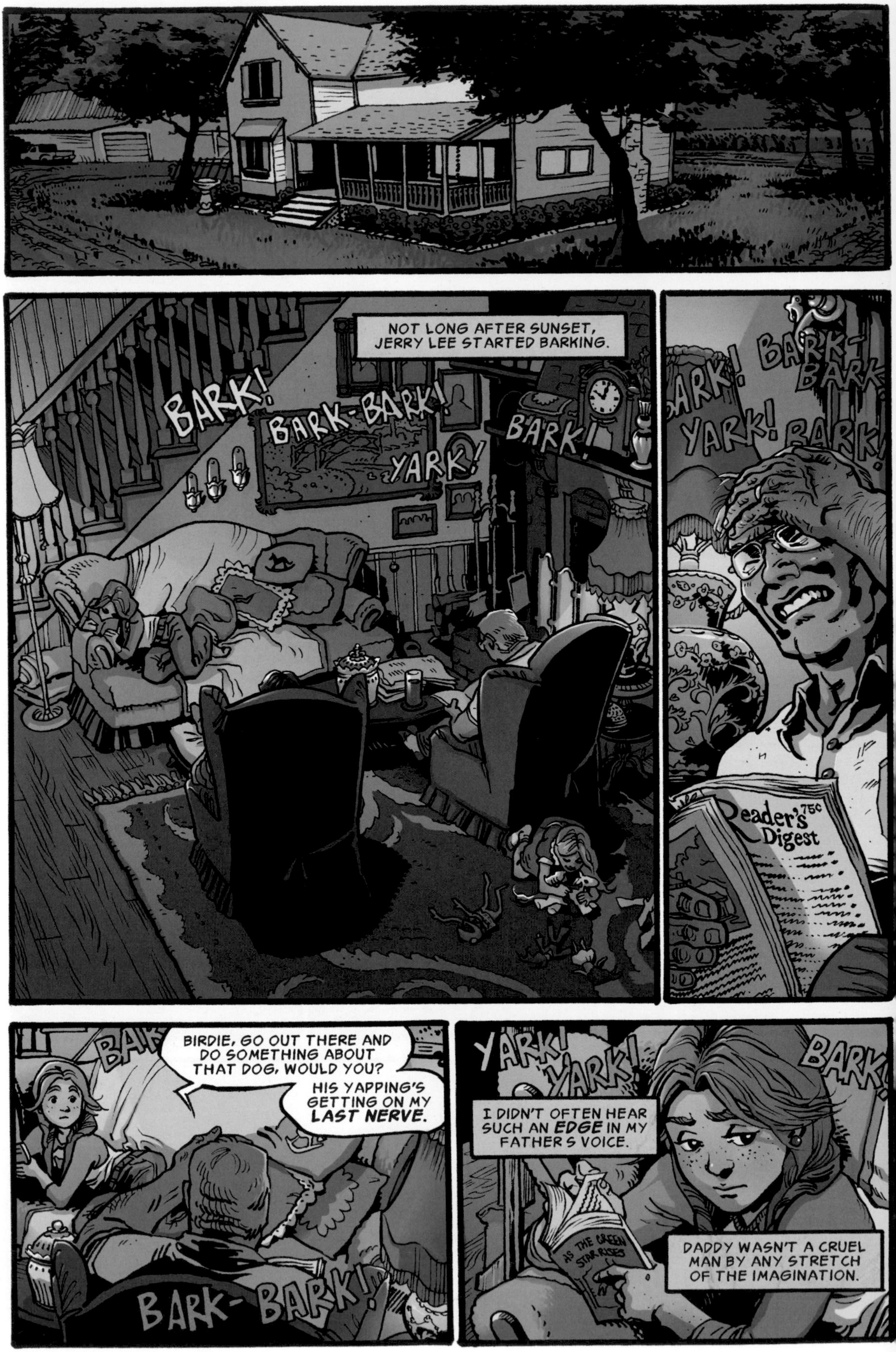
NOT LONG AFTER SUNSET, JERRY LEE STARTED BARKING.
BARK!
BARK-BARK!
YARK!
BARK!
BARK! BARK-BARK!
YARK! BARK!
Reader's 75¢ Digest
BIRDIE, GO OUT THERE AND DO SOMETHING ABOUT THAT DOG, WOULD YOU?
HIS YAPPING'S GETTING ON MY **LAST NERVE**.
BARK-BARK!
YARK! YARK!
BARK!
I DIDN'T OFTEN HEAR SUCH AN *EDGE* IN MY FATHER'S VOICE.
AS THE GREEN STAR RISES
DADDY WASN'T A CRUEL MAN BY ANY STRETCH OF THE IMAGINATION.

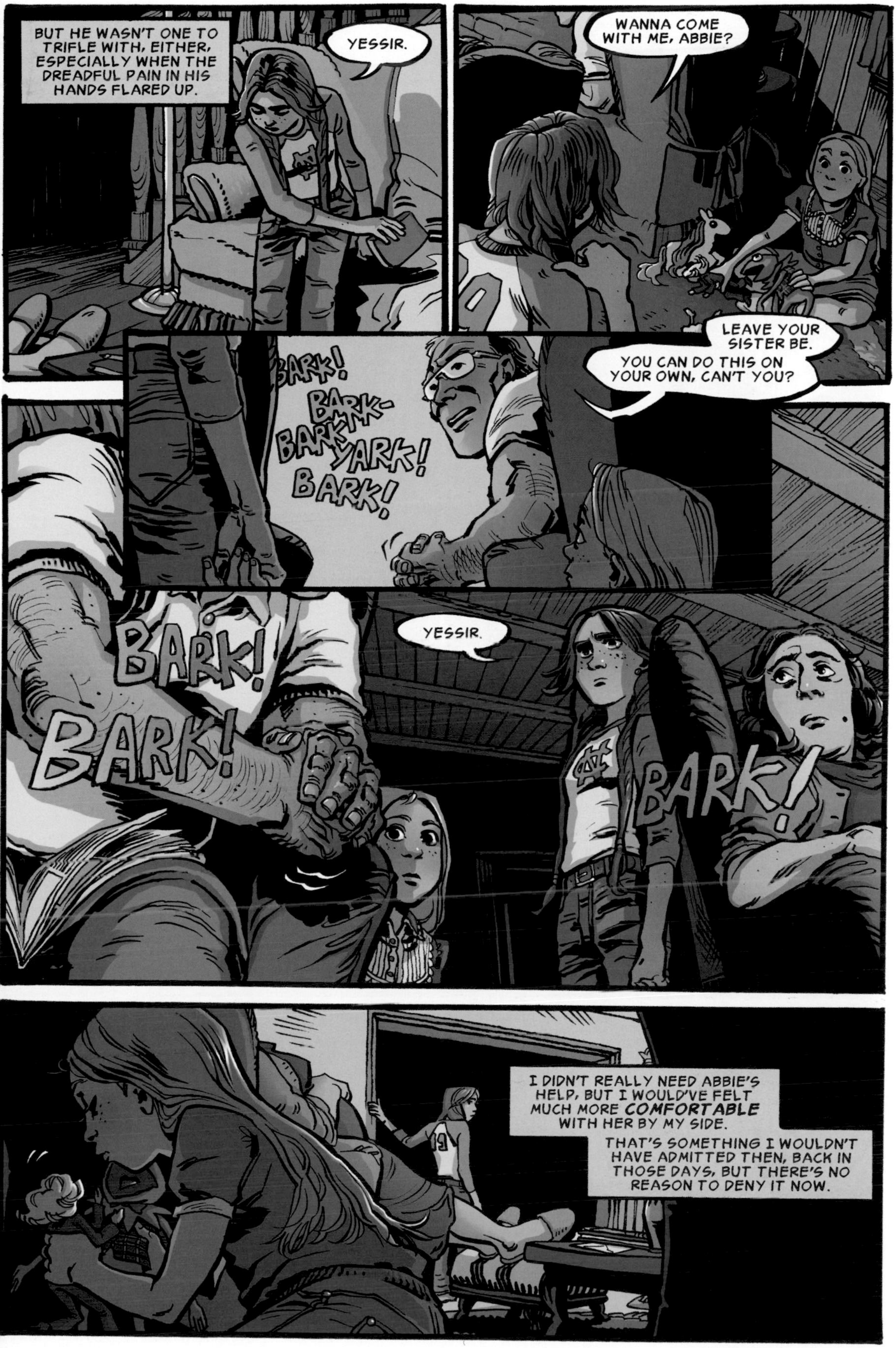
BUT HE WASN'T ONE TO TRIFLE WITH, EITHER, ESPECIALLY WHEN THE DREADFUL PAIN IN HIS HANDS FLARED UP.
YESSIR.
WANNA COME WITH ME, ABBIE?
LEAVE YOUR SISTER BE.
YOU CAN DO THIS ON YOUR OWN, CAN'T YOU?
BARK!
BARK-BARK
YARK!
BARK!
YESSIR.
BARK!
BARK!
BARK!
I DIDN'T REALLY NEED ABBIE'S HELP, BUT I WOULD'VE FELT MUCH MORE COMFORTABLE WITH HER BY MY SIDE.
THAT'S SOMETHING I WOULDN'T HAVE ADMITTED THEN, BACK IN THOSE DAYS, BUT THERE'S NO REASON TO DENY IT NOW.

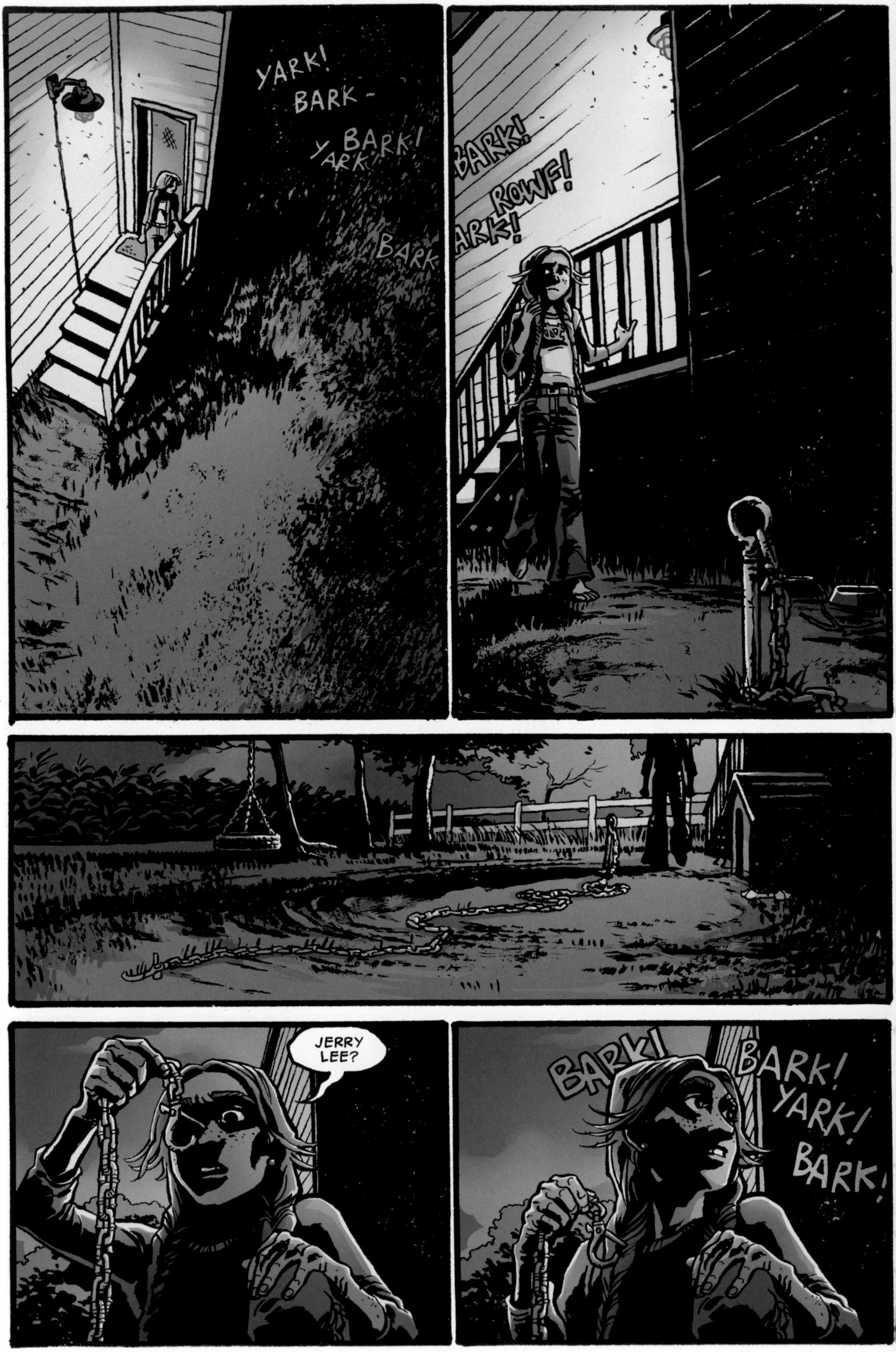
YARK!
BARK-
BARK!
YARK!
BARK
BARK!
ROWF!
ARK!
JERRY LEE?
BARK!
BARK!
YARK!
BARK!

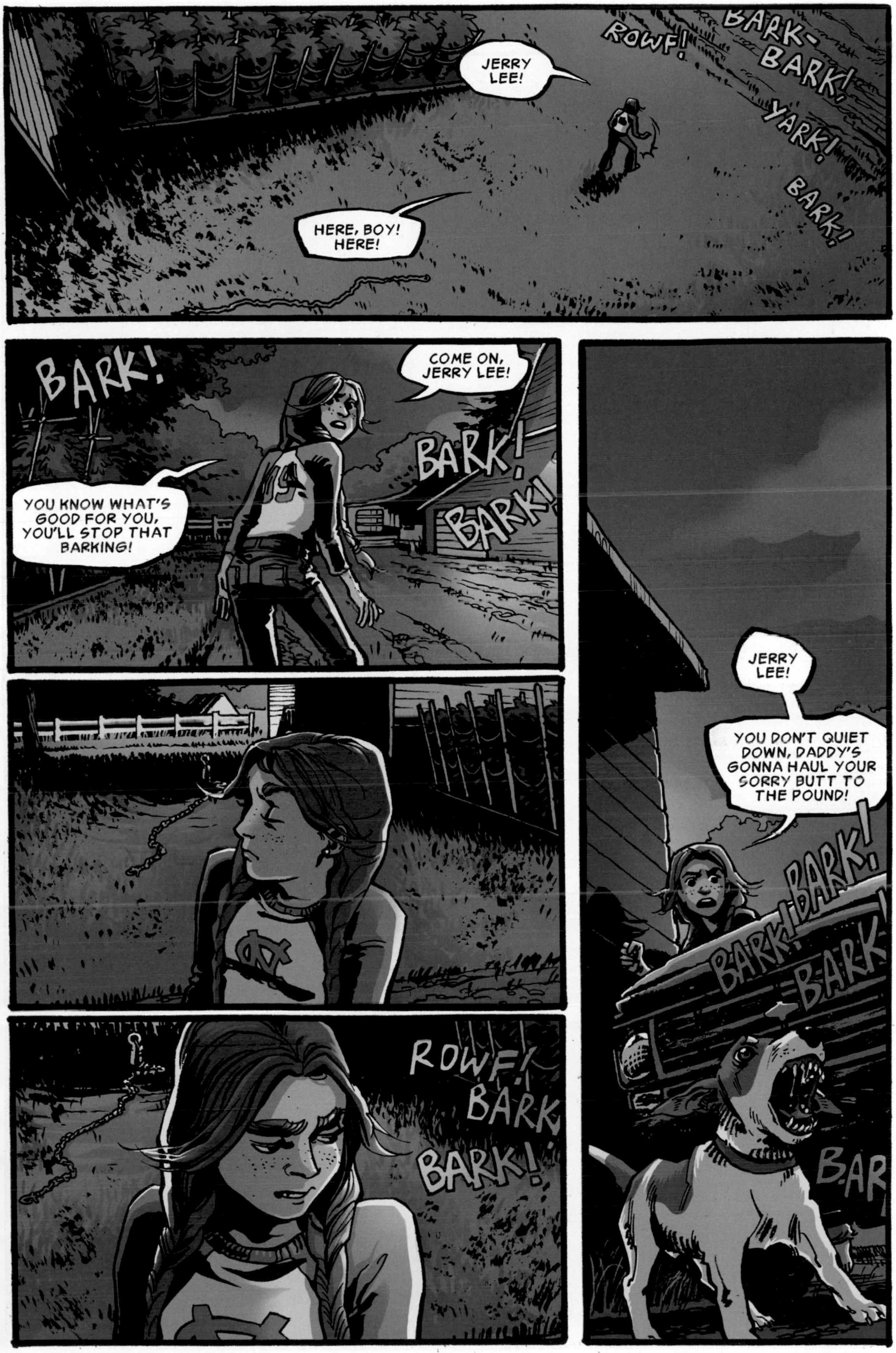
JERRY LEE!
ROWF!
BARK-BARK!
YARK!
BARK!
HERE, BOY! HERE!
BARK!
COME ON, JERRY LEE!
BARK!
BARK!
YOU KNOW WHAT'S GOOD FOR YOU, YOU'LL STOP THAT BARKING!
ROWF!
BARK
BARK!
JERRY LEE!
YOU DON'T QUIET DOWN, DADDY'S GONNA HAUL YOUR SORRY BUTT TO THE POUND!
BARK!
BARK!
BARK!
BARK
BAR

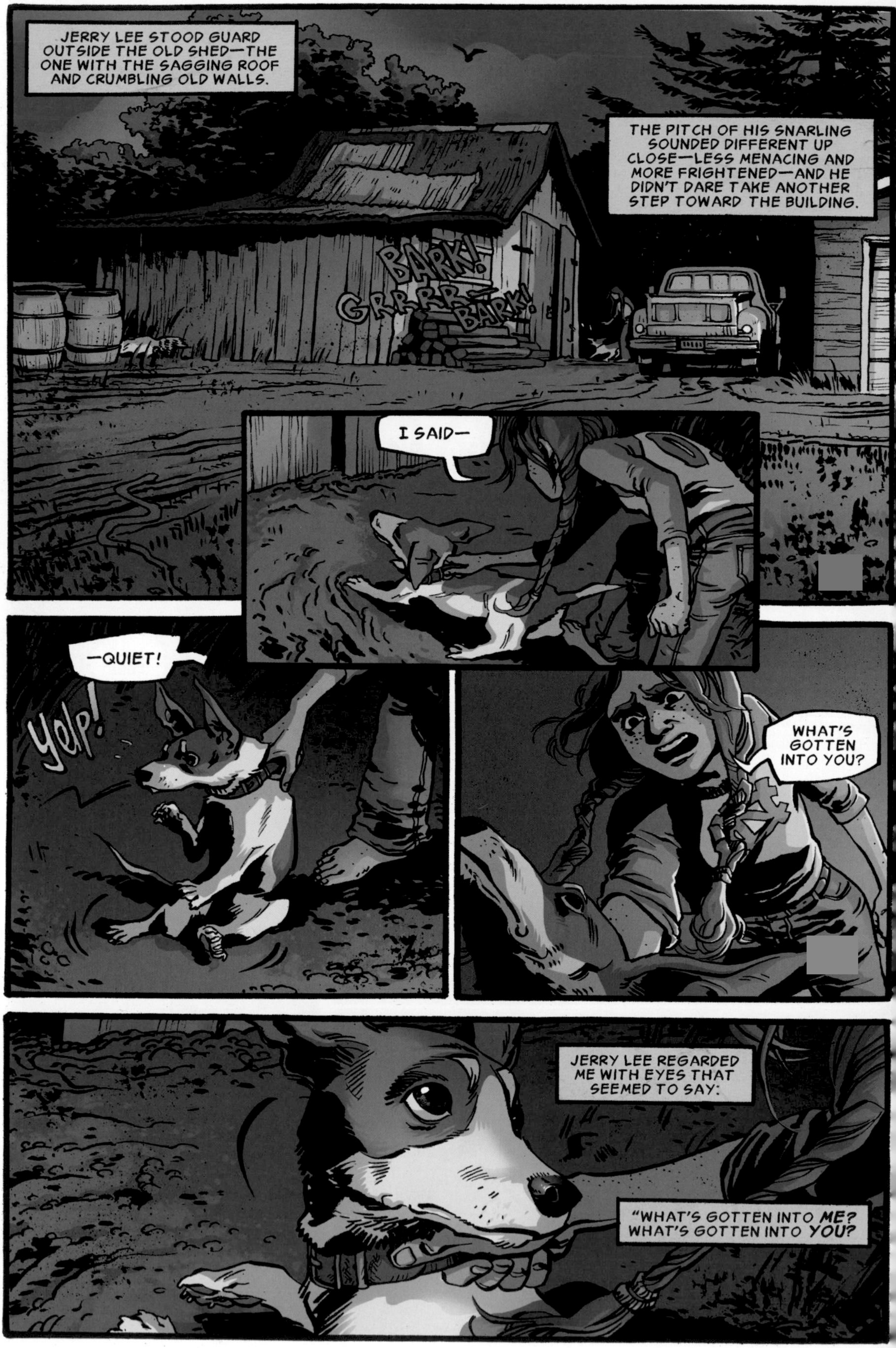
JERRY LEE STOOD GUARD OUTSIDE THE OLD SHED—THE ONE WITH THE SAGGING ROOF AND CRUMBLING OLD WALLS.
THE PITCH OF HIS SNARLING SOUNDED DIFFERENT UP CLOSE—LESS MENACING AND MORE FRIGHTENED—AND HE DIDN'T DARE TAKE ANOTHER STEP TOWARD THE BUILDING.
BARK!
GRRRRR—
BARK!
I SAID—
—QUIET!
YELP!
WHAT'S GOTTEN INTO YOU?
JERRY LEE REGARDED ME WITH EYES THAT SEEMED TO SAY:
"WHAT'S GOTTEN INTO *ME*? WHAT'S GOTTEN INTO *YOU*?

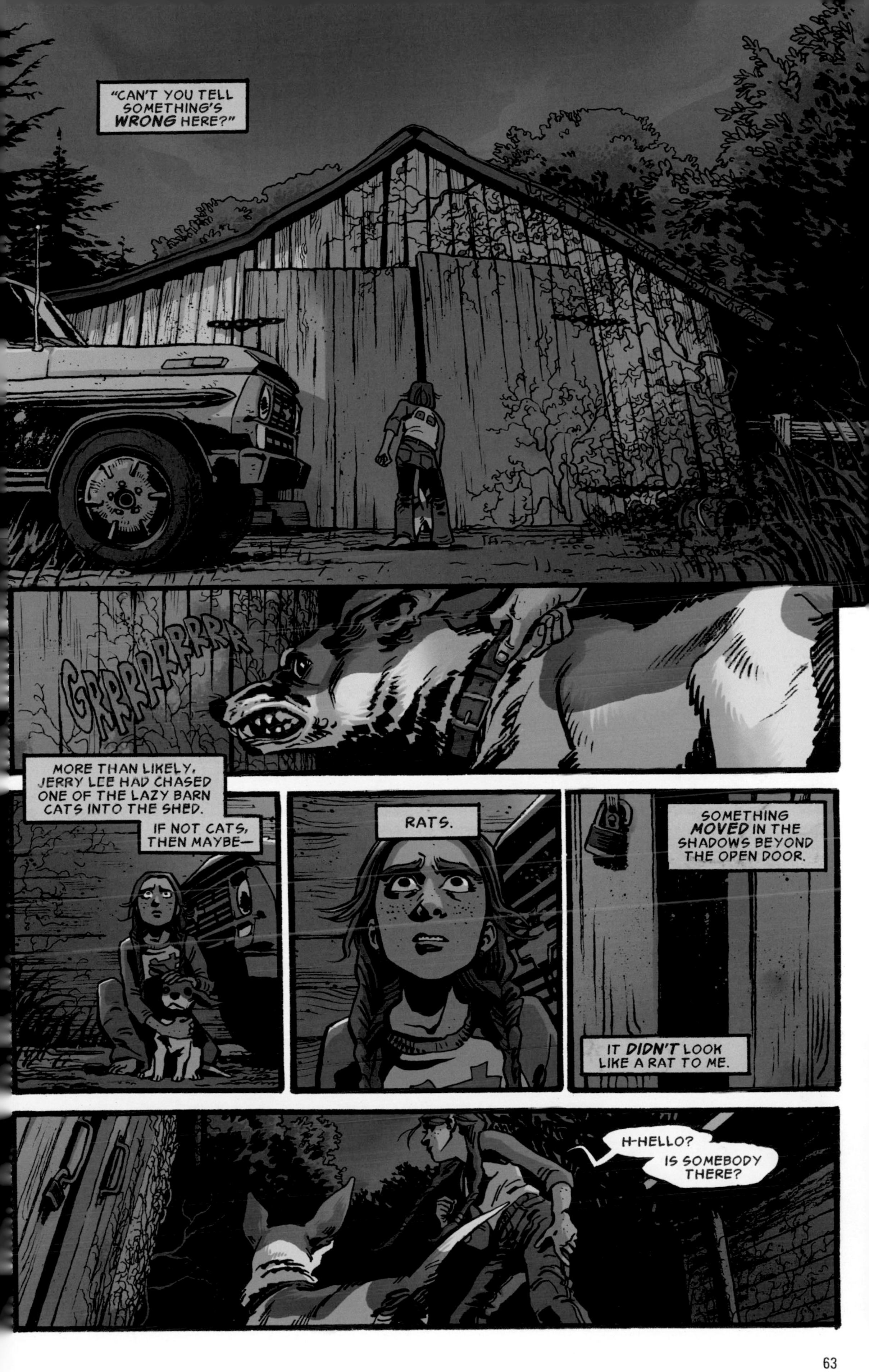
"CAN'T YOU TELL SOMETHING'S WRONG HERE?"
GRRRRRRRRA
MORE THAN LIKELY, JERRY LEE HAD CHASED ONE OF THE LAZY BARN CATS INTO THE SHED.
IF NOT CATS, THEN MAYBE—
RATS.
SOMETHING MOVED IN THE SHADOWS BEYOND THE OPEN DOOR.
IT DIDN'T LOOK LIKE A RAT TO ME.
H-HELLO?
IS SOMEBODY THERE?

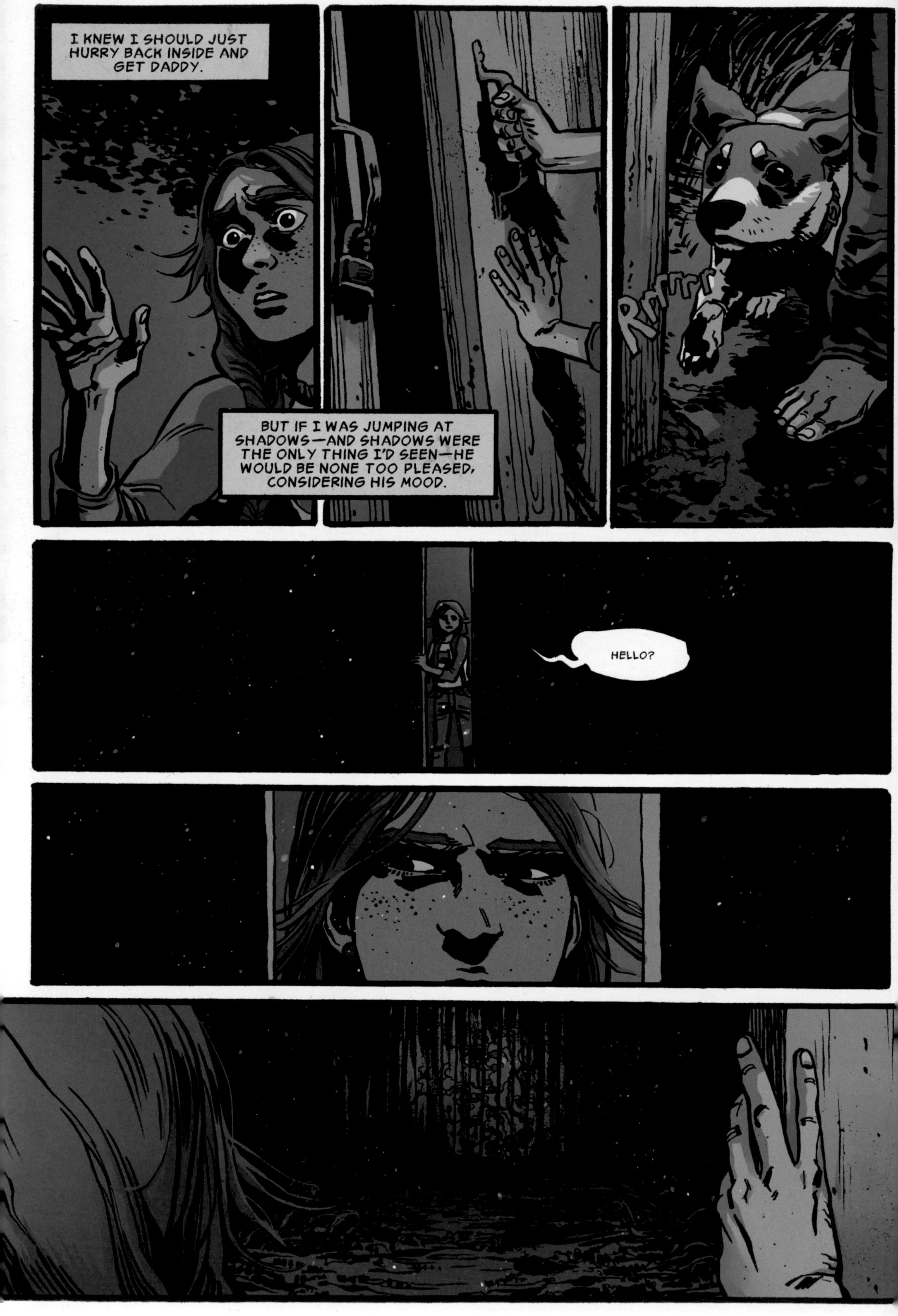
I KNEW I SHOULD JUST HURRY BACK INSIDE AND GET DADDY.
BUT IF I WAS JUMPING AT SHADOWS—AND SHADOWS WERE THE ONLY THING I'D SEEN—HE WOULD BE NONE TOO PLEASED, CONSIDERING HIS MOOD.
Rrrrrr
HELLO?

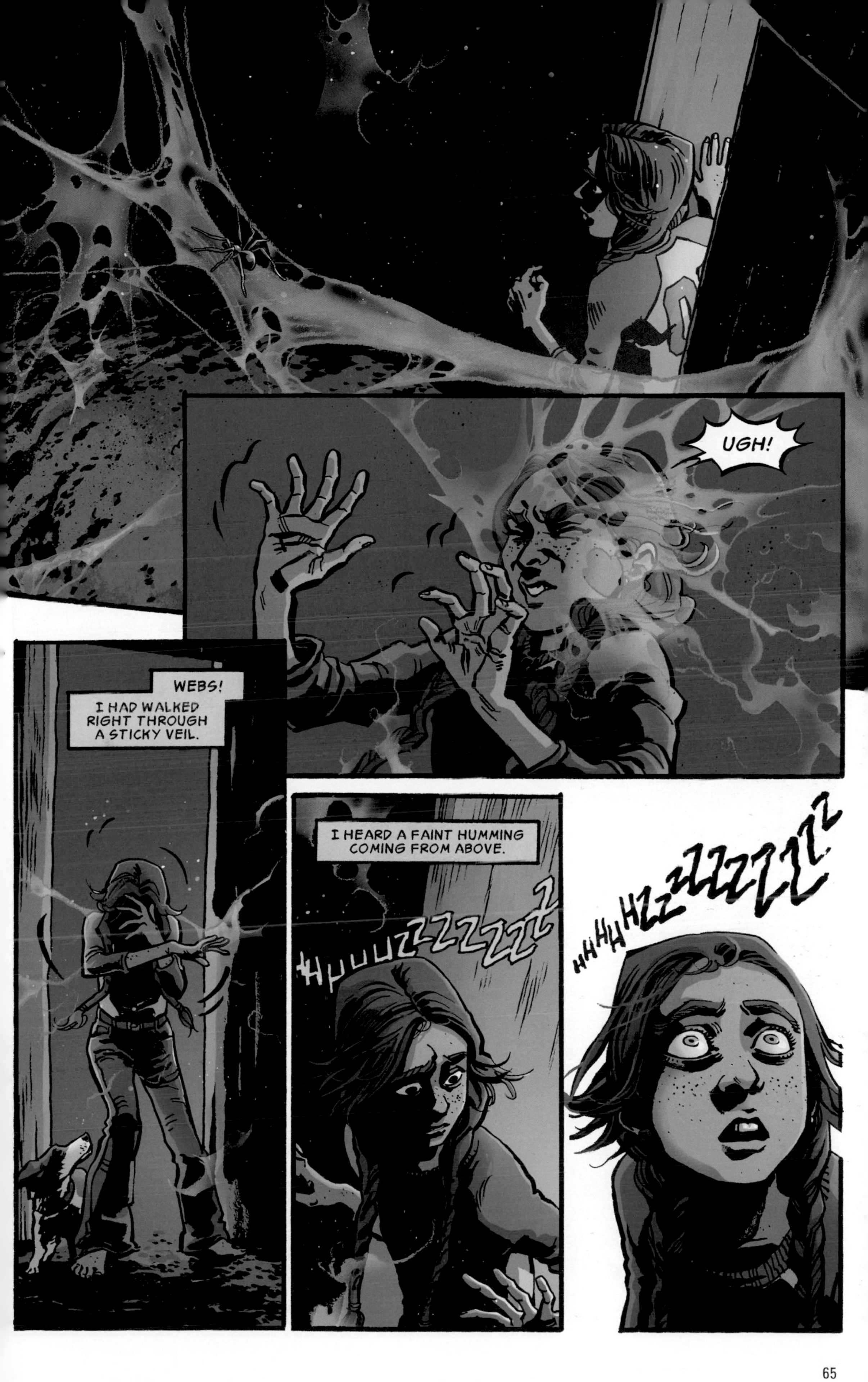
UGH!
WEBS!
I HAD WALKED RIGHT THROUGH A STICKY VEIL.
I HEARD A FAINT HUMMING COMING FROM ABOVE.
HMMMZZZZZZZZ
HHHHHZZZZZZZZZZZ

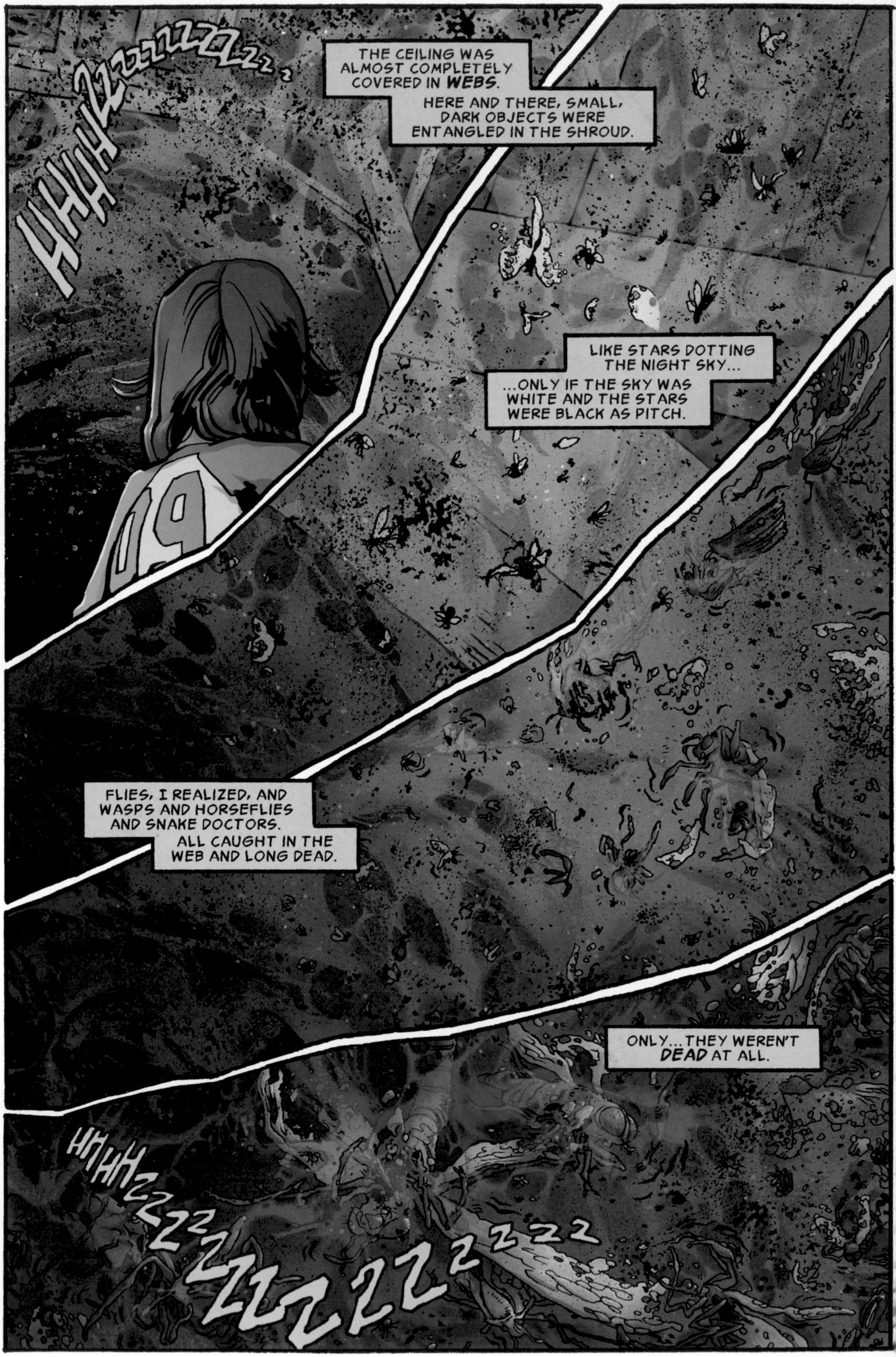
HHHHZZZZZZZZZZzzzz
THE CEILING WAS ALMOST COMPLETELY COVERED IN WEBS.
HERE AND THERE, SMALL, DARK OBJECTS WERE ENTANGLED IN THE SHROUD.
LIKE STARS DOTTING THE NIGHT SKY...
...ONLY IF THE SKY WAS WHITE AND THE STARS WERE BLACK AS PITCH.
FLIES, I REALIZED, AND WASPS AND HORSEFLIES AND SNAKE DOCTORS.
ALL CAUGHT IN THE WEB AND LONG DEAD.
ONLY...THEY WEREN'T DEAD AT ALL.
HHHHZZZZZZZZZZZZZZ

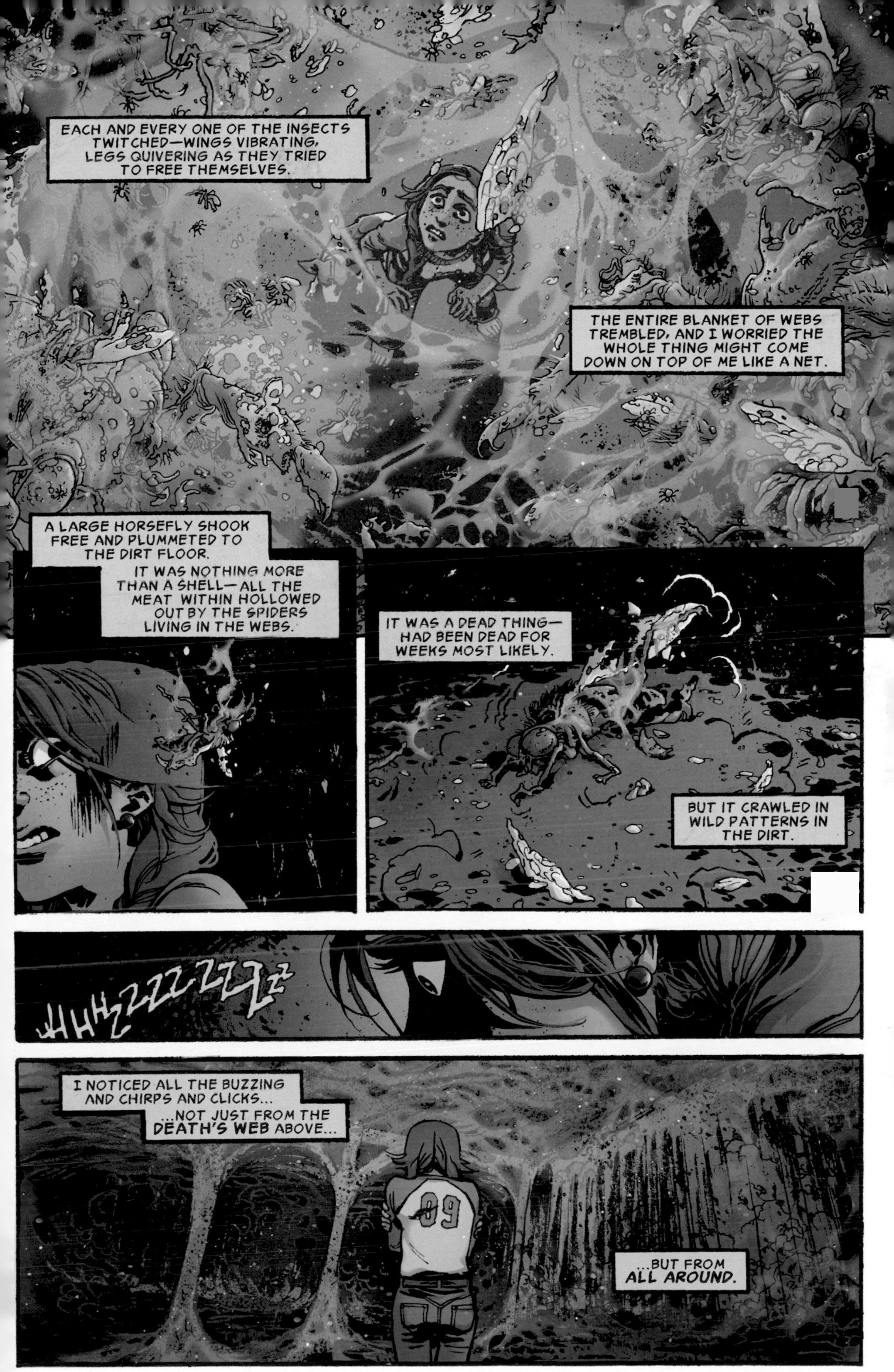
EACH AND EVERY ONE OF THE INSECTS TWITCHED—WINGS VIBRATING, LEGS QUIVERING AS THEY TRIED TO FREE THEMSELVES.
THE ENTIRE BLANKET OF WEBS TREMBLED, AND I WORRIED THE WHOLE THING MIGHT COME DOWN ON TOP OF ME LIKE A NET.
A LARGE HORSEFLY SHOOK FREE AND PLUMMETED TO THE DIRT FLOOR.
IT WAS NOTHING MORE THAN A SHELL—ALL THE MEAT WITHIN HOLLOWED OUT BY THE SPIDERS LIVING IN THE WEBS.
IT WAS A DEAD THING—HAD BEEN DEAD FOR WEEKS MOST LIKELY.
BUT IT CRAWLED IN WILD PATTERNS IN THE DIRT.
HHHzzzzzzzzz
I NOTICED ALL THE BUZZING AND CHIRPS AND CLICKS...
...NOT JUST FROM THE DEATH'S WEB ABOVE...
09
...BUT FROM ALL AROUND.

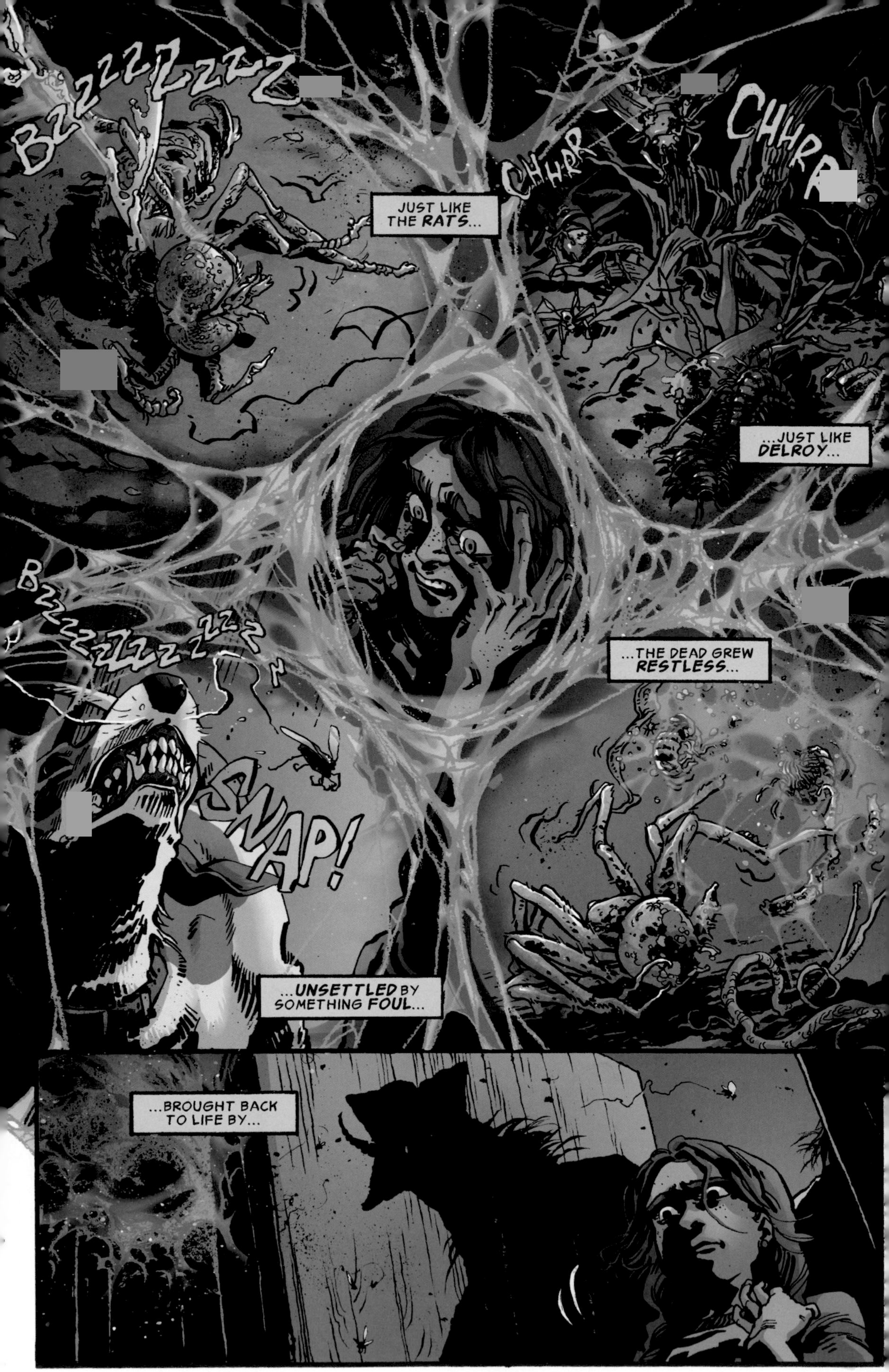
BZZZZZZZZZ
CHHRR
CHHRR
JUST LIKE THE RATS...
...JUST LIKE DELROY...
BZZZZZZZZZZZ
SNAP!
...THE DEAD GREW RESTLESS...
...UNSETTLED BY SOMETHING FOUL...
...BROUGHT BACK TO LIFE BY...

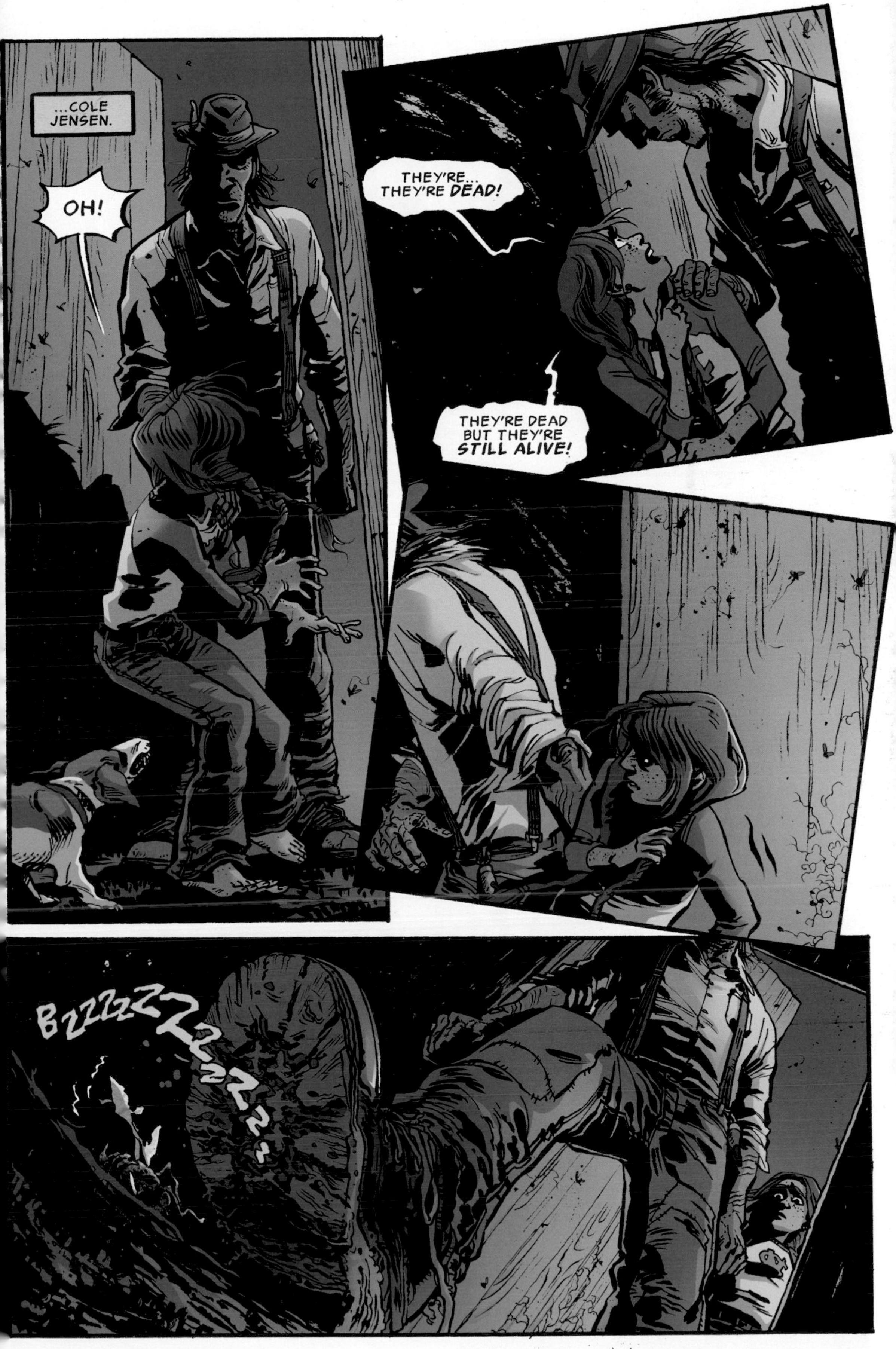
...COLE JENSEN.
OH!
THEY'RE... THEY'RE DEAD!
THEY'RE DEAD BUT THEY'RE STILL ALIVE!
BZZZZZZZZZZZZ

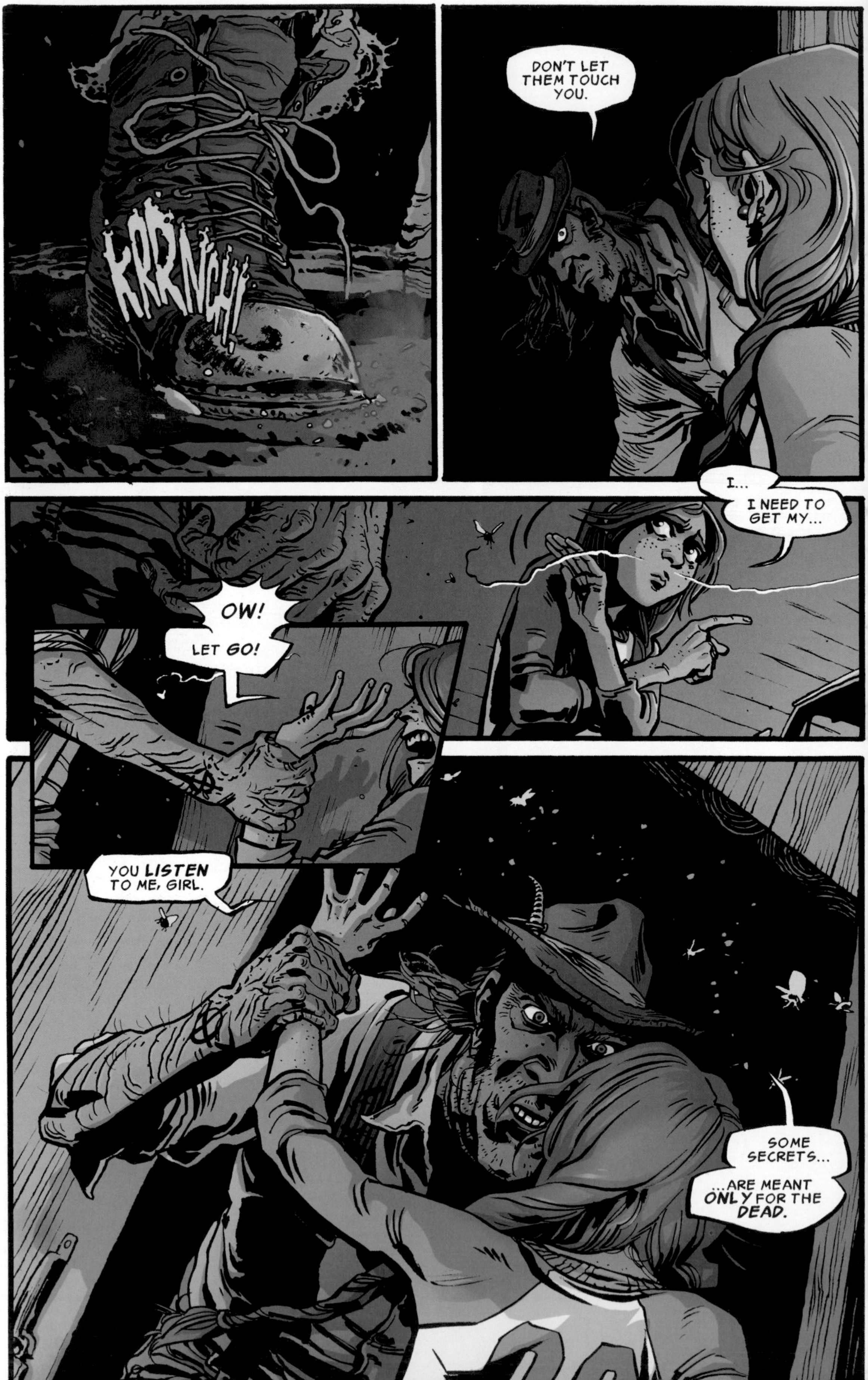
KRRNCH!
DON'T LET THEM TOUCH YOU.
I...
I NEED TO GET MY...
OW!
LET GO!
YOU LISTEN TO ME, GIRL.
SOME SECRETS...
...ARE MEANT ONLY FOR THE DEAD.

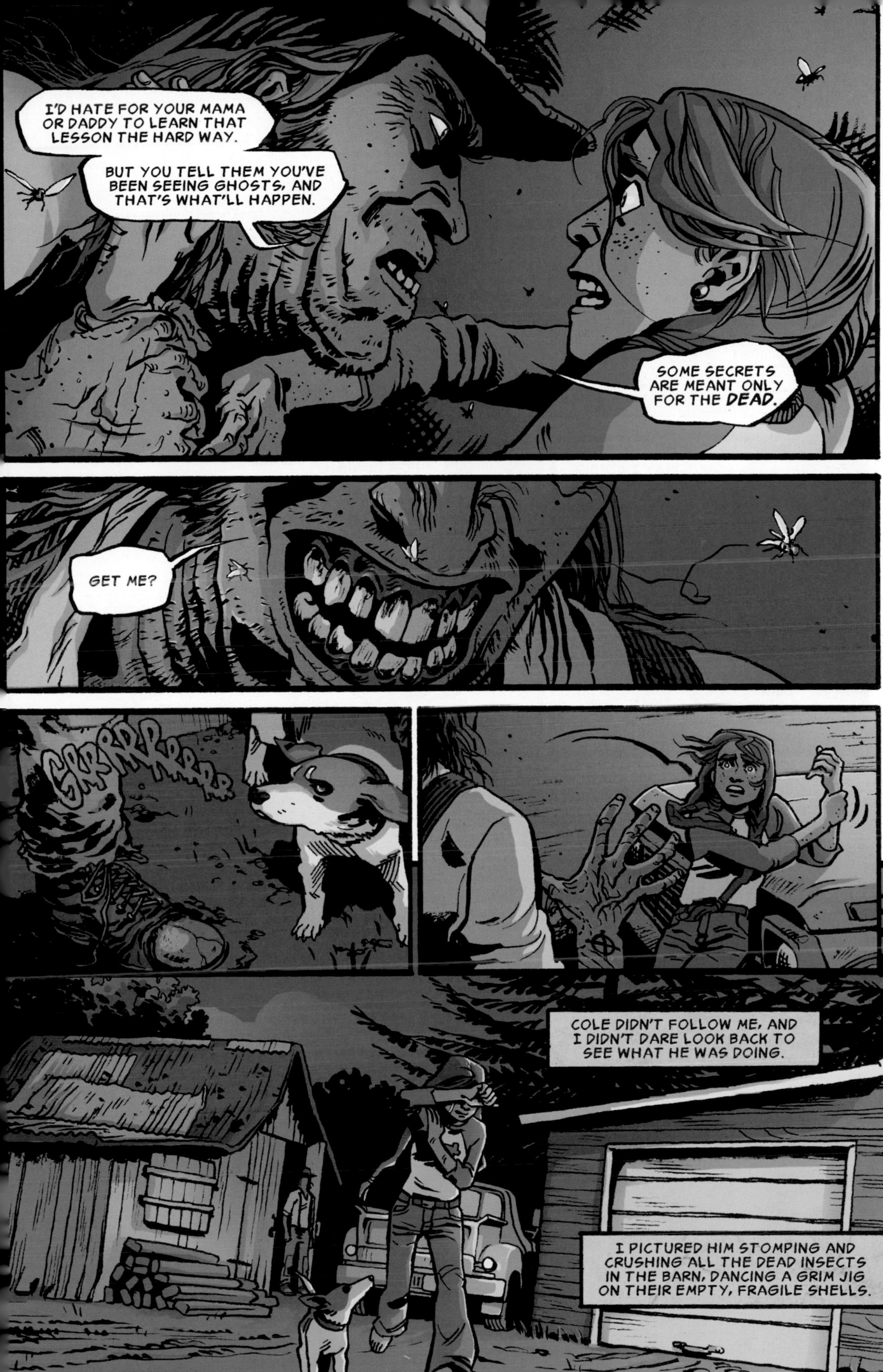
I'D HATE FOR YOUR MAMA OR DADDY TO LEARN THAT LESSON THE HARD WAY.
BUT YOU TELL THEM YOU'VE BEEN SEEING GHOSTS, AND THAT'S WHAT'LL HAPPEN.
SOME SECRETS ARE MEANT ONLY FOR THE DEAD.
GET ME?
GRRRRrrrr
COLE DIDN'T FOLLOW ME, AND I DIDN'T DARE LOOK BACK TO SEE WHAT HE WAS DOING.
I PICTURED HIM STOMPING AND CRUSHING ALL THE DEAD INSECTS IN THE BARN, DANCING A GRIM JIG ON THEIR EMPTY, FRAGILE SHELLS.

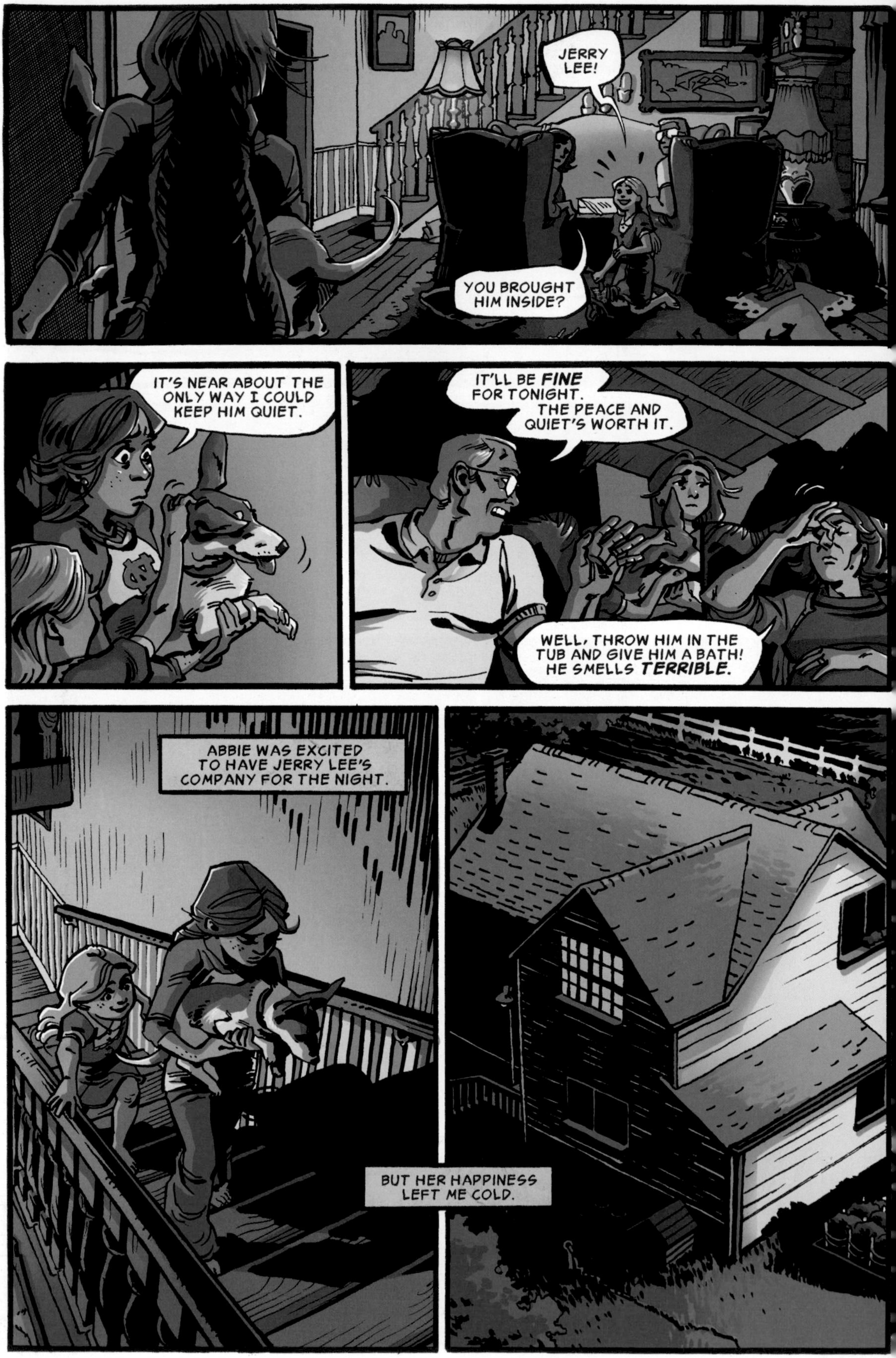
JERRY LEE!
YOU BROUGHT HIM INSIDE?
IT'S NEAR ABOUT THE ONLY WAY I COULD KEEP HIM QUIET.
IT'LL BE FINE FOR TONIGHT. THE PEACE AND QUIET'S WORTH IT.
WELL, THROW HIM IN THE TUB AND GIVE HIM A BATH! HE SMELLS TERRIBLE.
ABBIE WAS EXCITED TO HAVE JERRY LEE'S COMPANY FOR THE NIGHT.
BUT HER HAPPINESS LEFT ME COLD.

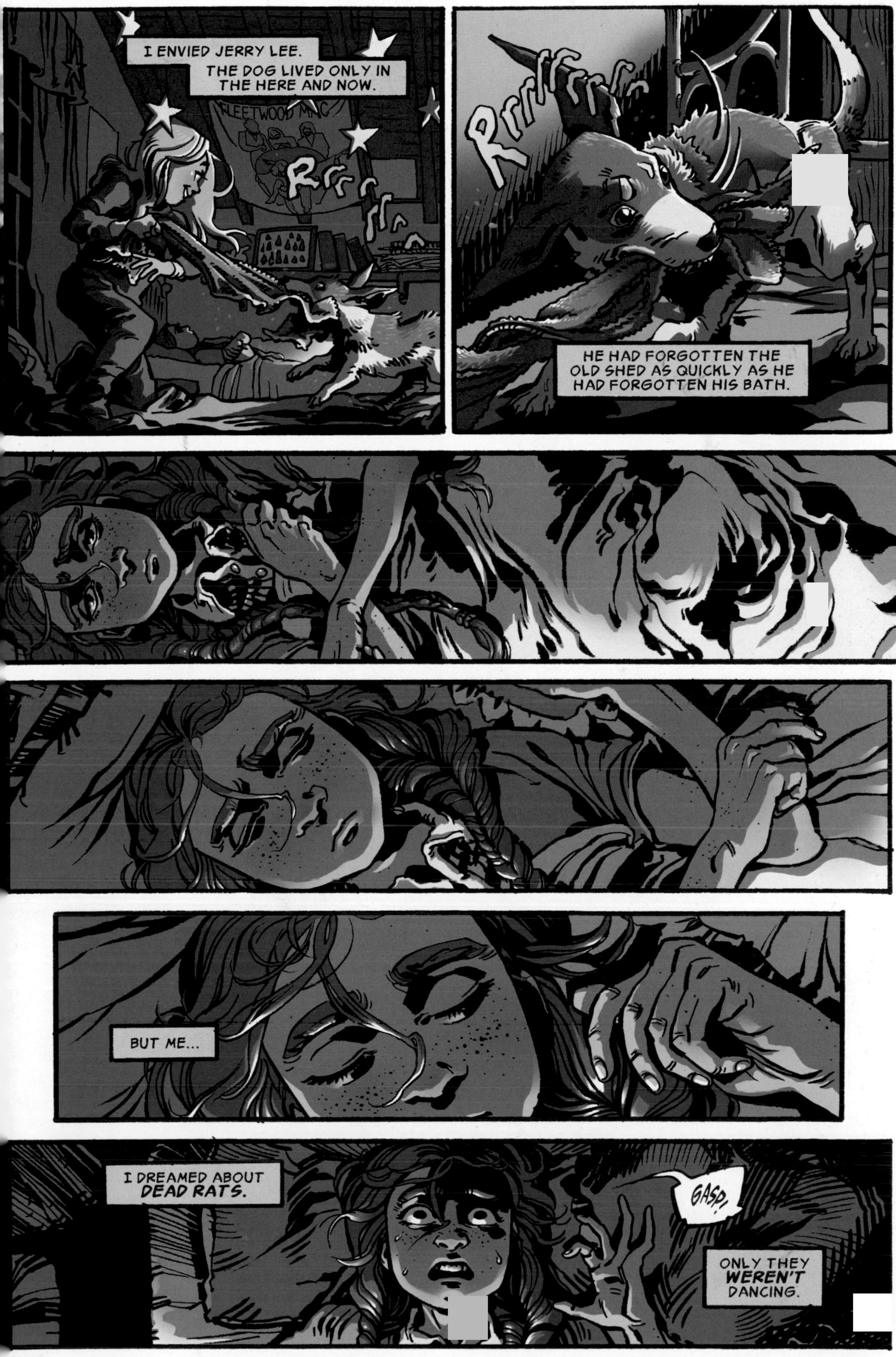
I ENVIED JERRY LEE.
THE DOG LIVED ONLY IN THE HERE AND NOW.
FLEETWOOD MAC
HE HAD FORGOTTEN THE OLD SHED AS QUICKLY AS HE HAD FORGOTTEN HIS BATH.
BUT ME...
I DREAMED ABOUT DEAD RATS.
GASP!
ONLY THEY WEREN'T DANCING.

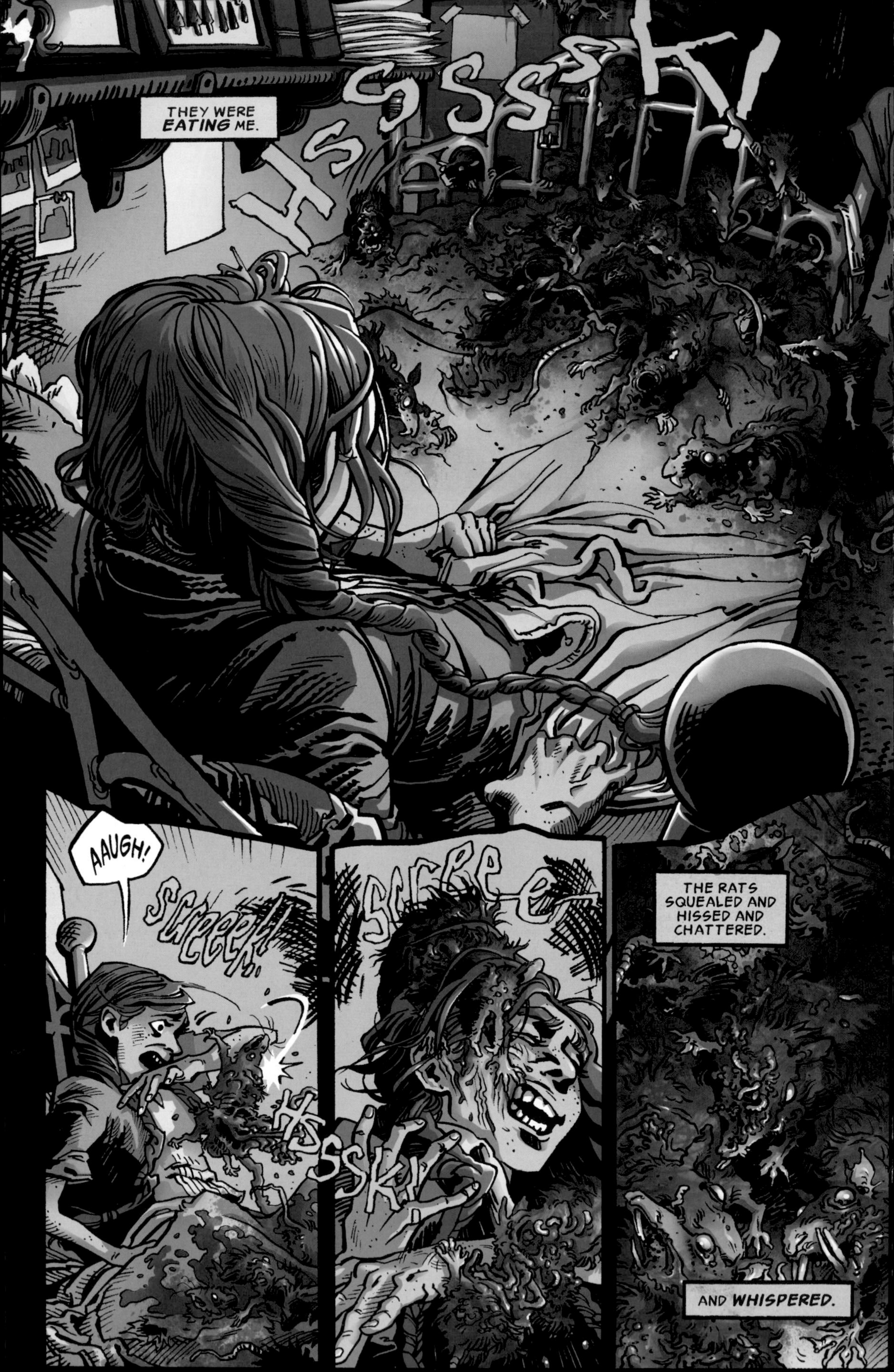
THEY WERE EATING ME.
HSSSSSKK!
AAUGH!
SCREEK!
SCREE-E
HSSSK!
THE RATS SQUEALED AND HISSED AND CHATTERED.
AND WHISPERED.

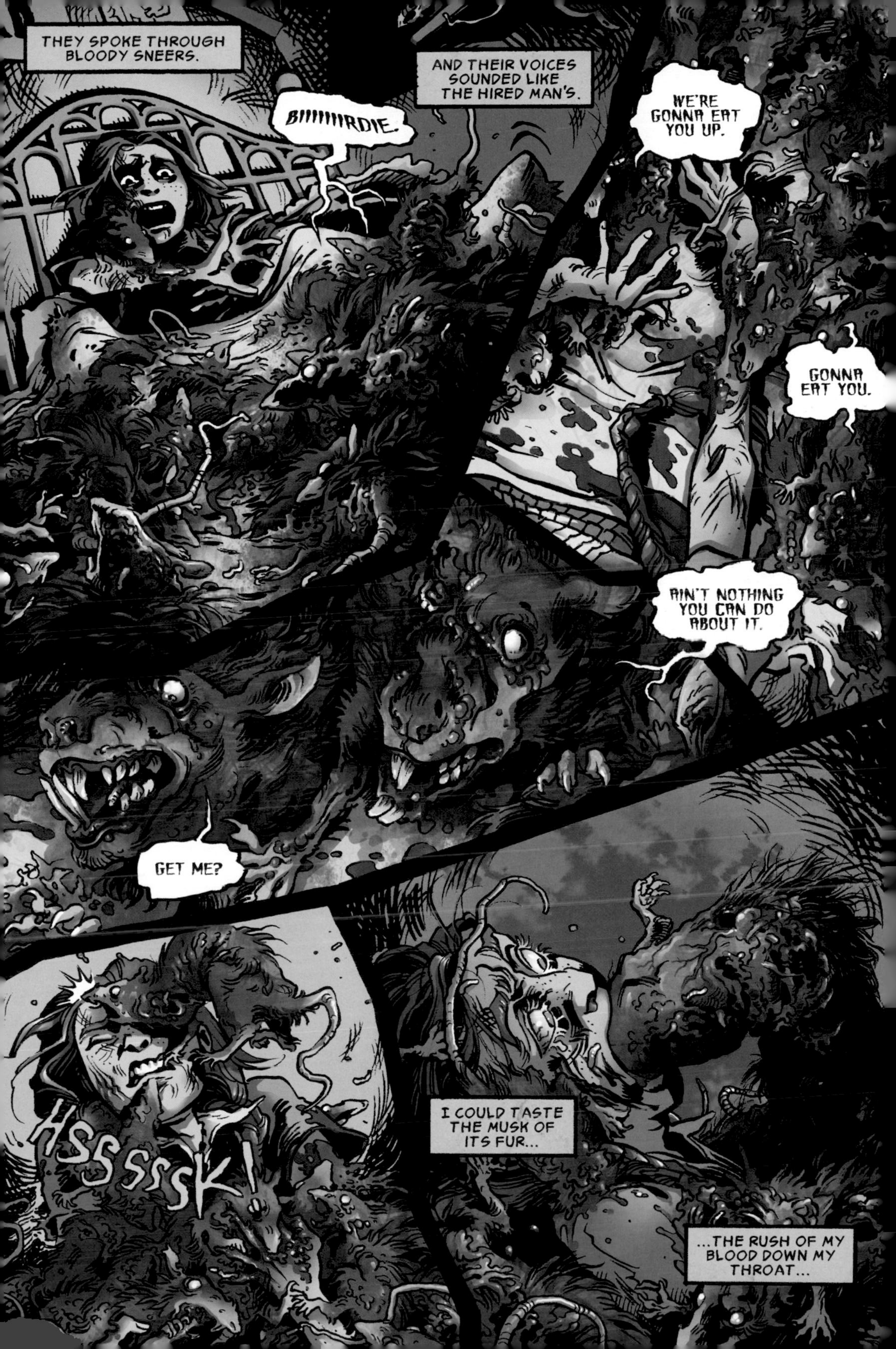
THEY SPOKE THROUGH BLOODY SNEERS.
AND THEIR VOICES SOUNDED LIKE THE HIRED MAN'S.
BIIIIIIRDIE.
WE'RE GONNA EAT YOU UP.
GONNA EAT YOU.
AIN'T NOTHING YOU CAN DO ABOUT IT.
GET ME?
HSSSSSK!
I COULD TASTE THE MUSK OF ITS FUR...
...THE RUSH OF MY BLOOD DOWN MY THROAT...

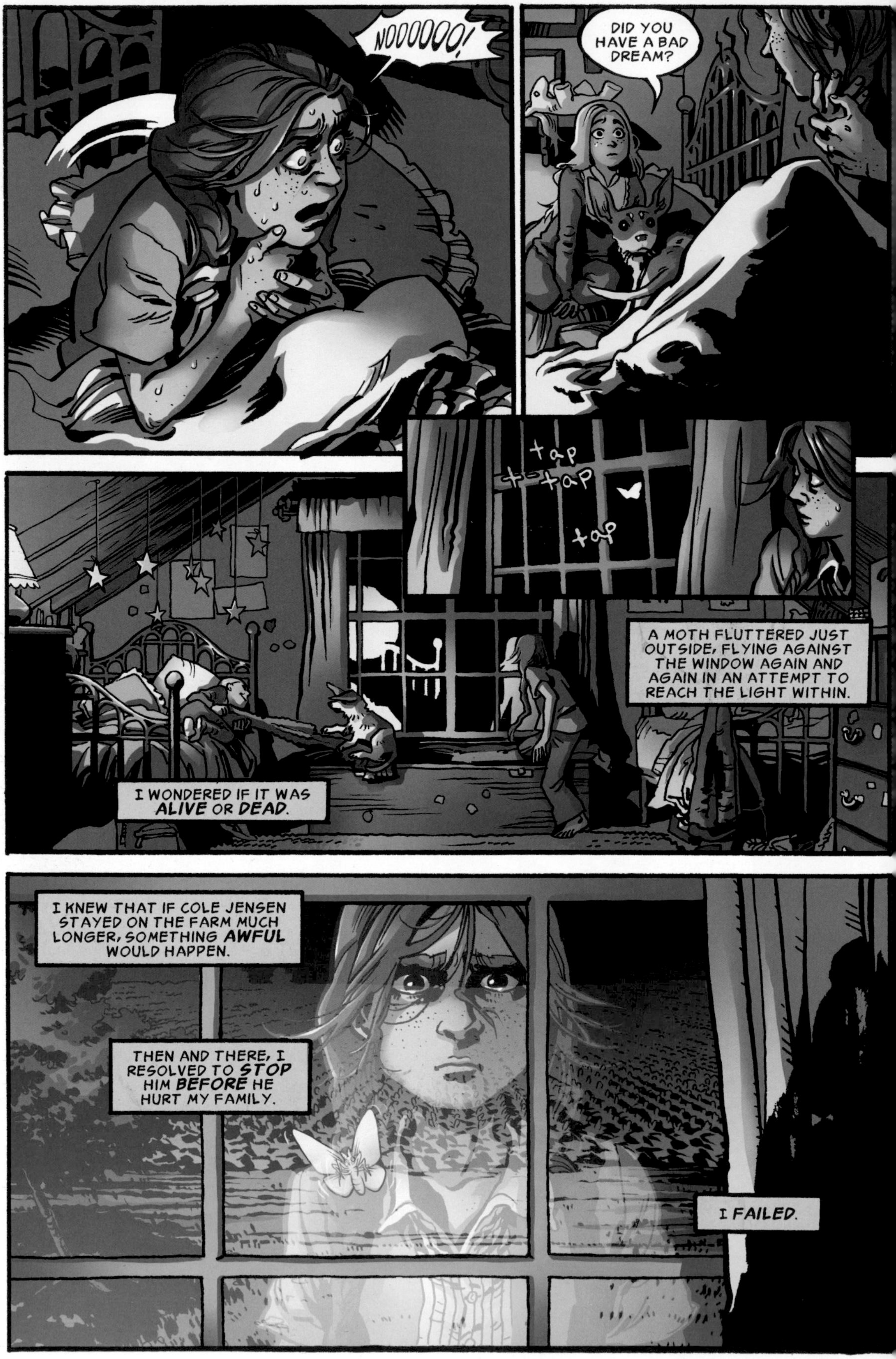
NOOOOOO!
DID YOU HAVE A BAD DREAM?
tap
tap-tap
tap
A MOTH FLUTTERED JUST OUTSIDE, FLYING AGAINST THE WINDOW AGAIN AND AGAIN IN AN ATTEMPT TO REACH THE LIGHT WITHIN.
I WONDERED IF IT WAS **ALIVE** OR **DEAD**.
I KNEW THAT IF COLE JENSEN STAYED ON THE FARM MUCH LONGER, SOMETHING **AWFUL** WOULD HAPPEN.
THEN AND THERE, I RESOLVED TO **STOP** HIM **BEFORE** HE HURT MY FAMILY.
I **FAILED**.

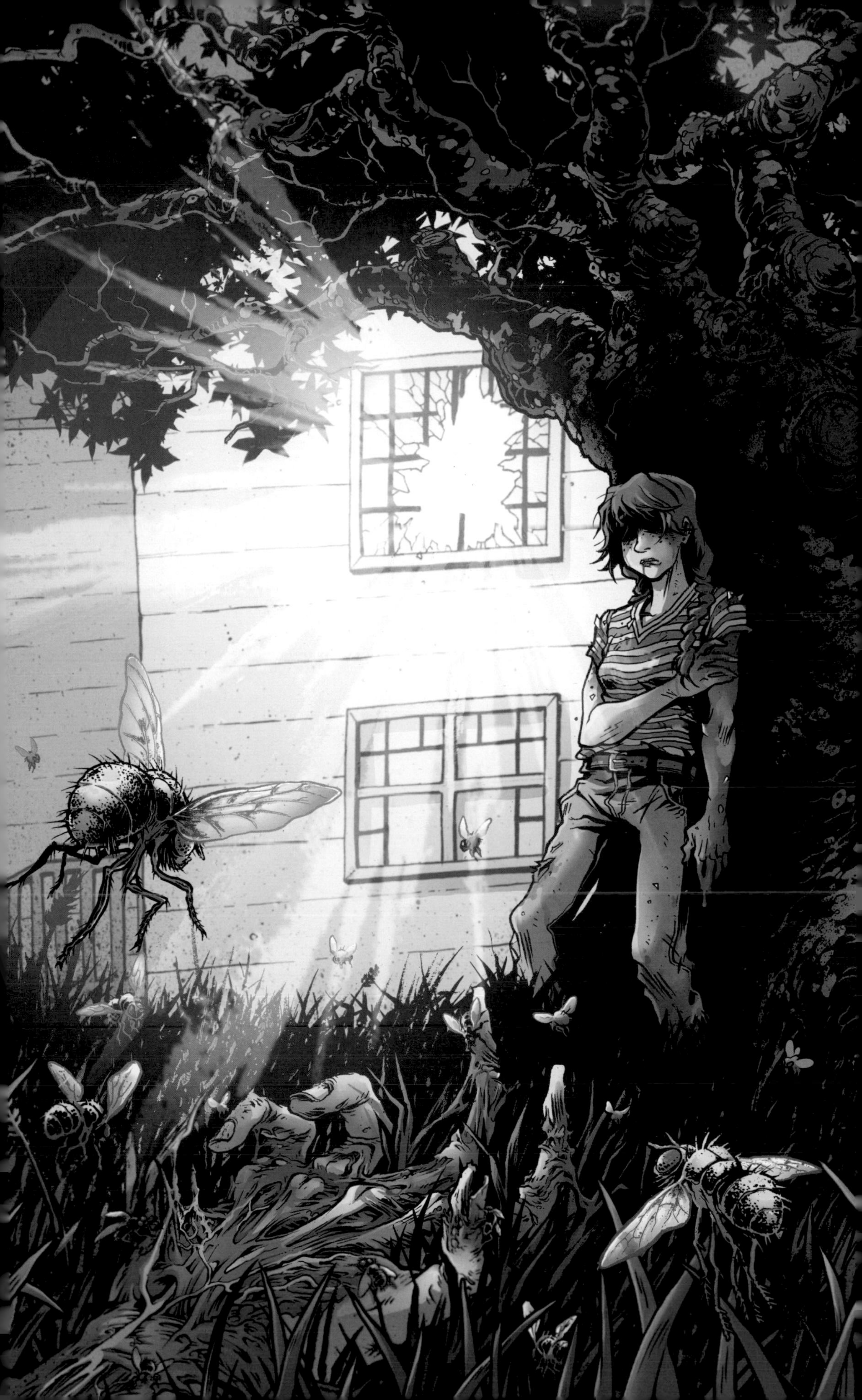

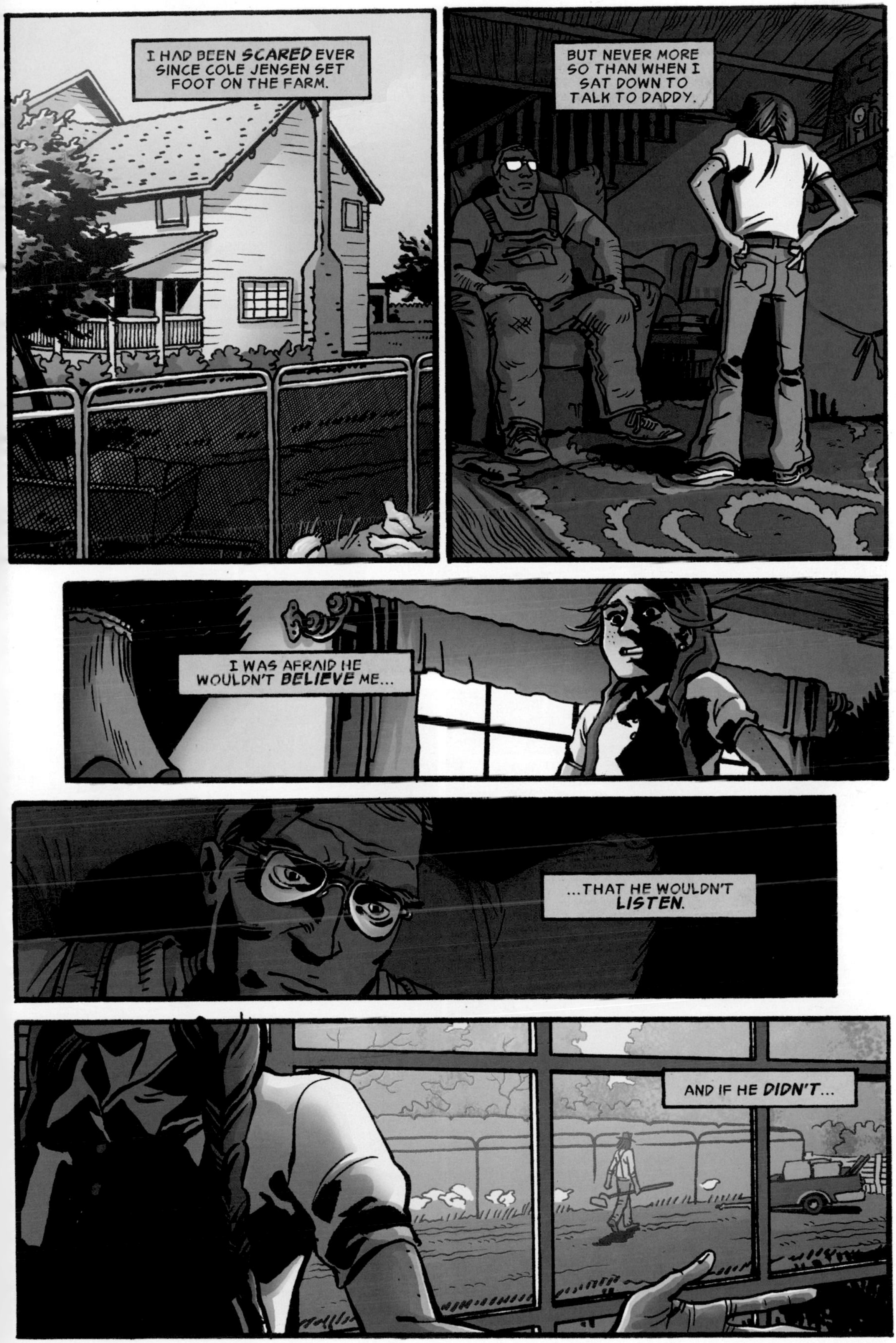
I HAD BEEN SCARED EVER SINCE COLE JENSEN SET FOOT ON THE FARM.
BUT NEVER MORE SO THAN WHEN I SAT DOWN TO TALK TO DADDY.
I WAS AFRAID HE WOULDN'T BELIEVE ME...
...THAT HE WOULDN'T LISTEN.
AND IF HE DIDN'T...

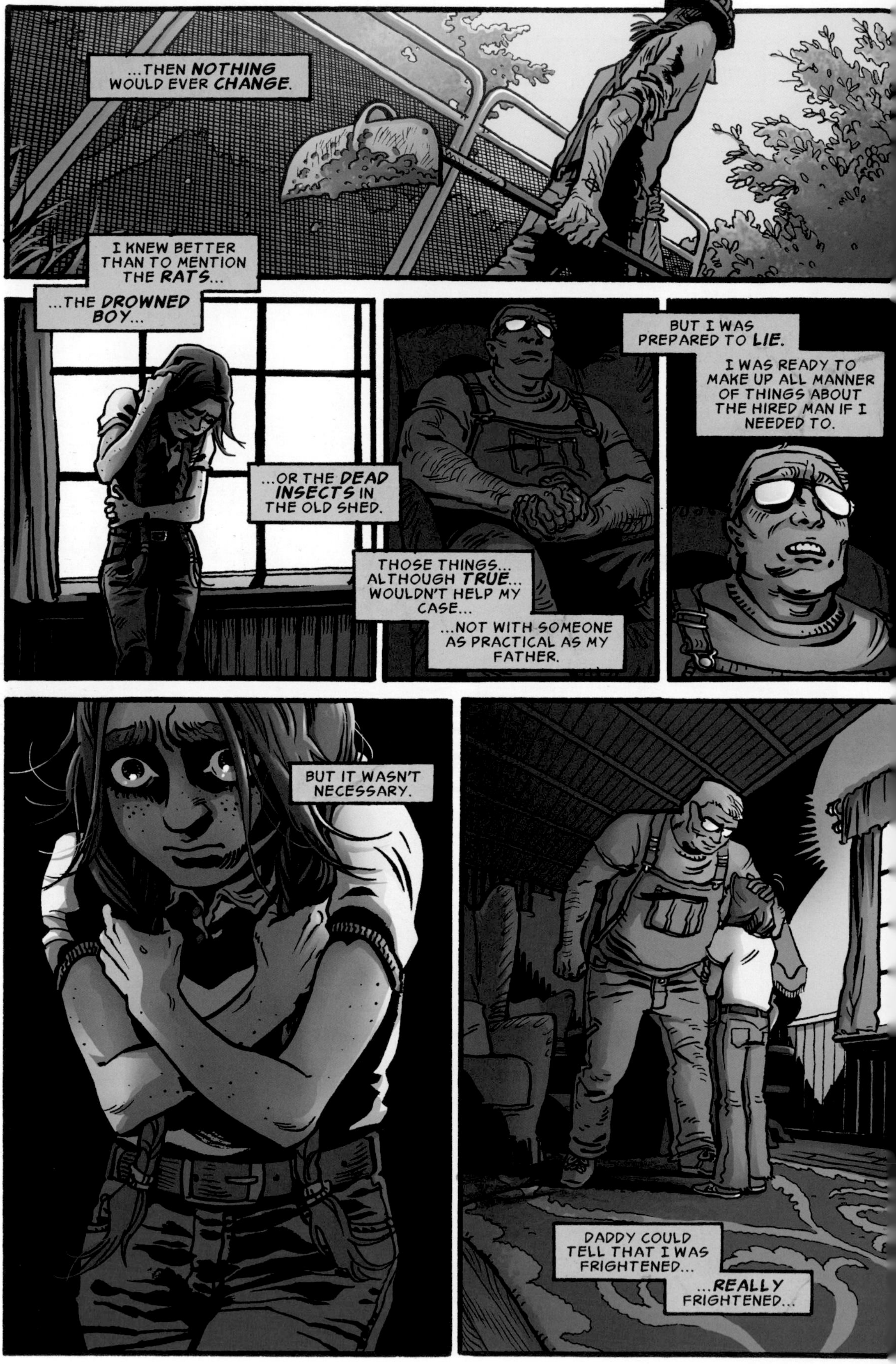

...THEN NOTHING WOULD EVER CHANGE.
I KNEW BETTER THAN TO MENTION THE RATS...
...THE DROWNED BOY...
...OR THE DEAD INSECTS IN THE OLD SHED.
THOSE THINGS... ALTHOUGH TRUE... WOULDN'T HELP MY CASE...
...NOT WITH SOMEONE AS PRACTICAL AS MY FATHER.
BUT I WAS PREPARED TO LIE.
I WAS READY TO MAKE UP ALL MANNER OF THINGS ABOUT THE HIRED MAN IF I NEEDED TO.
BUT IT WASN'T NECESSARY.
DADDY COULD TELL THAT I WAS FRIGHTENED...
...REALLY FRIGHTENED...

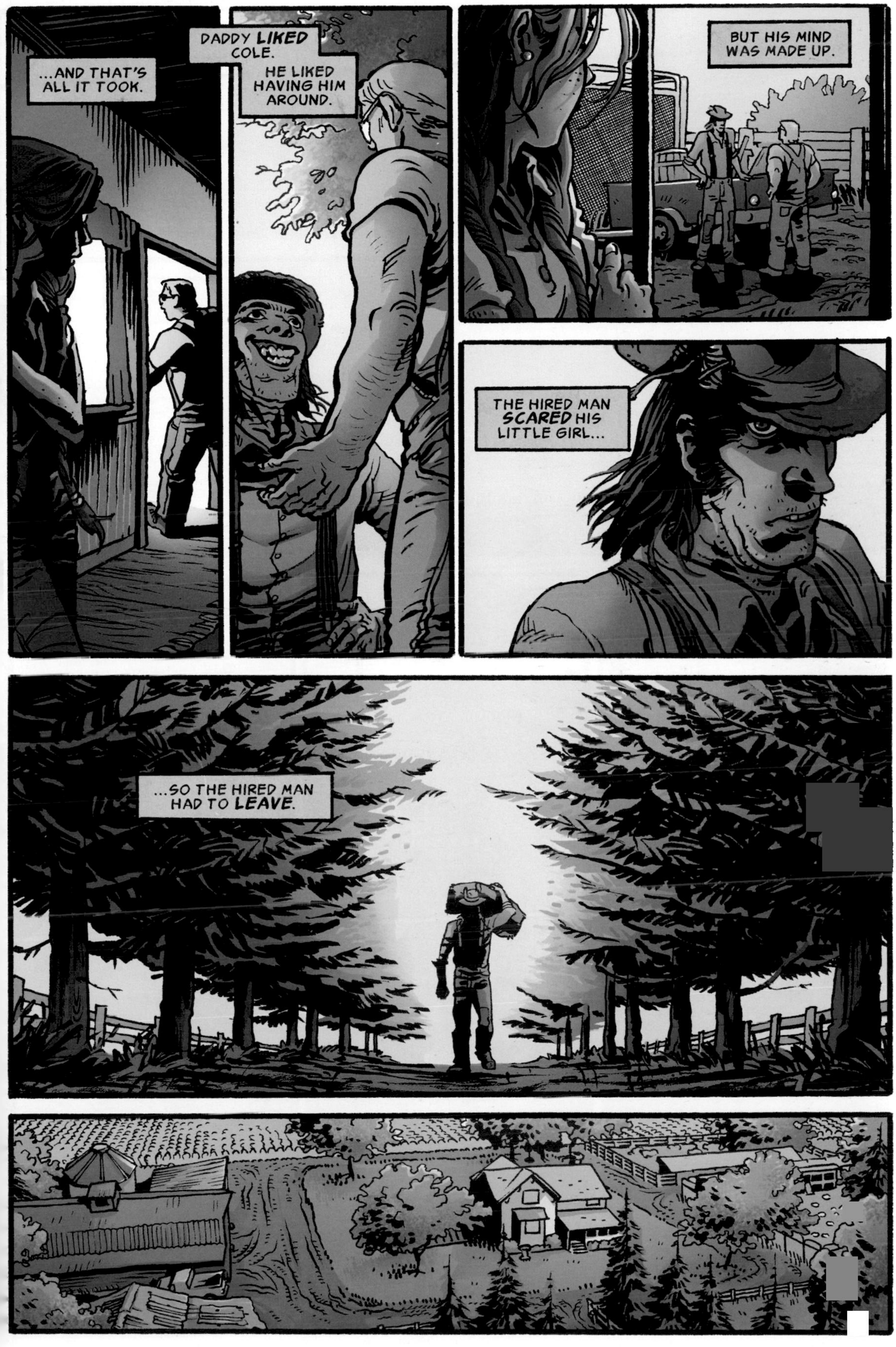
...AND THAT'S ALL IT TOOK.
DADDY LIKED COLE.
HE LIKED HAVING HIM AROUND.
BUT HIS MIND WAS MADE UP.
THE HIRED MAN SCARED HIS LITTLE GIRL...
...SO THE HIRED MAN HAD TO LEAVE.

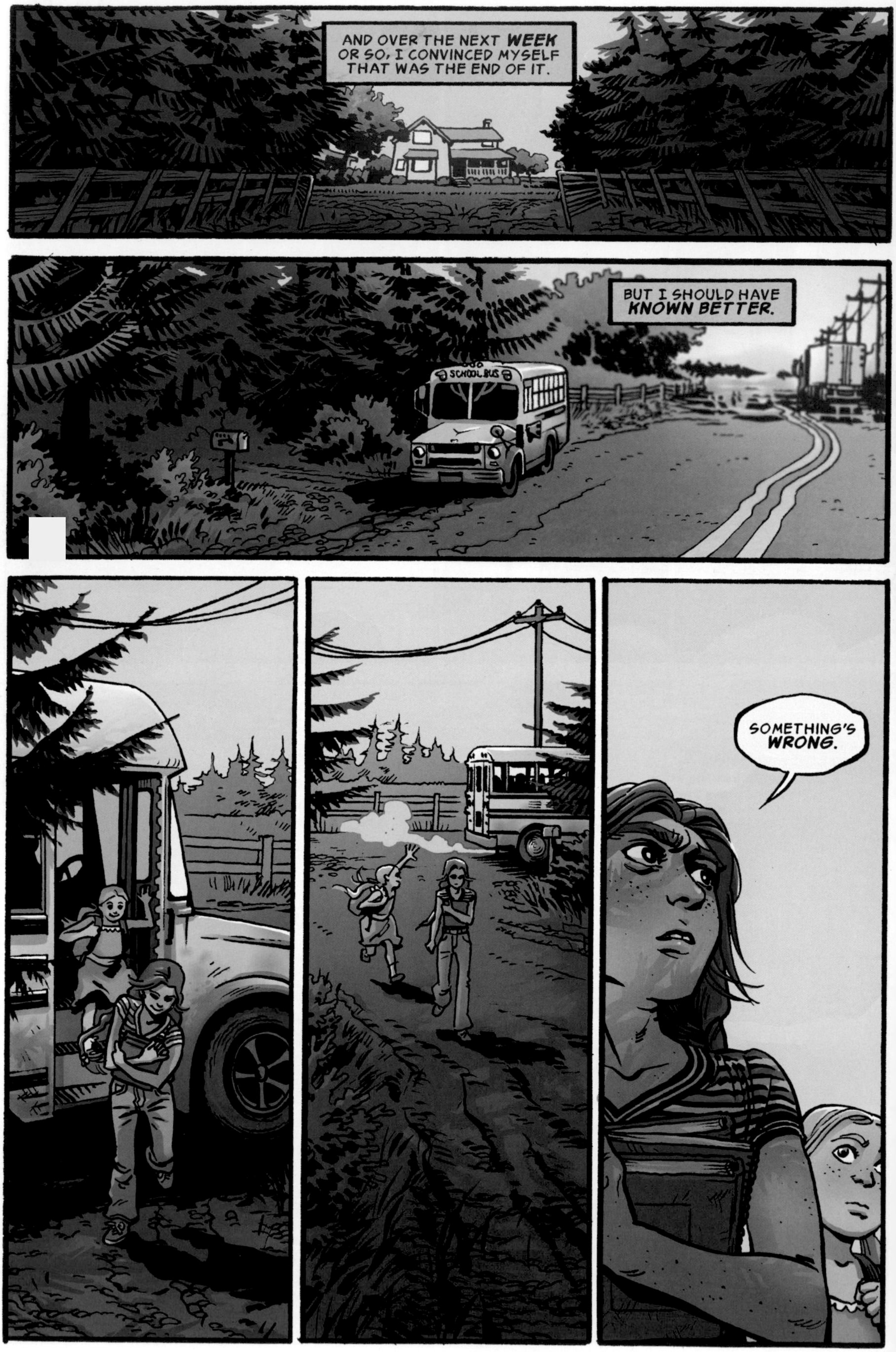
AND OVER THE NEXT WEEK OR SO, I CONVINCED MYSELF THAT WAS THE END OF IT.
SCHOOL BUS
BUT I SHOULD HAVE KNOWN BETTER.
SOMETHING'S WRONG.

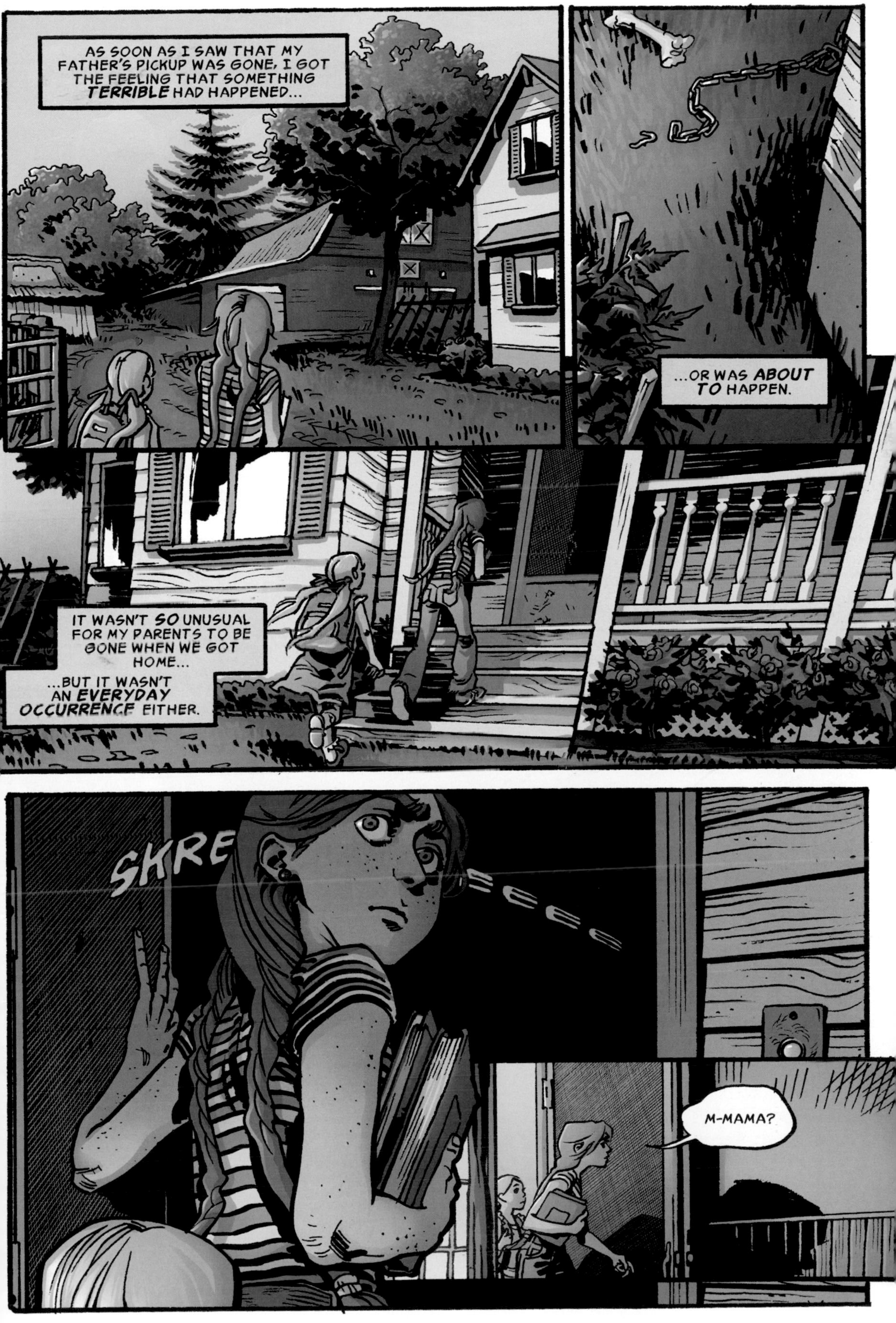
AS SOON AS I SAW THAT MY FATHER'S PICKUP WAS GONE, I GOT THE FEELING THAT SOMETHING *TERRIBLE* HAD HAPPENED...
...OR WAS *ABOUT TO* HAPPEN.
IT WASN'T *SO* UNUSUAL FOR MY PARENTS TO BE GONE WHEN WE GOT HOME...
...BUT IT WASN'T AN *EVERYDAY OCCURRENCE* EITHER.
SKREEEEE
M-MAMA?

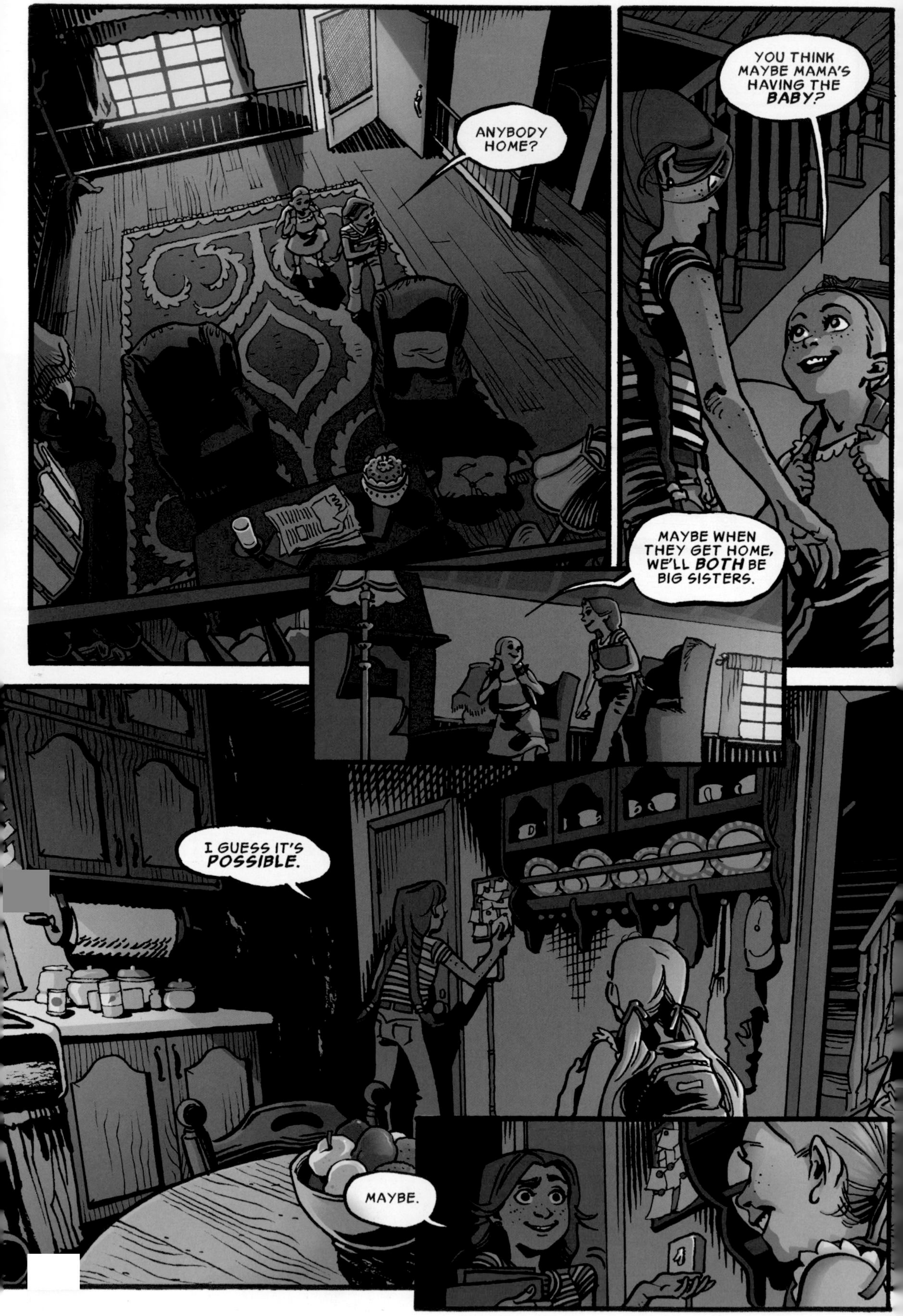
ANYBODY HOME?
YOU THINK MAYBE MAMA'S HAVING THE *BABY?*
MAYBE WHEN THEY GET HOME, WE'LL *BOTH* BE BIG SISTERS.
I GUESS IT'S *POSSIBLE.*
MAYBE.

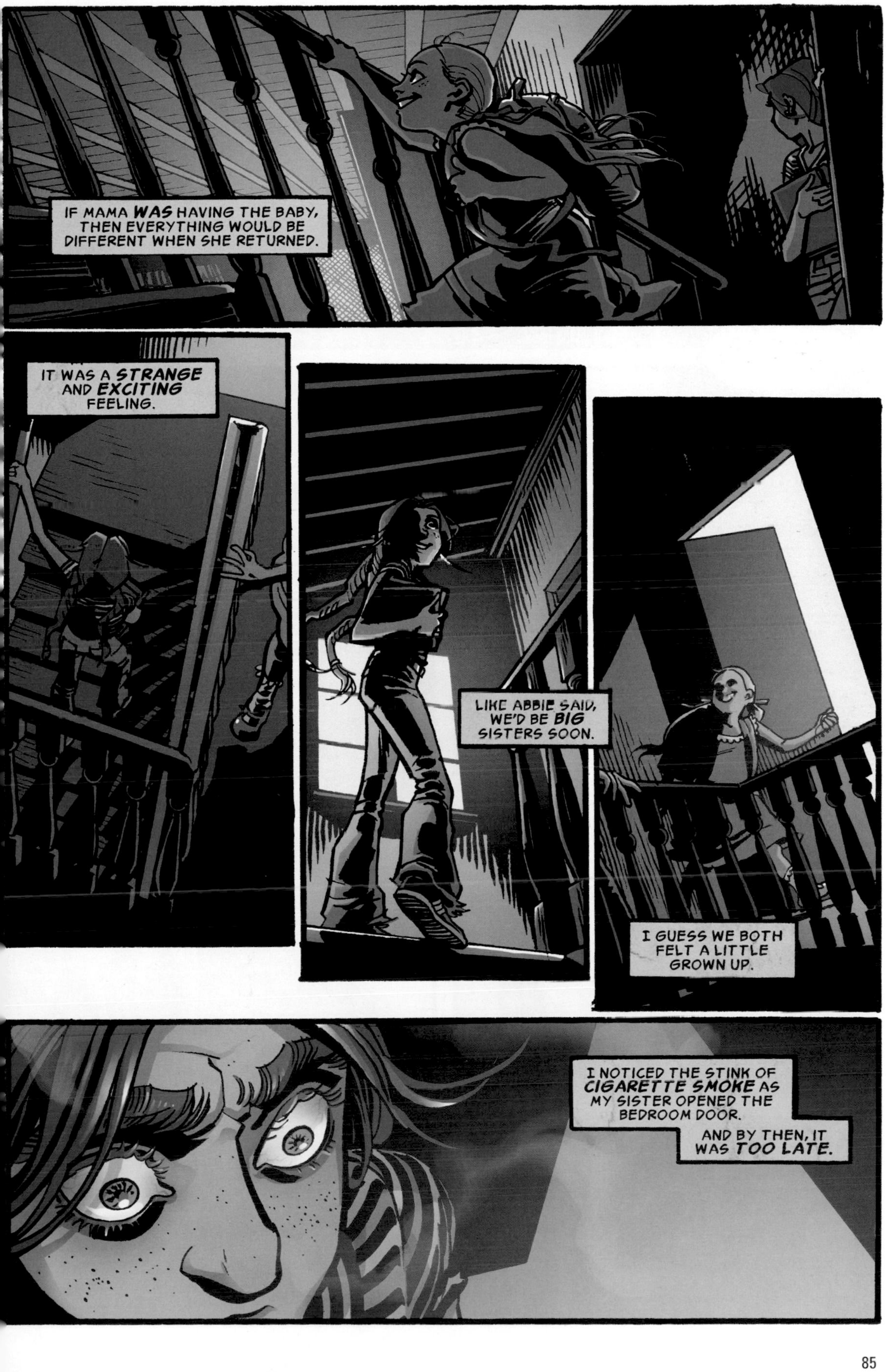
IF MAMA WAS HAVING THE BABY, THEN EVERYTHING WOULD BE DIFFERENT WHEN SHE RETURNED.
IT WAS A STRANGE AND EXCITING FEELING.
LIKE ABBIE SAID, WE'D BE BIG SISTERS SOON.
I GUESS WE BOTH FELT A LITTLE GROWN UP.
I NOTICED THE STINK OF CIGARETTE SMOKE AS MY SISTER OPENED THE BEDROOM DOOR.
AND BY THEN, IT WAS TOO LATE.

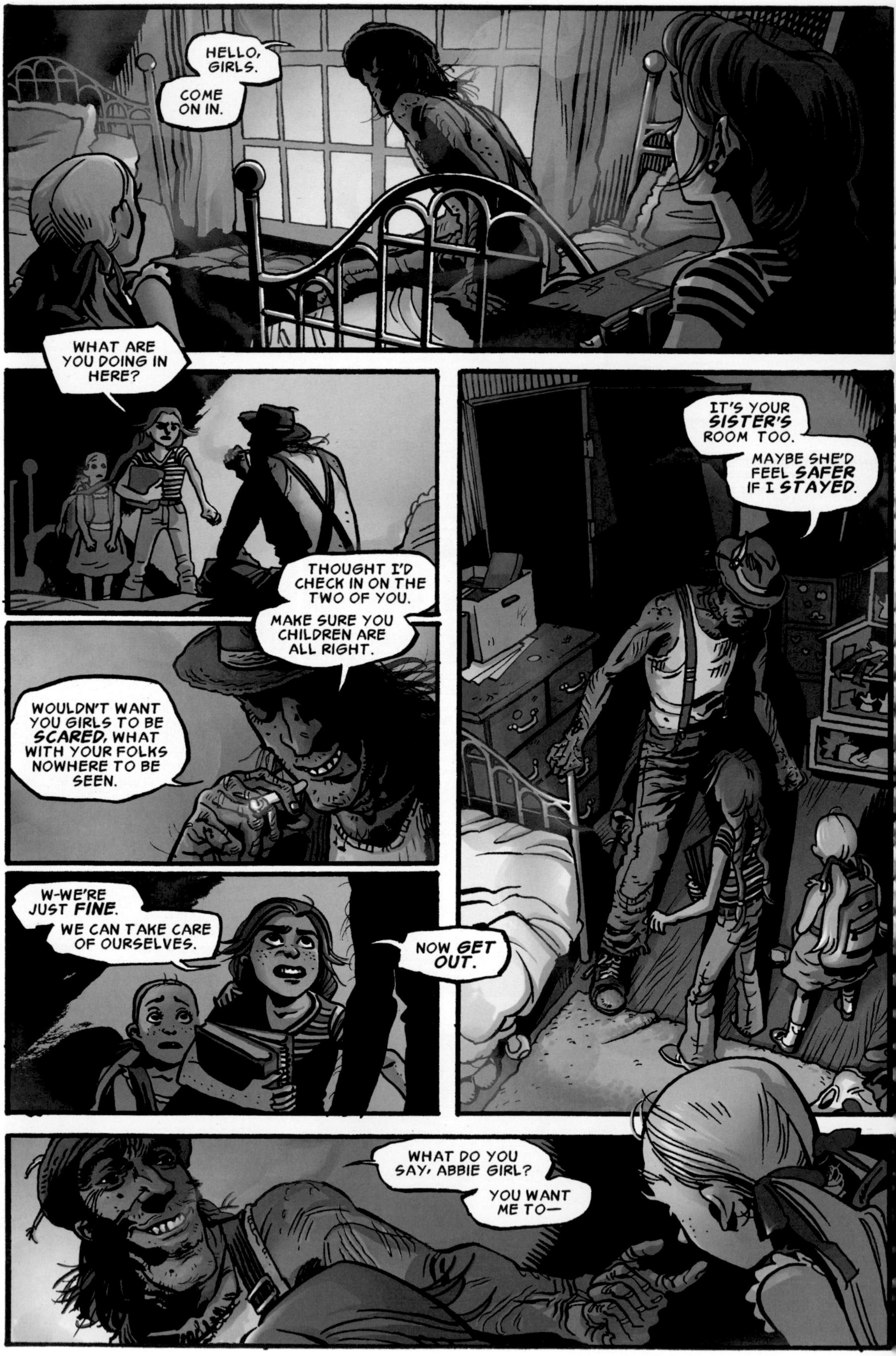
HELLO, GIRLS.
COME ON IN.
WHAT ARE YOU DOING IN HERE?
THOUGHT I'D CHECK IN ON THE TWO OF YOU.
MAKE SURE YOU CHILDREN ARE ALL RIGHT.
WOULDN'T WANT YOU GIRLS TO BE SCARED, WHAT WITH YOUR FOLKS NOWHERE TO BE SEEN.
W-WE'RE JUST FINE.
WE CAN TAKE CARE OF OURSELVES.
NOW GET OUT.
IT'S YOUR SISTER'S ROOM TOO.
MAYBE SHE'D FEEL SAFER IF I STAYED.
WHAT DO YOU SAY, ABBIE GIRL?
YOU WANT ME TO—

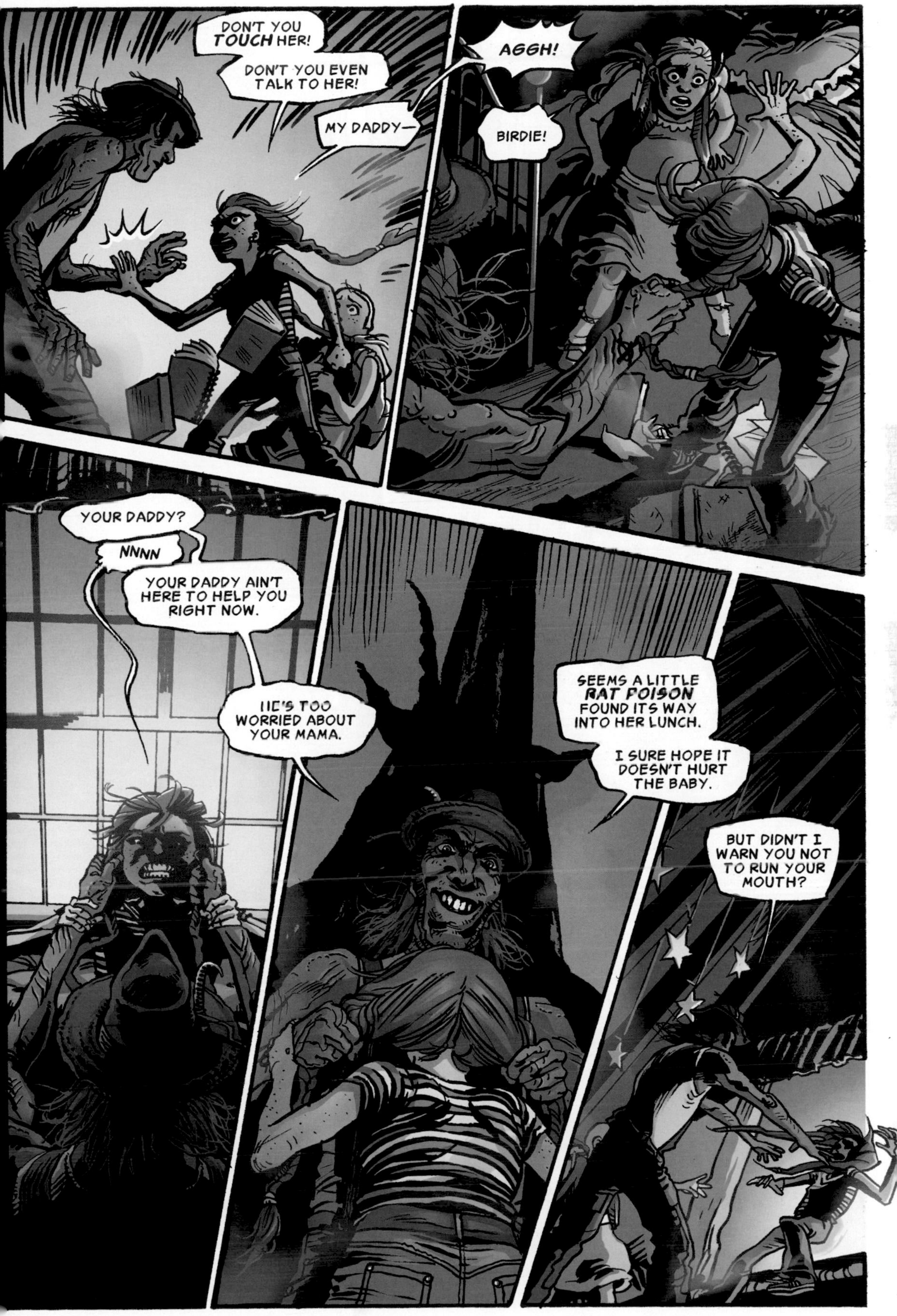

DON'T YOU TOUCH HER!
DON'T YOU EVEN TALK TO HER!
MY DADDY—
AGGH!
BIRDIE!
YOUR DADDY?
NNNN
YOUR DADDY AIN'T HERE TO HELP YOU RIGHT NOW.
HE'S TOO WORRIED ABOUT YOUR MAMA.
SEEMS A LITTLE RAT POISON FOUND ITS WAY INTO HER LUNCH.
I SURE HOPE IT DOESN'T HURT THE BABY.
BUT DIDN'T I WARN YOU NOT TO RUN YOUR MOUTH?

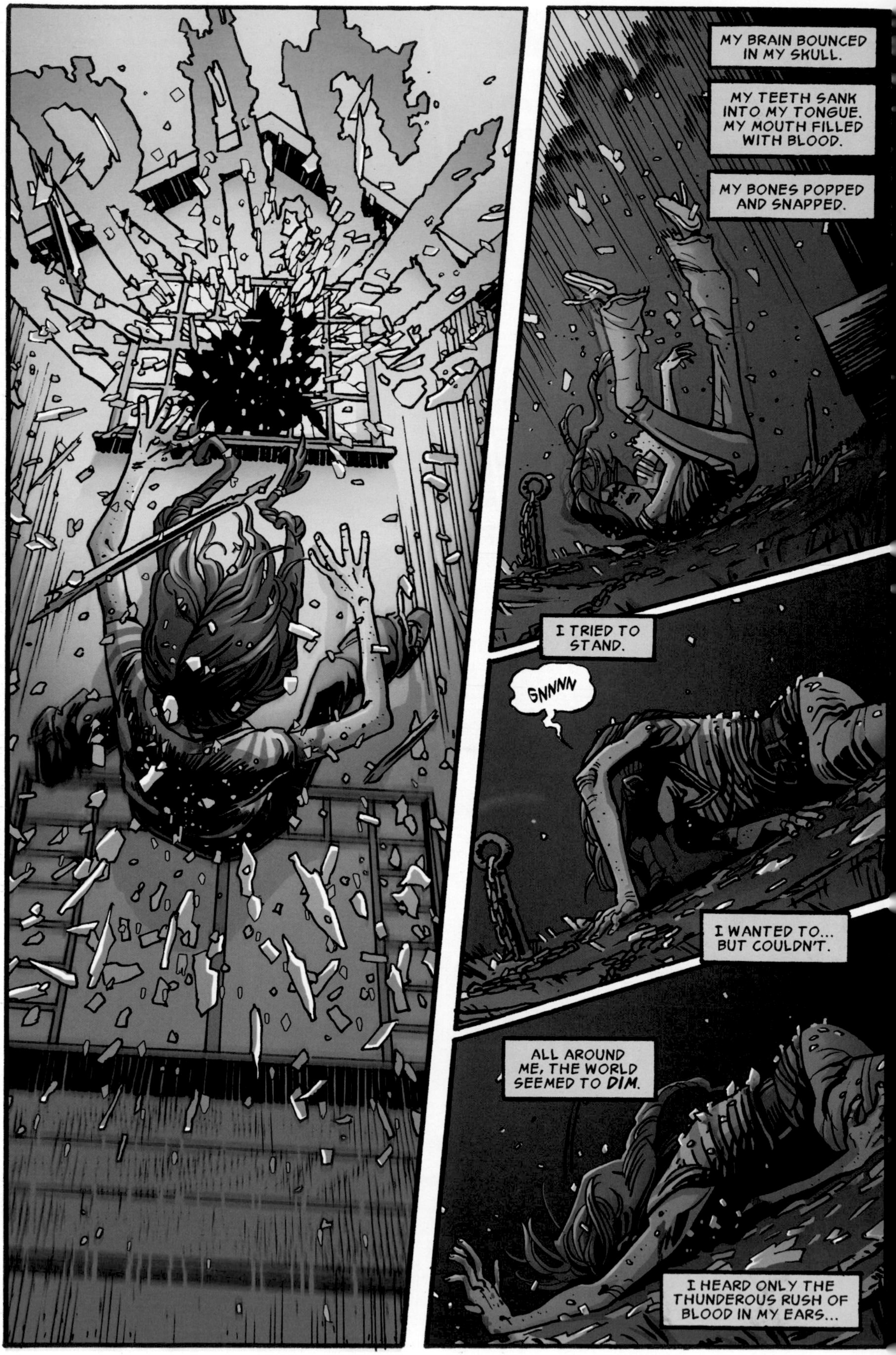

MY BRAIN BOUNCED IN MY SKULL.
MY TEETH SANK INTO MY TONGUE. MY MOUTH FILLED WITH BLOOD.
MY BONES POPPED AND SNAPPED.
I TRIED TO STAND.
GNNNN
I WANTED TO... BUT COULDN'T.
ALL AROUND ME, THE WORLD SEEMED TO DIM.
I HEARD ONLY THE THUNDEROUS RUSH OF BLOOD IN MY EARS...

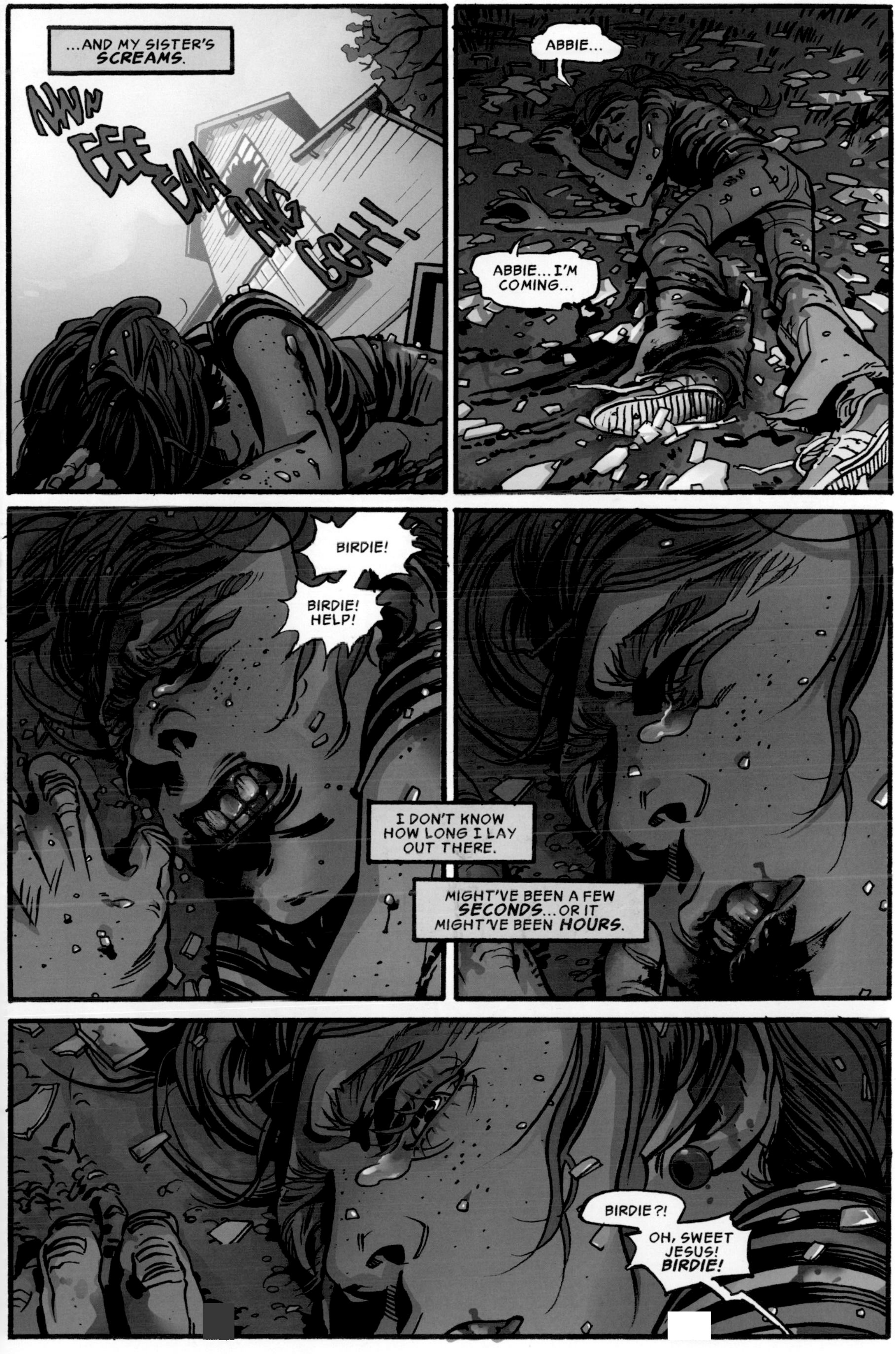
...AND MY SISTER'S SCREAMS.
NNN EEE EAA AAG GGH!
ABBIE...
ABBIE... I'M COMING...
BIRDIE!
BIRDIE! HELP!
I DON'T KNOW HOW LONG I LAY OUT THERE.
MIGHT'VE BEEN A FEW SECONDS... OR IT MIGHT'VE BEEN HOURS.
BIRDIE?!
OH, SWEET JESUS! BIRDIE!

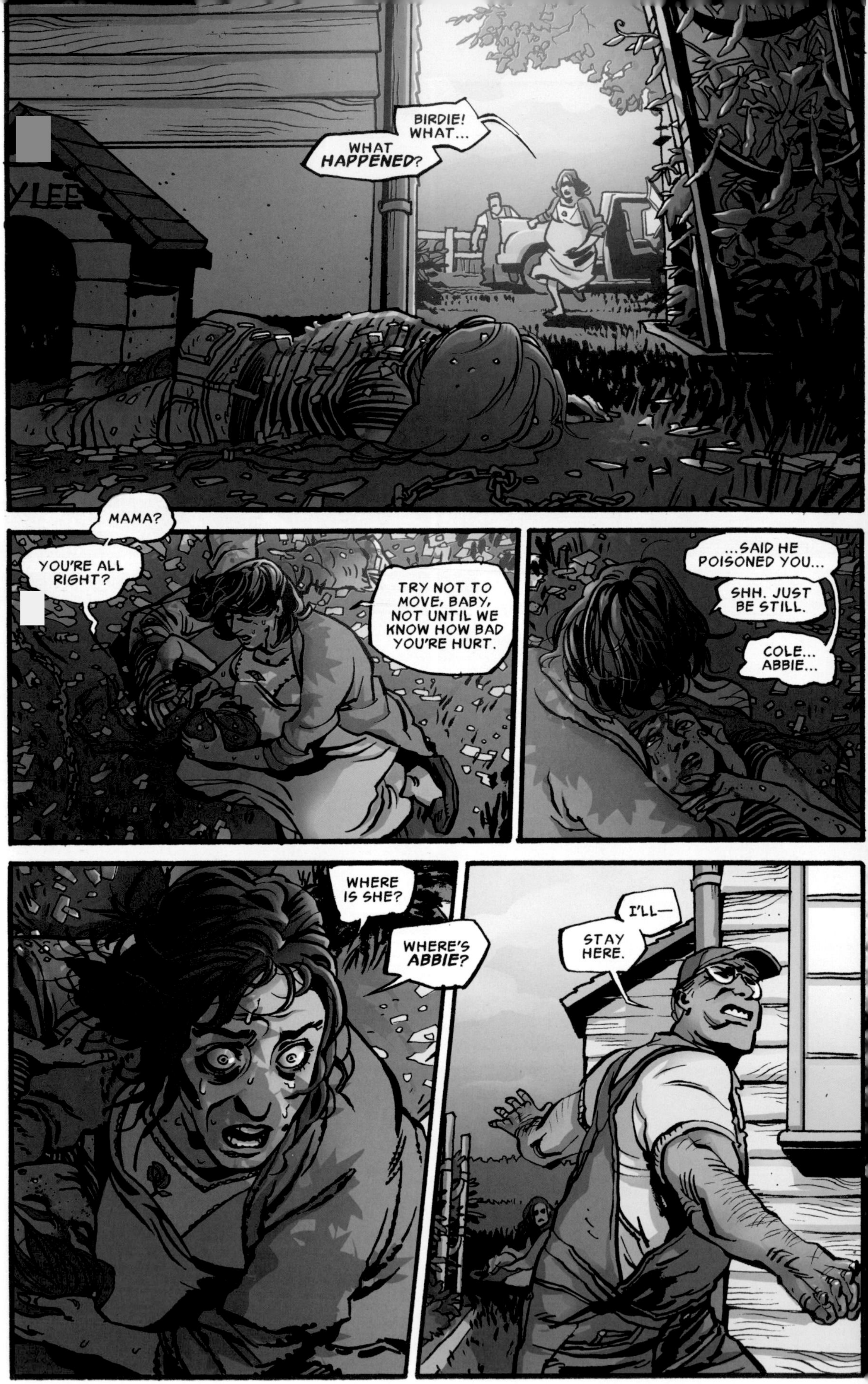

BIRDIE! WHAT...
WHAT HAPPENED?
MAMA?
YOU'RE ALL RIGHT?
TRY NOT TO MOVE, BABY, NOT UNTIL WE KNOW HOW BAD YOU'RE HURT.
...SAID HE POISONED YOU...
SHH. JUST BE STILL.
COLE... ABBIE...
WHERE IS SHE?
WHERE'S ABBIE?
I'LL—
STAY HERE.

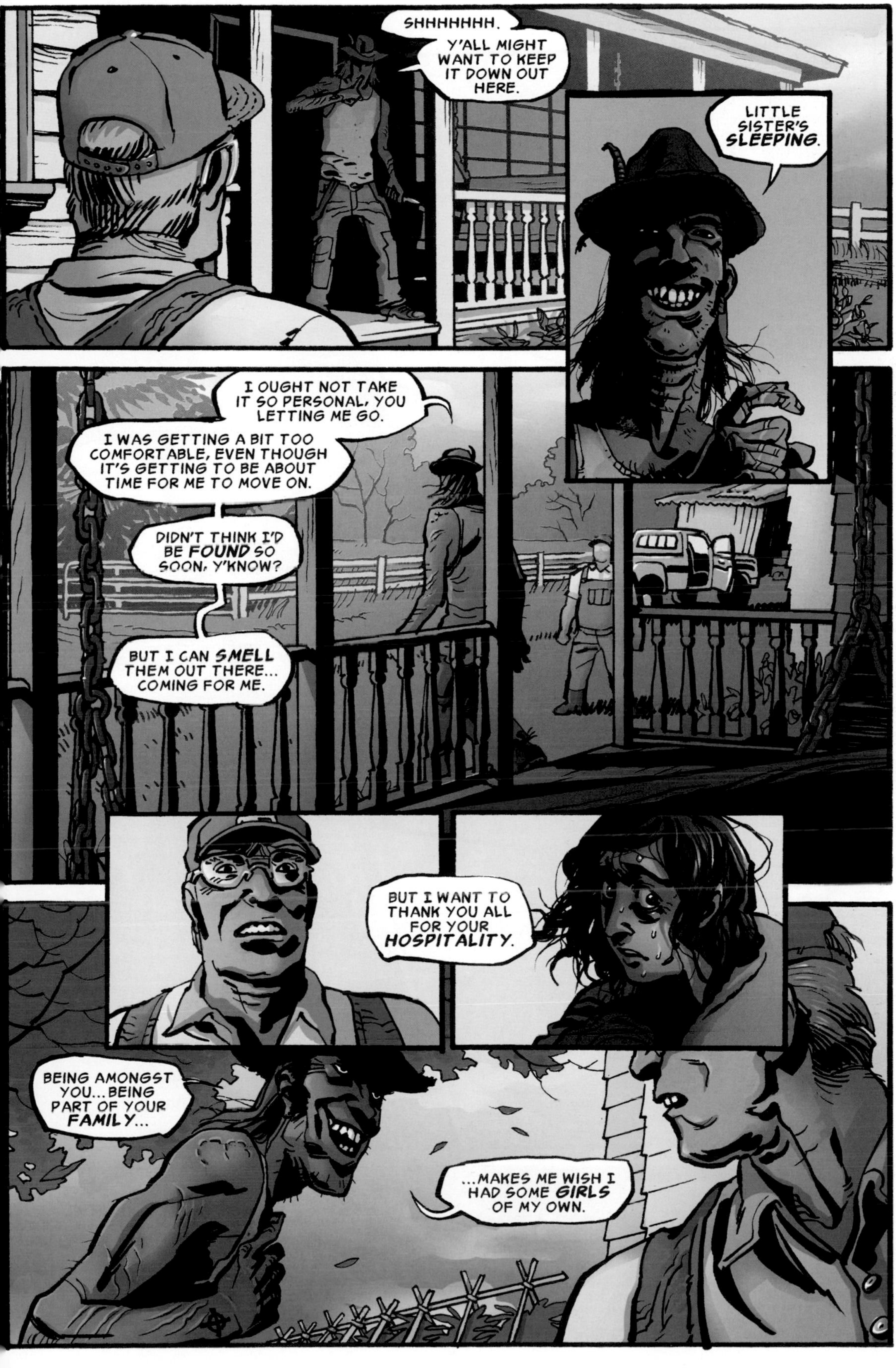
SHHHHHHH.
Y'ALL MIGHT WANT TO KEEP IT DOWN OUT HERE.
LITTLE SISTER'S SLEEPING.
I OUGHT NOT TAKE IT SO PERSONAL, YOU LETTING ME GO.
I WAS GETTING A BIT TOO COMFORTABLE, EVEN THOUGH IT'S GETTING TO BE ABOUT TIME FOR ME TO MOVE ON.
DIDN'T THINK I'D BE FOUND SO SOON, Y'KNOW?
BUT I CAN SMELL THEM OUT THERE... COMING FOR ME.
BUT I WANT TO THANK YOU ALL FOR YOUR HOSPITALITY.
BEING AMONGST YOU... BEING PART OF YOUR FAMILY...
...MAKES ME WISH I HAD SOME GIRLS OF MY OWN.

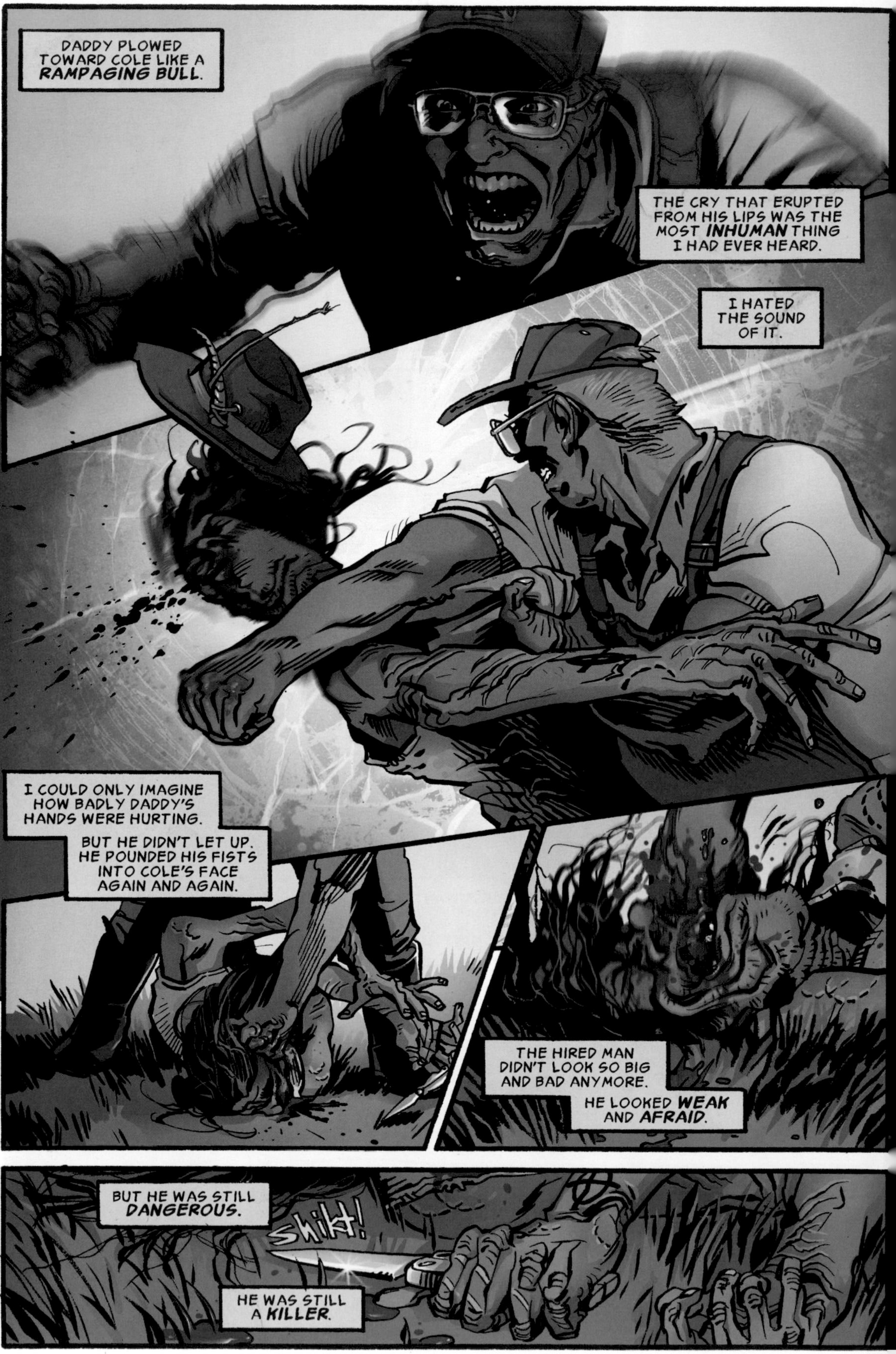
DADDY PLOWED TOWARD COLE LIKE A **RAMPAGING BULL**.
THE CRY THAT ERUPTED FROM HIS LIPS WAS THE MOST **INHUMAN** THING I HAD EVER HEARD.
I HATED THE SOUND OF IT.
I COULD ONLY IMAGINE HOW BADLY DADDY'S HANDS WERE HURTING.
BUT HE DIDN'T LET UP. HE POUNDED HIS FISTS INTO COLE'S FACE AGAIN AND AGAIN.
THE HIRED MAN DIDN'T LOOK SO BIG AND BAD ANYMORE.
HE LOOKED **WEAK** AND **AFRAID**.
BUT HE WAS STILL **DANGEROUS**.
SHIKT!
HE WAS STILL A **KILLER**.

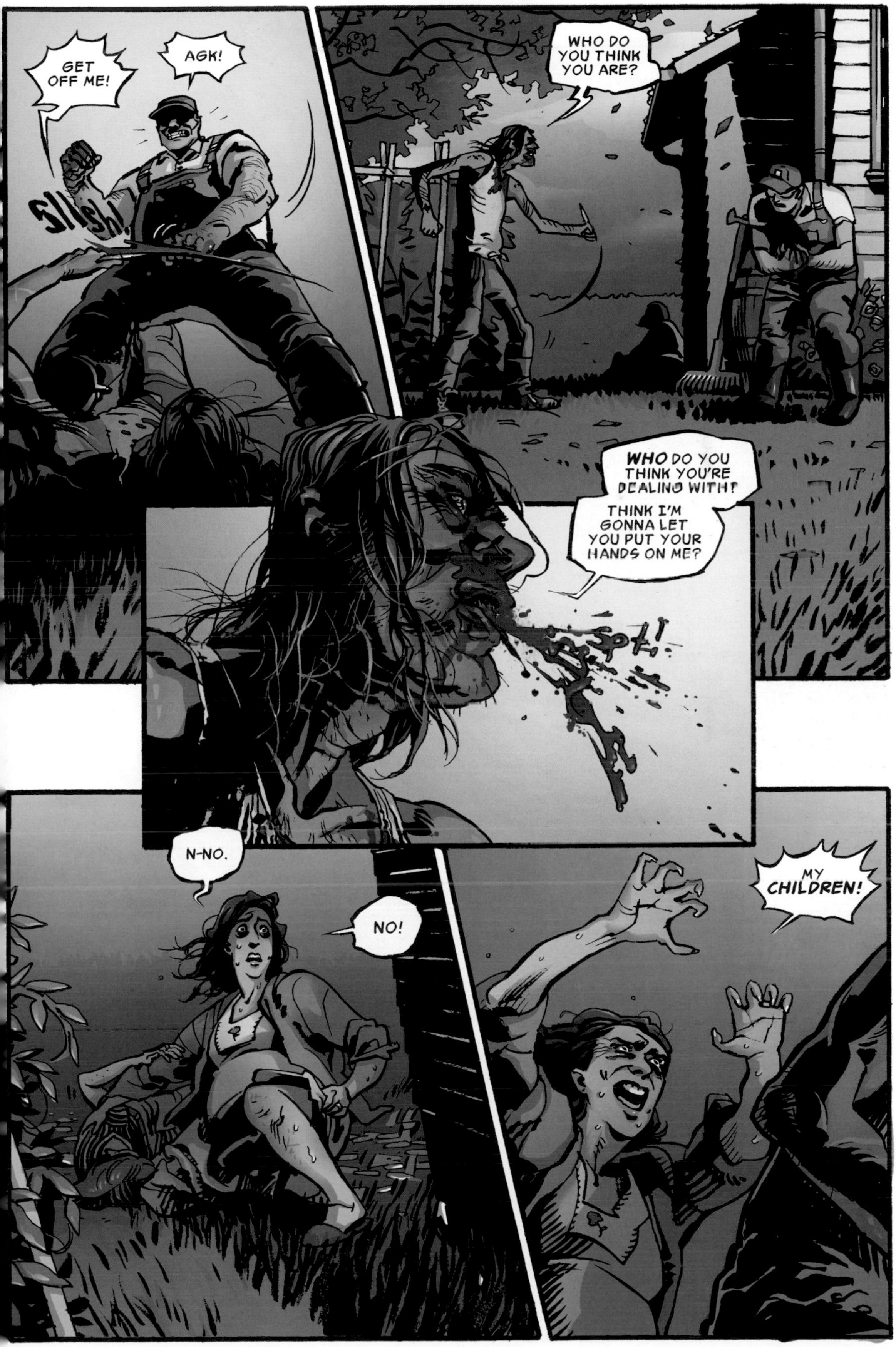
GET OFF ME!
AGK!
SLISH!
WHO DO YOU THINK YOU ARE?
WHO DO YOU THINK YOU'RE DEALING WITH?
THINK I'M GONNA LET YOU PUT YOUR HANDS ON ME?
SPT!
N-NO.
NO!
MY CHILDREN!

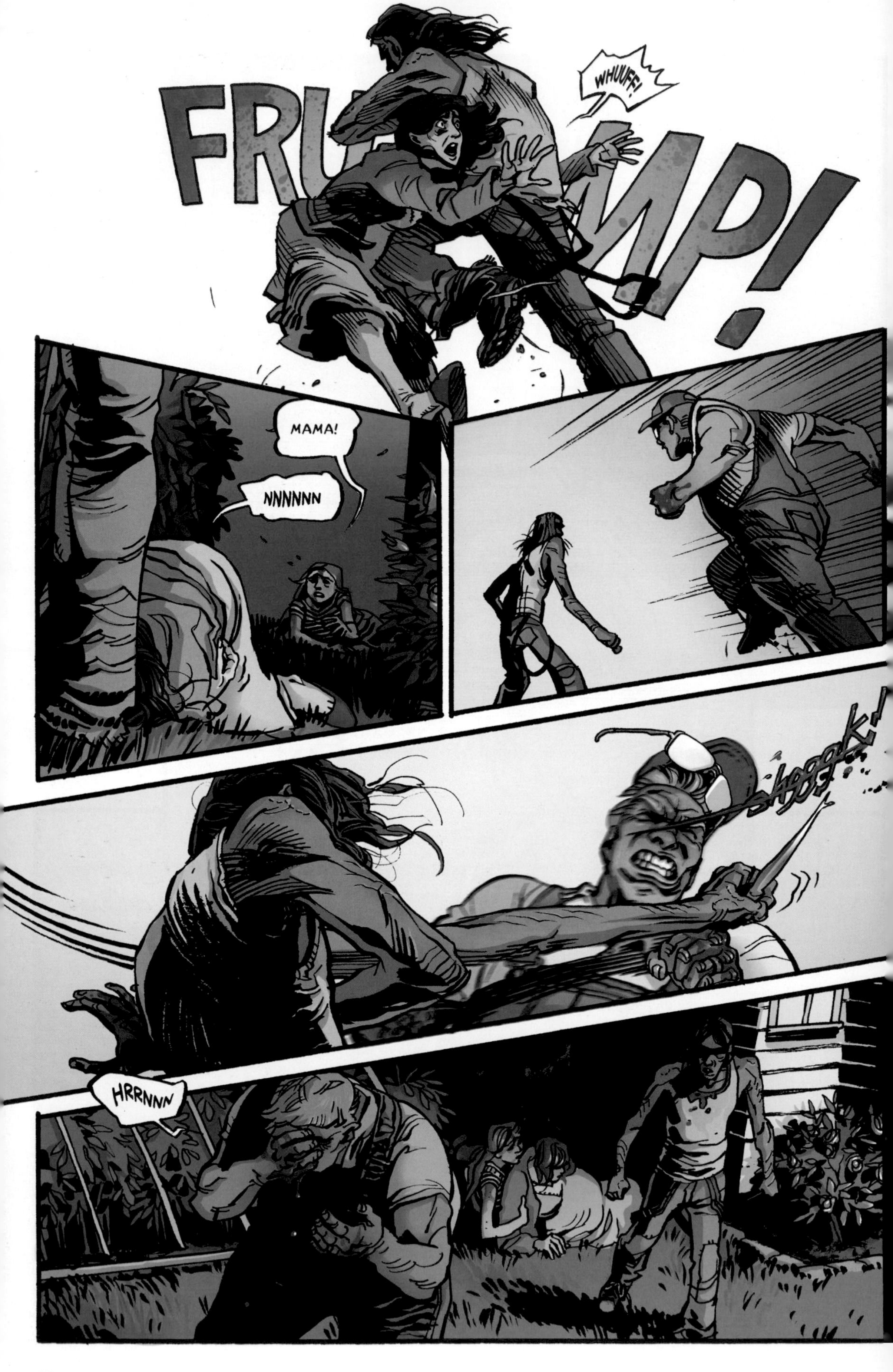
FRUMP!
WHUUFF!
MAMA!
NNNNNN
shhggk!
HRRNNN

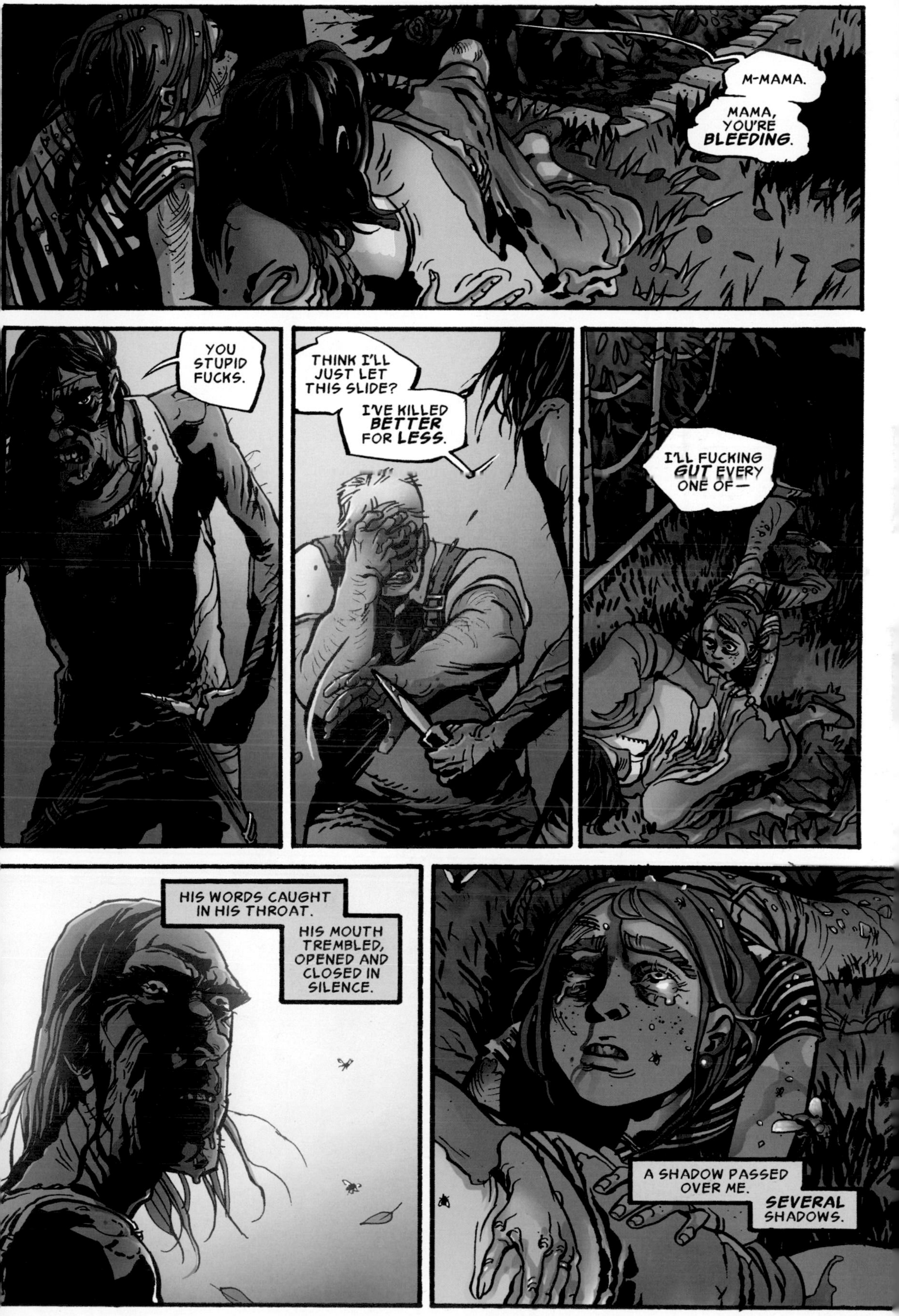
M-MAMA.
MAMA, YOU'RE BLEEDING.
YOU STUPID FUCKS.
THINK I'LL JUST LET THIS SLIDE?
I'VE KILLED BETTER FOR LESS.
I'LL FUCKING GUT EVERY ONE OF—
HIS WORDS CAUGHT IN HIS THROAT.
HIS MOUTH TREMBLED, OPENED AND CLOSED IN SILENCE.
A SHADOW PASSED OVER ME.
SEVERAL SHADOWS.

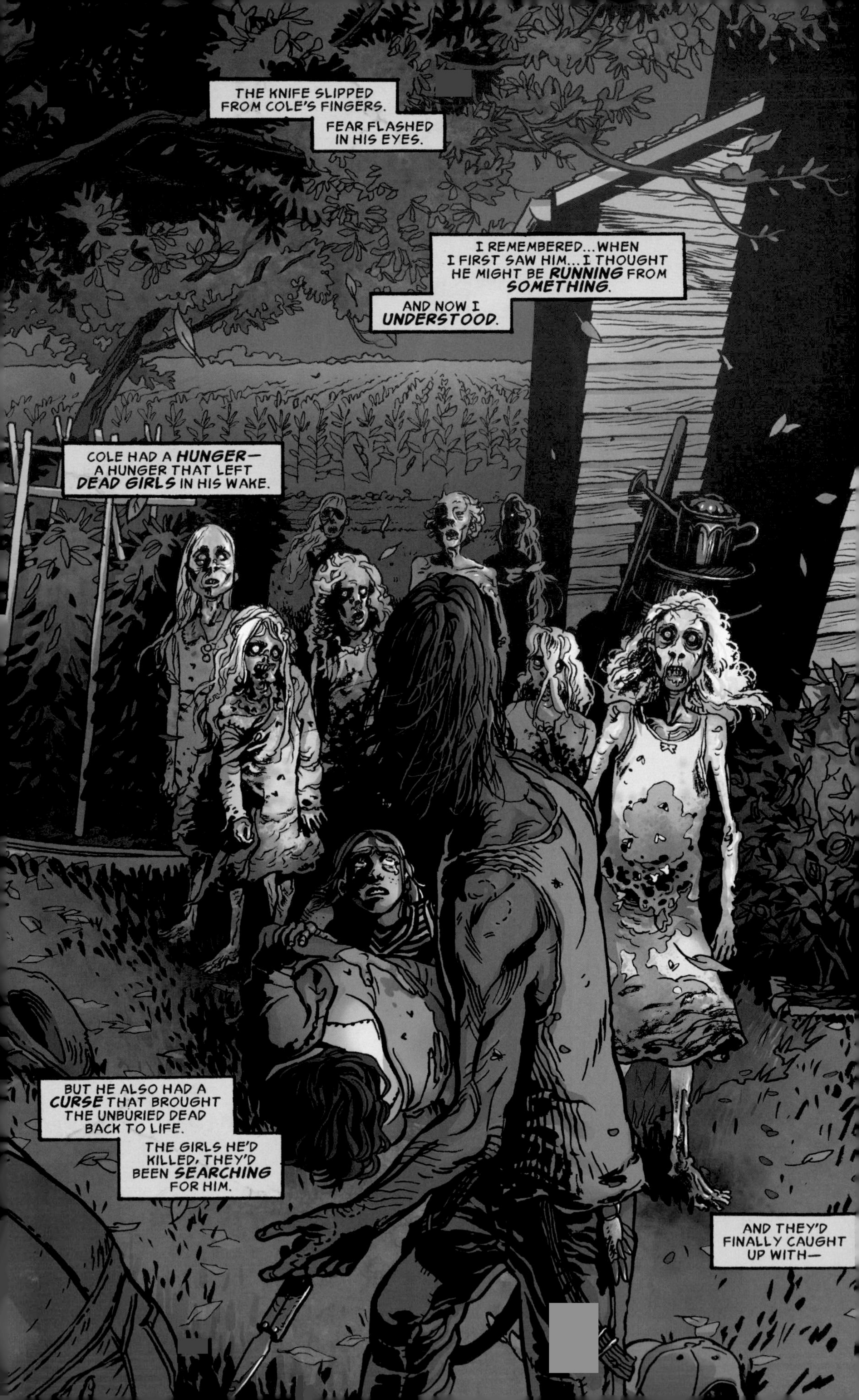
THE KNIFE SLIPPED FROM COLE'S FINGERS.
FEAR FLASHED IN HIS EYES.
I REMEMBERED...WHEN I FIRST SAW HIM...I THOUGHT HE MIGHT BE RUNNING FROM SOMETHING.
AND NOW I UNDERSTOOD.
COLE HAD A HUNGER— A HUNGER THAT LEFT DEAD GIRLS IN HIS WAKE.
BUT HE ALSO HAD A CURSE THAT BROUGHT THE UNBURIED DEAD BACK TO LIFE.
THE GIRLS HE'D KILLED, THEY'D BEEN SEARCHING FOR HIM.
AND THEY'D FINALLY CAUGHT UP WITH—

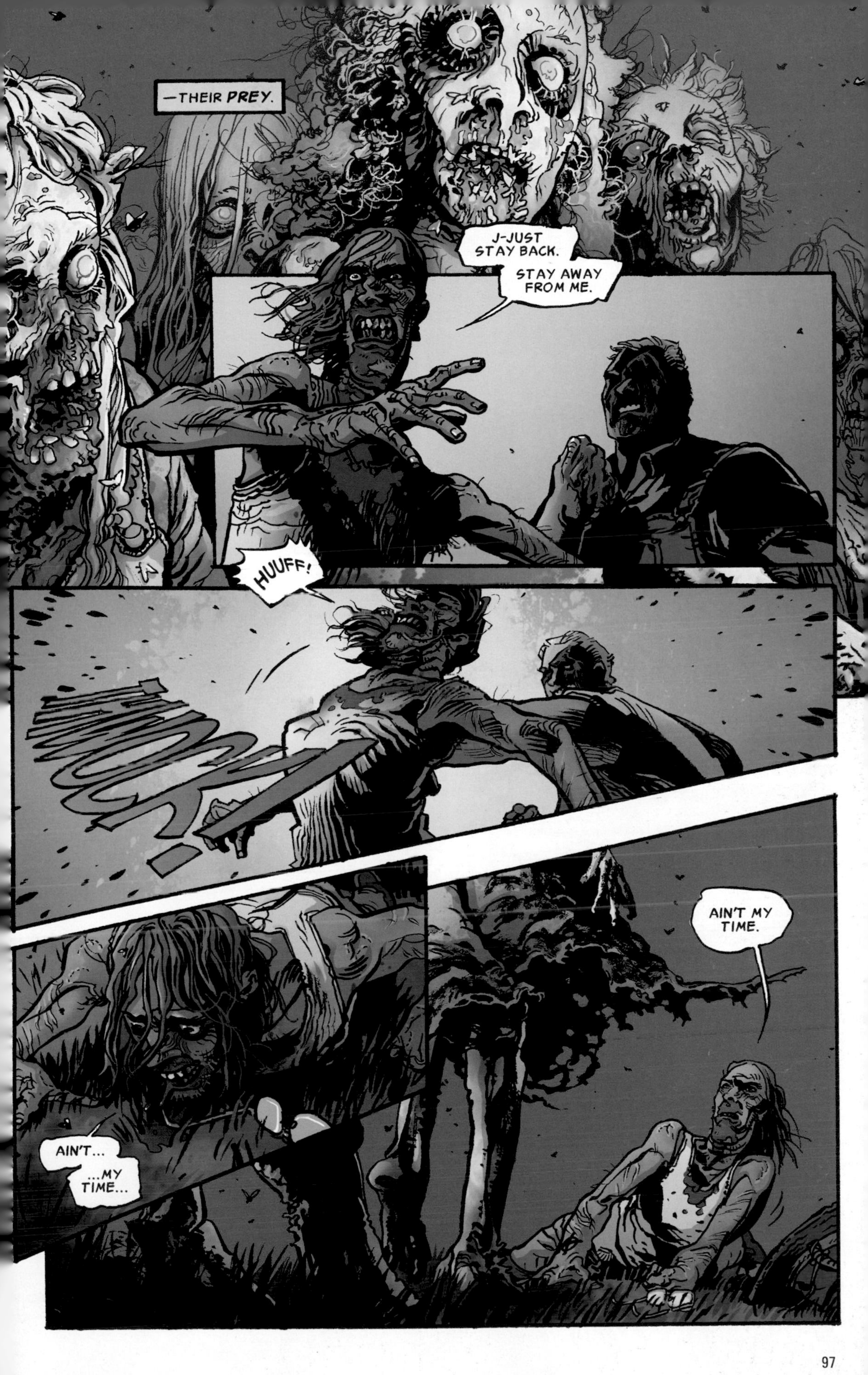

—THEIR PREY.
J-JUST STAY BACK.
STAY AWAY FROM ME.
HUUFF!
AIN'T...
...MY TIME...
AIN'T MY TIME.

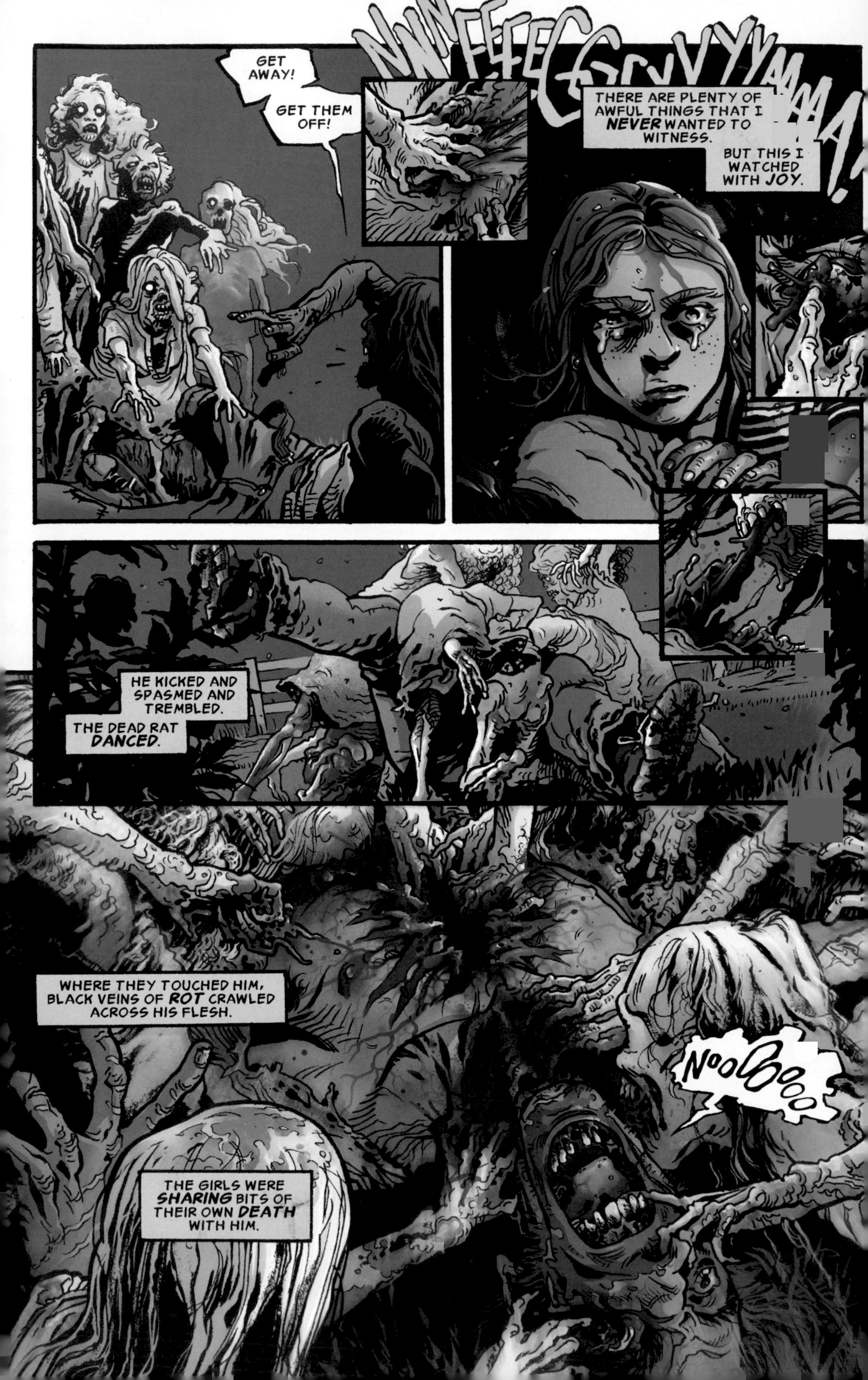
GET AWAY!
GET THEM OFF!
THERE ARE PLENTY OF AWFUL THINGS THAT I NEVER WANTED TO WITNESS.
BUT THIS I WATCHED WITH JOY.
HE KICKED AND SPASMED AND TREMBLED.
THE DEAD RAT DANCED.
WHERE THEY TOUCHED HIM, BLACK VEINS OF ROT CRAWLED ACROSS HIS FLESH.
THE GIRLS WERE SHARING BITS OF THEIR OWN DEATH WITH HIM.

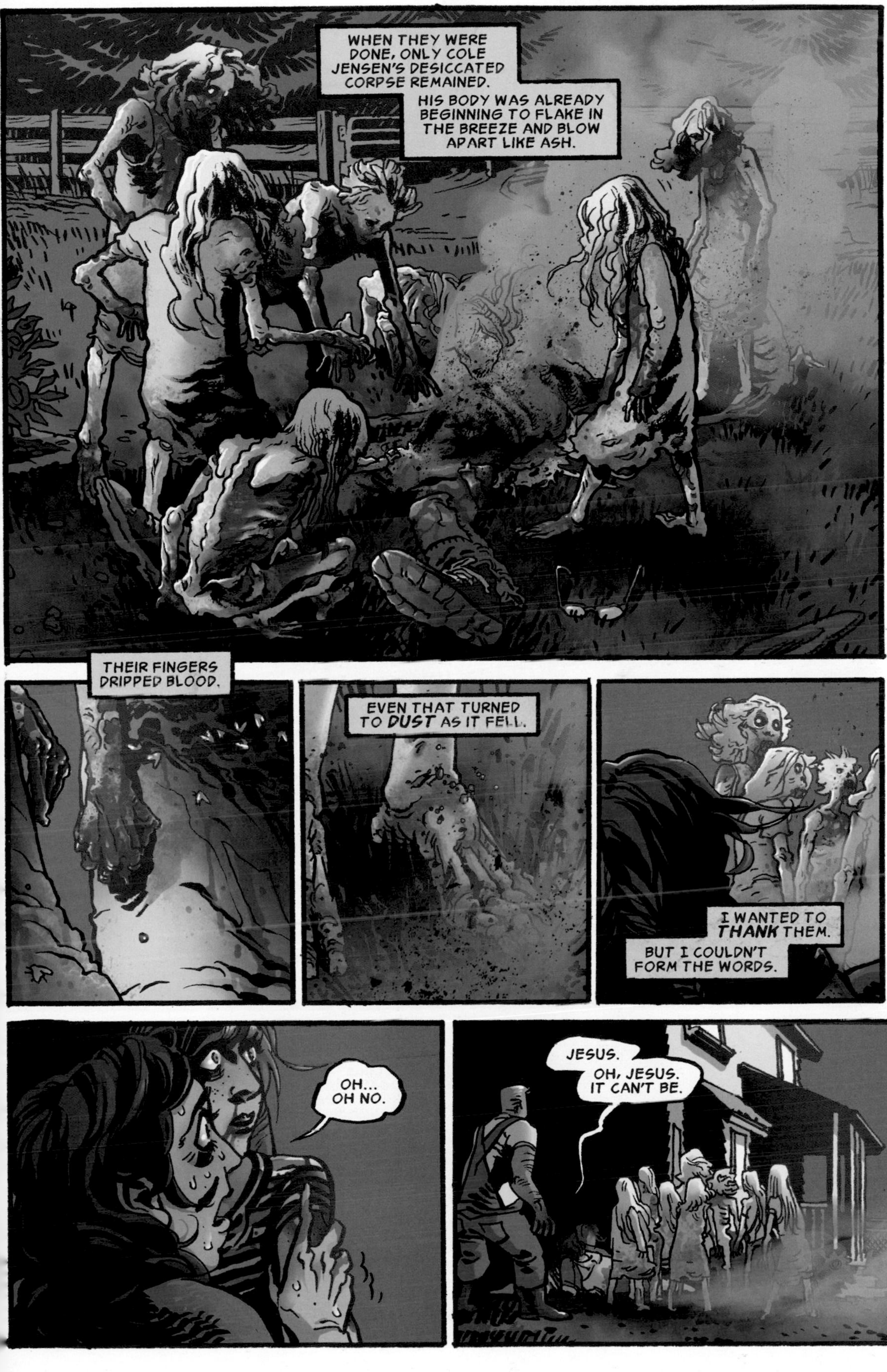
WHEN THEY WERE DONE, ONLY COLE JENSEN'S DESICCATED CORPSE REMAINED.
HIS BODY WAS ALREADY BEGINNING TO FLAKE IN THE BREEZE AND BLOW APART LIKE ASH.
THEIR FINGERS DRIPPED BLOOD.
EVEN THAT TURNED TO DUST AS IT FELL.
I WANTED TO THANK THEM.
BUT I COULDN'T FORM THE WORDS.
OH... OH NO.
JESUS.
OH, JESUS. IT CAN'T BE.

ABBIE?

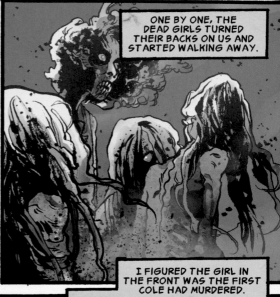

ONE BY ONE, THE DEAD GIRLS TURNED THEIR BACKS ON US AND STARTED WALKING AWAY.

I FIGURED THE GIRL IN THE FRONT WAS THE FIRST COLE HAD MURDERED. THE *LAST* GIRL...

...WAS MY *SISTER.*

I LIKE TO THINK ABBIE LOOKED BACK AT US, EVEN FOR A SECOND, BEFORE SHE VANISHED FROM SIGHT.

BUT I COULDN'T BE SURE.

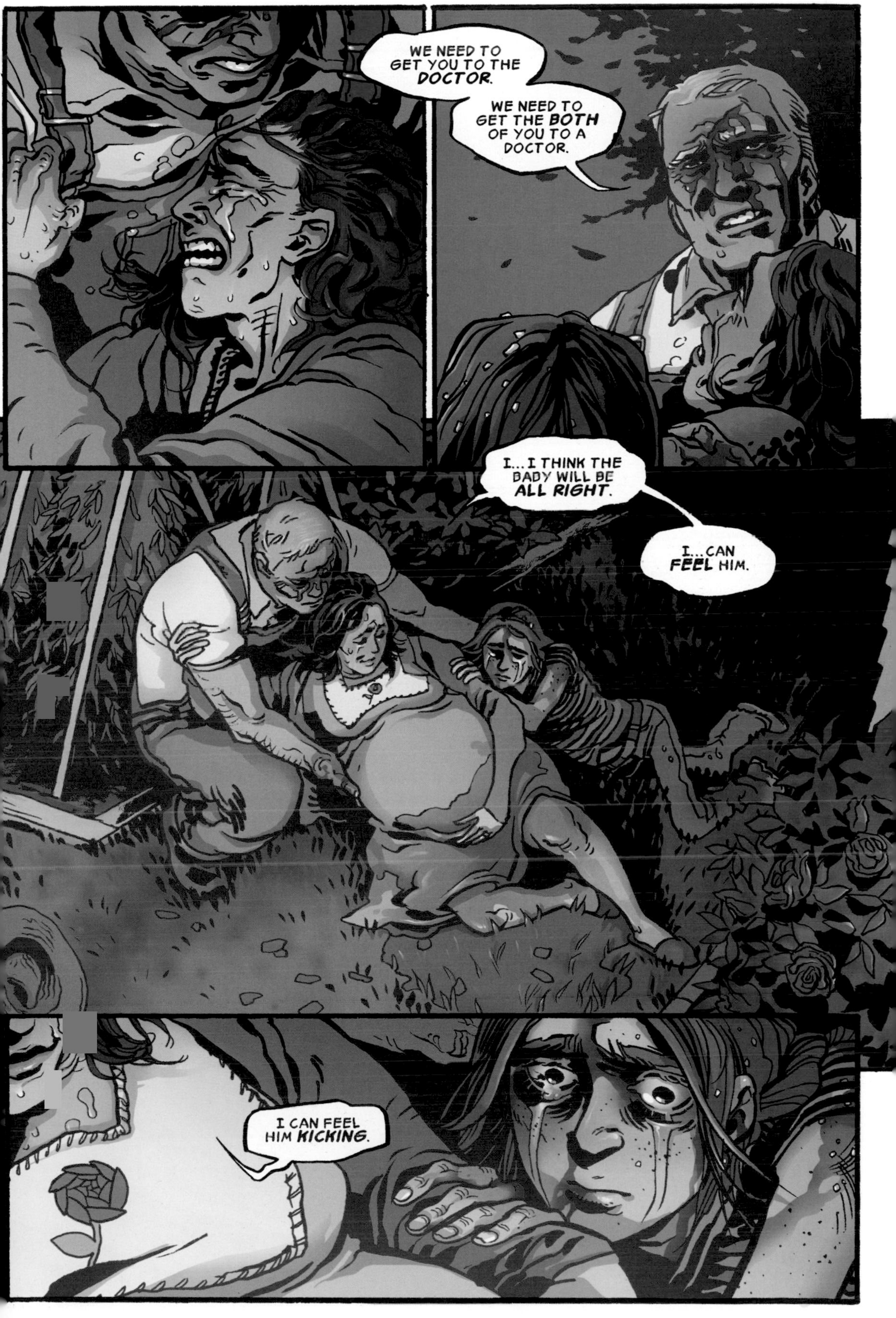
WE NEED TO GET YOU TO THE DOCTOR.
WE NEED TO GET THE BOTH OF YOU TO A DOCTOR.
I... I THINK THE BABY WILL BE ALL RIGHT.
I... CAN FEEL HIM.
I CAN FEEL HIM KICKING.

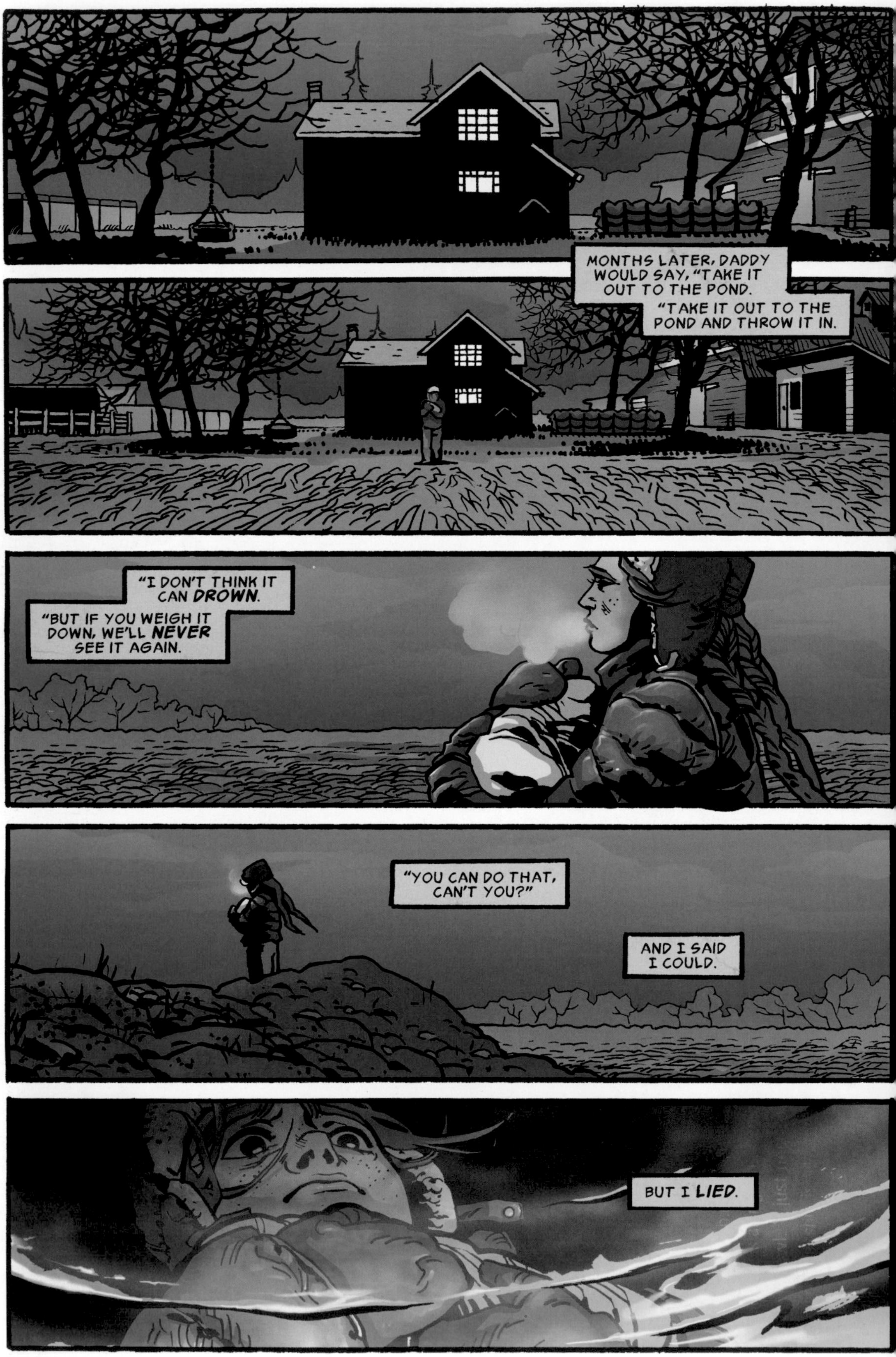
MONTHS LATER, DADDY WOULD SAY, "TAKE IT OUT TO THE POND.
"TAKE IT OUT TO THE POND AND THROW IT IN.
"I DON'T THINK IT CAN DROWN.
"BUT IF YOU WEIGH IT DOWN, WE'LL NEVER SEE IT AGAIN.
"YOU CAN DO THAT, CAN'T YOU?"
AND I SAID I COULD.
BUT I LIED.

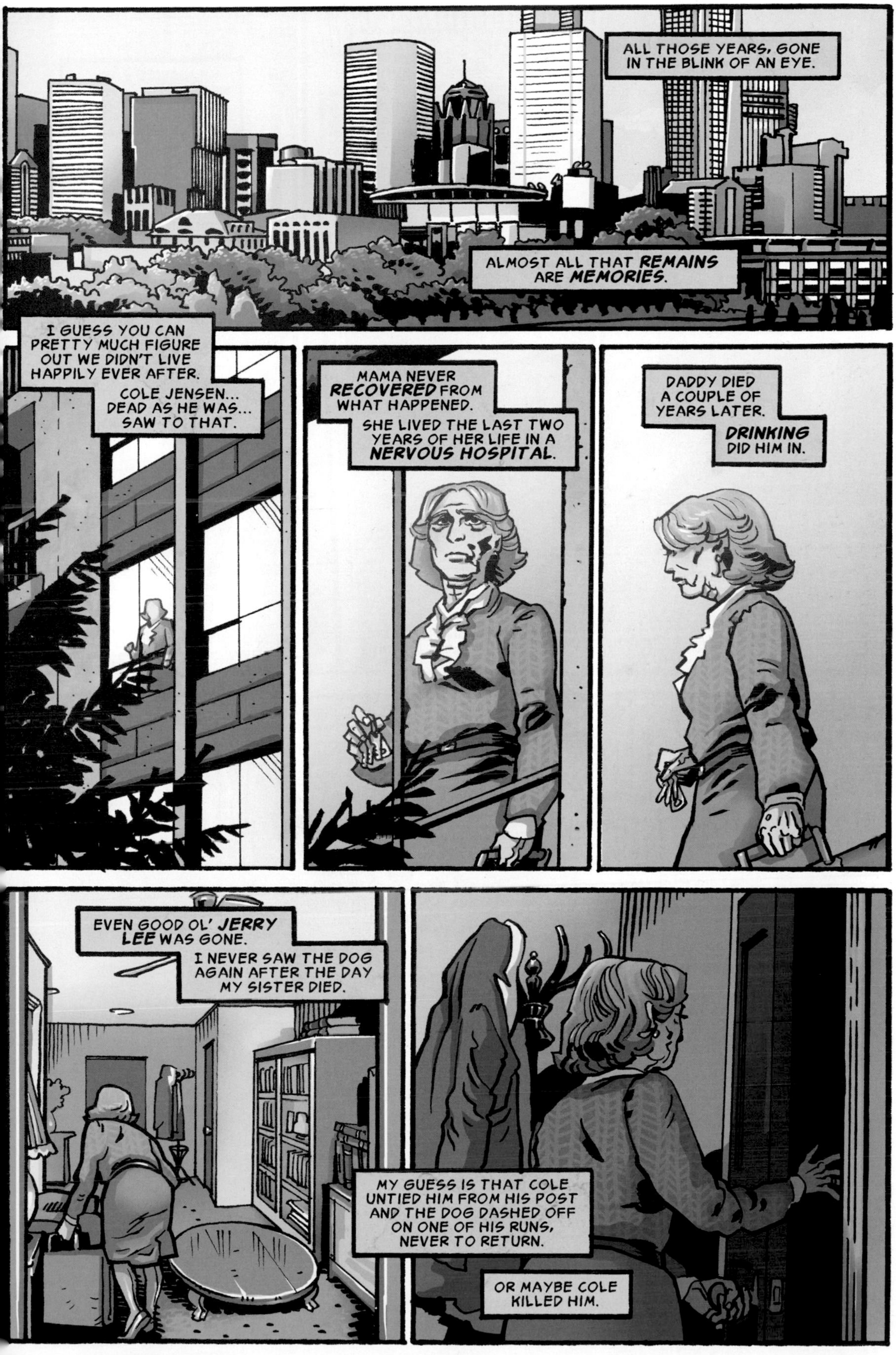
ALL THOSE YEARS, GONE IN THE BLINK OF AN EYE.
ALMOST ALL THAT REMAINS ARE MEMORIES.
I GUESS YOU CAN PRETTY MUCH FIGURE OUT WE DIDN'T LIVE HAPPILY EVER AFTER.
COLE JENSEN... DEAD AS HE WAS... SAW TO THAT.
MAMA NEVER RECOVERED FROM WHAT HAPPENED.
SHE LIVED THE LAST TWO YEARS OF HER LIFE IN A NERVOUS HOSPITAL.
DADDY DIED A COUPLE OF YEARS LATER.
DRINKING DID HIM IN.
EVEN GOOD OL' JERRY LEE WAS GONE.
I NEVER SAW THE DOG AGAIN AFTER THE DAY MY SISTER DIED.
MY GUESS IS THAT COLE UNTIED HIM FROM HIS POST AND THE DOG DASHED OFF ON ONE OF HIS RUNS, NEVER TO RETURN.
OR MAYBE COLE KILLED HIM.

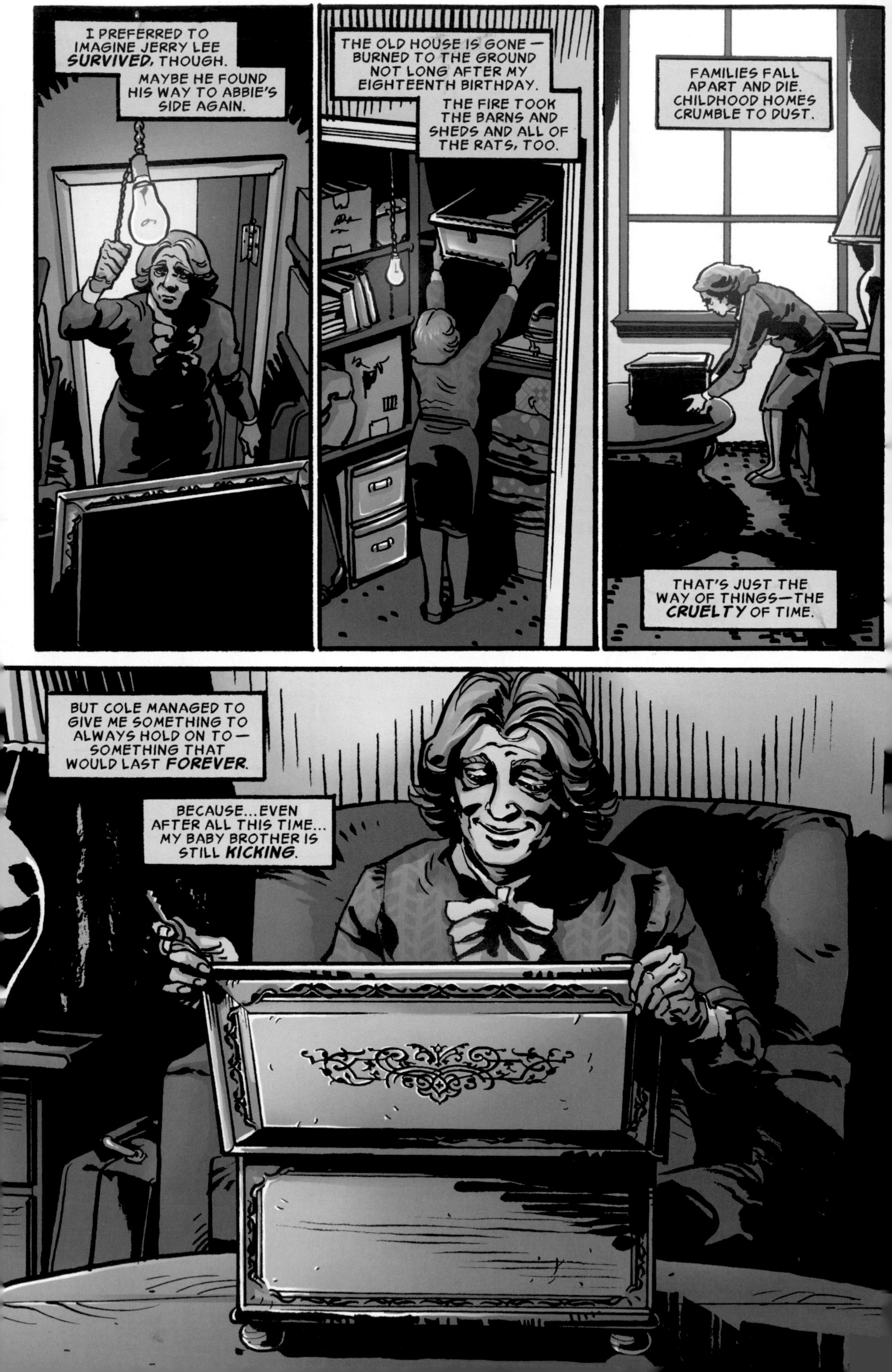

I PREFERRED TO IMAGINE JERRY LEE SURVIVED, THOUGH.
MAYBE HE FOUND HIS WAY TO ABBIE'S SIDE AGAIN.
THE OLD HOUSE IS GONE—BURNED TO THE GROUND NOT LONG AFTER MY EIGHTEENTH BIRTHDAY.
THE FIRE TOOK THE BARNS AND SHEDS AND ALL OF THE RATS, TOO.
FAMILIES FALL APART AND DIE. CHILDHOOD HOMES CRUMBLE TO DUST.
THAT'S JUST THE WAY OF THINGS—THE CRUELTY OF TIME.
BUT COLE MANAGED TO GIVE ME SOMETHING TO ALWAYS HOLD ON TO—SOMETHING THAT WOULD LAST FOREVER.
BECAUSE...EVEN AFTER ALL THIS TIME... MY BABY BROTHER IS STILL KICKING.

SKETCHES

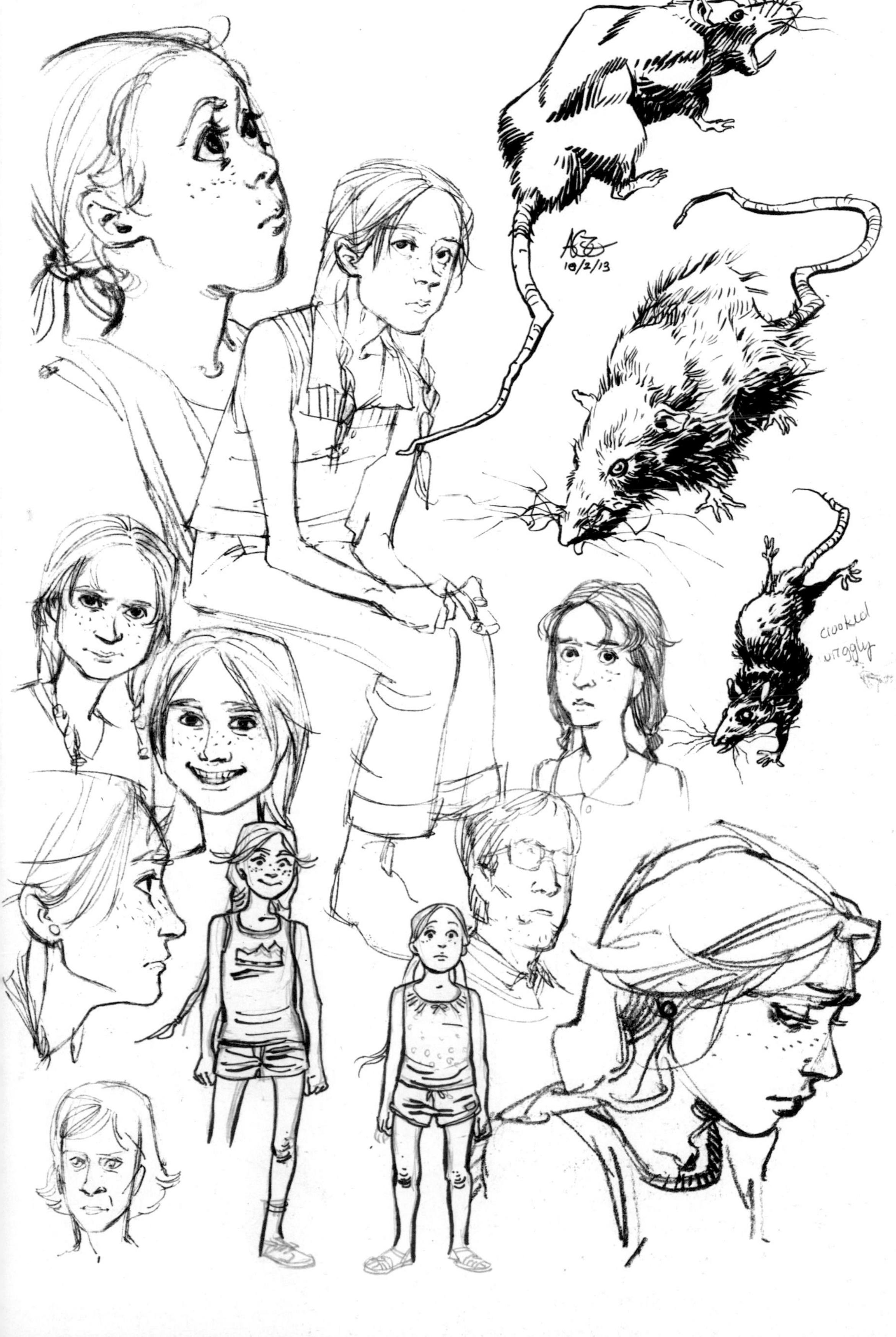

10/2/13
crooked
wriggly

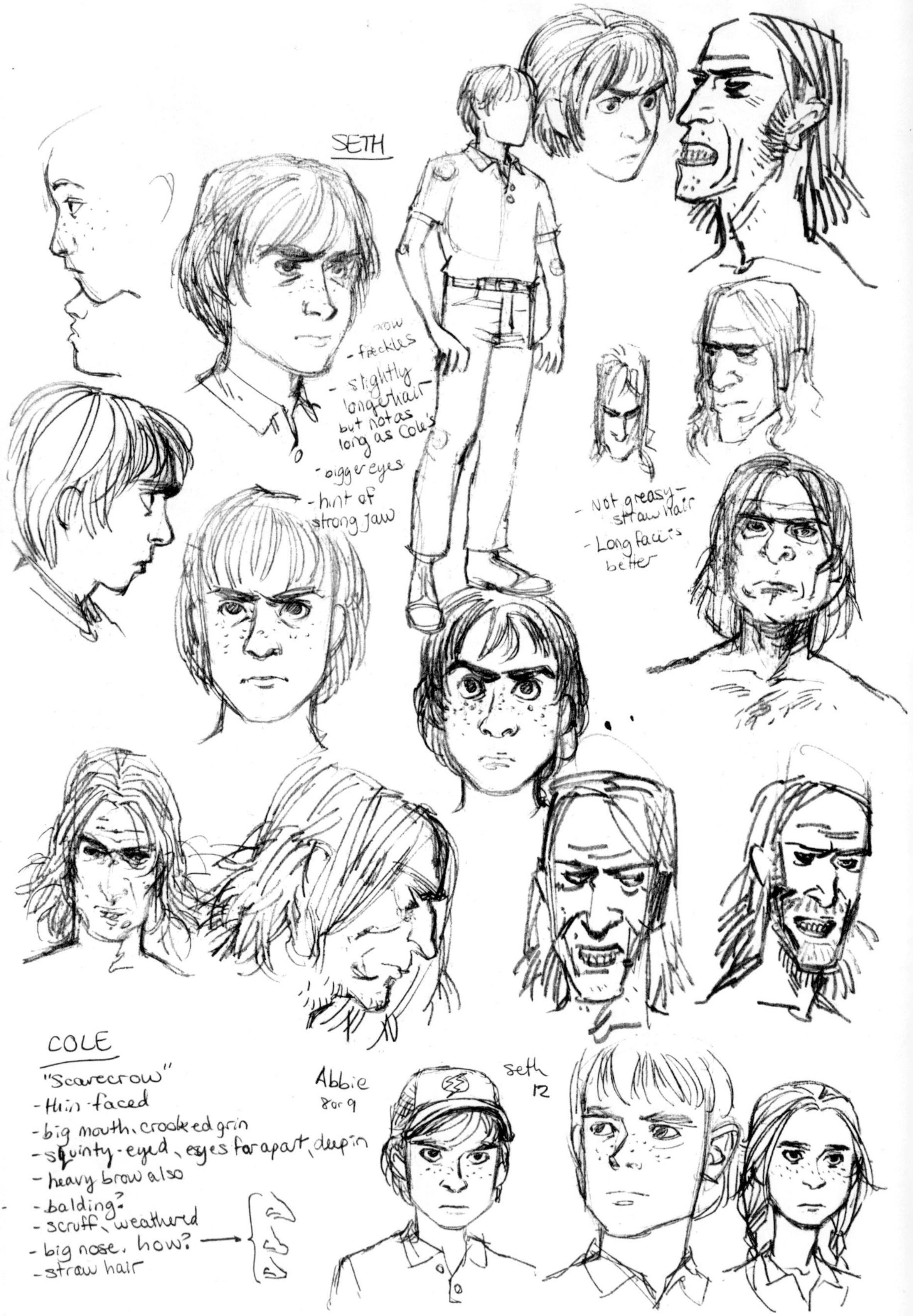
SETH
- freckles
- slightly longer hair but not as long as Cole's
- bigger eyes
- hint of strong jaw
- Not greasy - straw hair
- Long face is better
COLE
"Scarecrow"
- thin-faced
- big mouth, crooked grin
- squinty-eyed, eyes far apart, deep in
- heavy brow also
- balding?
- scruff, weathered
- big nose, how?
- straw hair
Abbie
8 or 9
Seth
12

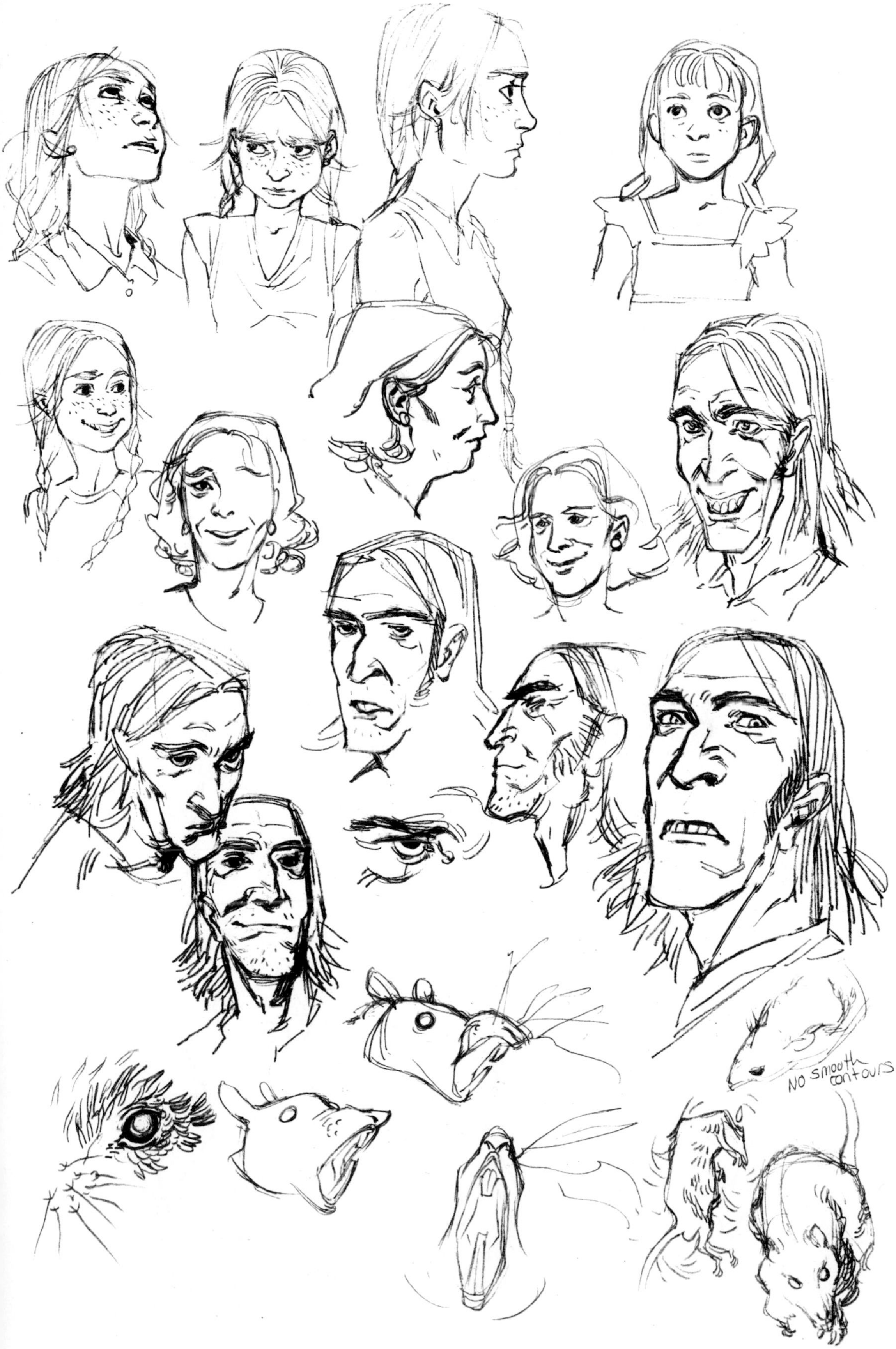
No smooth contours

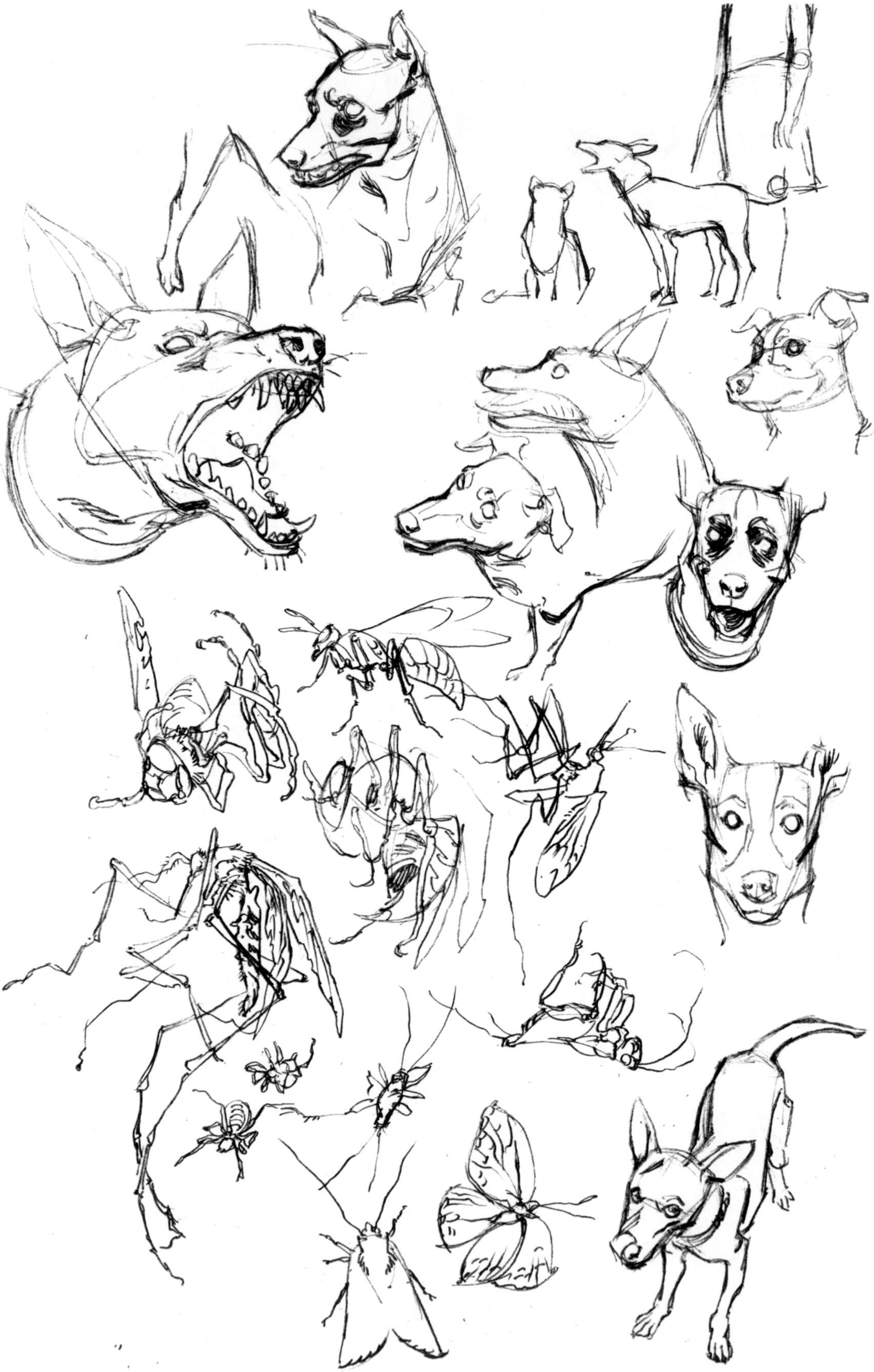

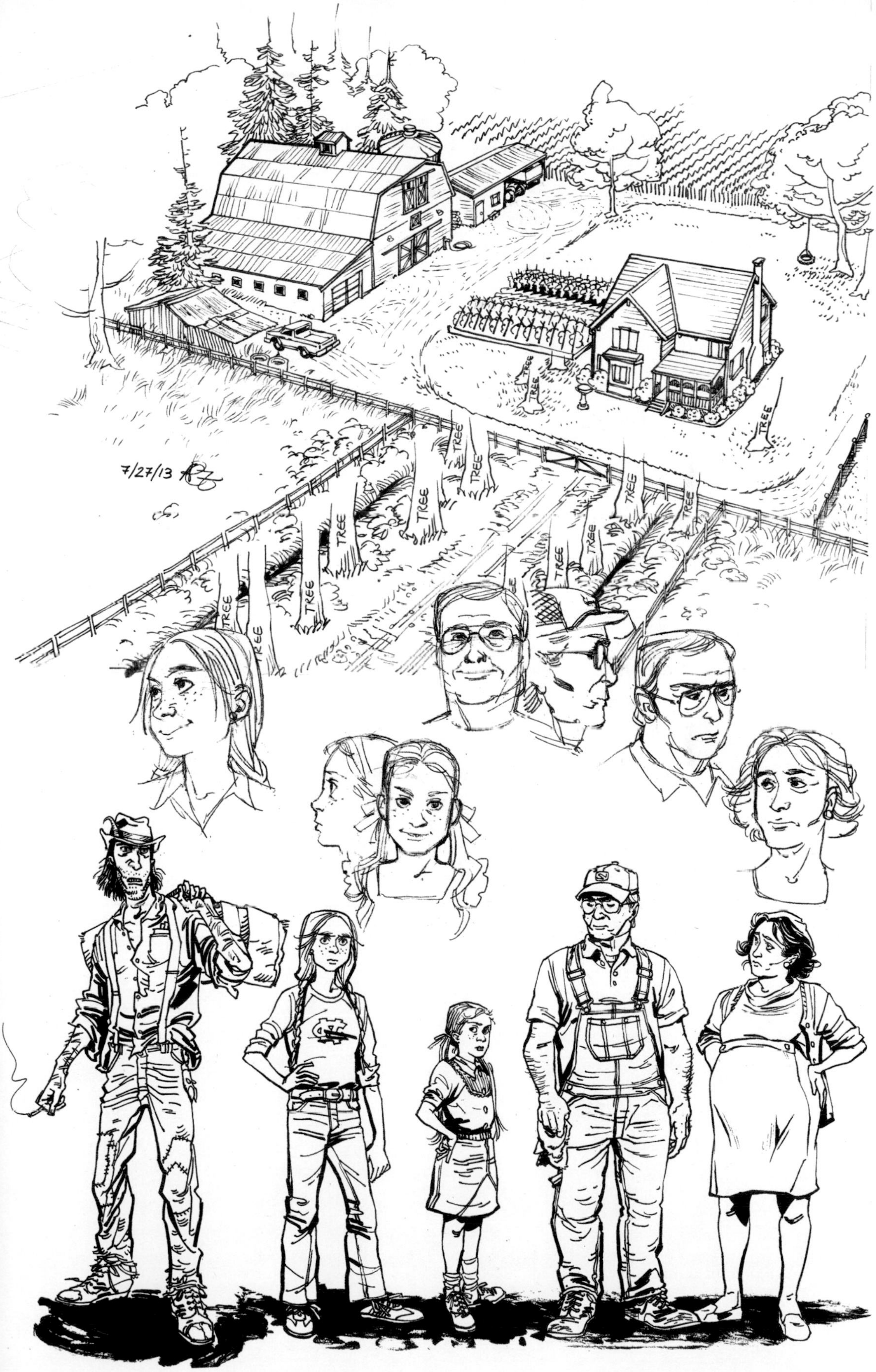

7/27/13
TREE

REMAINS

The original title of this book was *Remains* and was originally published online by Monkeybrain Comics. We decided to change the name for the print version because there already was a comic out there called *Remains* so we wanted to make sure Cullen's story had an original title for print. Like *Harrow County*, the earliest version of this tale existed as a prose story written by Cullen. Included here is the original prose tale where you will notice a few similarities and differences. Enjoy!

The dead rats danced the day the hired man came round.

My father, rest his soul, might have scolded me for saying such a foolish thing. He didn't care much for dreams and fancies—nightmares, either. But that's how it started, way back during those last warm weeks of September, more than thirty years ago.

With dead rats.

Dancing.

My little sister spotted the stranger before I did. I was shelling peas, like Mama had asked the both of us. Sitting on the warped front steps, I snapped pods, scraped peas into a large bowl, and tossed the husks into the yard for the chickens to squabble over. Abbie, on the other hand, did everything in her power to avoid anything remotely akin to a chore. I could hear her crawling around the crawlspace beneath the front porch.

"What are you doing?" I asked.

"I'm *busy*."

"Sure you are." I glanced at the bucket of unsnapped peas. The supply didn't appear to be diminished, despite my efforts. "You know, you're supposed to be helping."

"I'm *busy*," Abbie said again.

"Mama doesn't want you playing under there anyhow. You're gonna ruin your clothes, and there's spiders down there big enough to bite your fingers off."

I grabbed another snap from the bucket and cracked it open for emphasis. Abbie hated spiders, and I hoped to startle her out from under the porch. Considering how hardheaded my little sister could be, though, I should've known better.

"Ain't no spiders down here, Seth, not that I ever saw."

"You *sure* about that?"

"Yes, I am, thank you very much."

I sighed in defeat. Since scaring her didn't work, I decided to give guilt a try.

"Maybe not, but you should come on out of there anyhow. I wouldn't ever stick you with doing the chores all by yourself."

That was a lie, but as I hollowed out yet another shell, it felt like the truth.

Abbie started humming a lighthearted tune, partly to let me know our discussion was at an end. I halfway considered tattling on her, just to watch Mama drag her out from under the porch

jutted out through the latticework lining the porch. Through the holes in the trim, I saw her big blue eyes peering out from the shadows. "He looking for someone?"

He's on the run, I thought, *from the law . . . Or something worse*.

The idea just popped into my head. Unexpected thoughts like that often exploded through my noggin, and I'd been accused of letting my imagination get the better of me more than once. To hear my folks tell the tale, I read too many of those crime and horror comics Mr. Oswald stocked at the drugstore. Maybe I did, maybe I didn't. Either way, I'd learned to keep my lips sealed when it came to my wild notions.

But I didn't like the stranger from the moment I spotted him.

Something about him put me on edge.

He gave me the creeps.

"You just stay put." I rapped my knuckles against the porch, and Abbie pulled her fingers back into the shadows. "Stay quiet. Stay out of sight."

For once, Abbie didn't backtalk me. I figured the stranger spooked her as much as he did me. In its time, the filthy crawlspace beneath the porch had served as a fairy-tale castle and the Lone Ranger's base of operations, an army bunker and a mud-pie bakery. But today, Abbie used it as a hiding place.

I continued shelling peas, but I didn't take my eyes off the man as he tramped my way. I couldn't guess his age with any accuracy. He might have been in his late thirties or early forties. His face was weathered from countless hours wiled away in the sun, and his longish hair was more gray than black.

"Afternoon," he said. His voice was deep and gravelly, as if road grit coated his throat.

I nodded and scowled at him.

He shrugged his bag from his shoulder. The duffel *thunked* into the dirt. Placing one of his steel-toed work boots on the lowest porch step, the stranger leaned close and draped his arms over his knee. His sleeves were rolled up to his elbows, and I saw dozens of scars crisscrossing

and take a switch to her backside. But Abbie and me, we had an understanding—we didn't snitch, no matter what. Sometimes, the agreement bit me in the behind, but a deal's a deal. I kept on snapping peas, and before I knew it, I was humming right along with my sister.

I didn't notice the lone figure approaching our house, but eagle-eyed Abbie spotted him right away.

"Who's that?" It took me a second to realize she'd stopped humming. Her voice was hushed and muffled. "Somebody's coming this way."

I shaded my eyes from the sun and looked down the tree-lined path.

The stranger was tall and lean, dressed in dirty jeans and a button-up work shirt. He carried a bulky duffel bag slung over his shoulder. For some reason, he reminded me of a scarecrow that had crawled down from its perch in the cornfield. I couldn't really see his face, because the shadows from the trees seemed to cling to his features. He didn't so much walk as lope, like an animal, and every few steps he paused to glance over his shoulder, as if expecting to see someone following him.

"What's he doing?" Abbie's small fingers

the flesh of his forearms—some of them still pink and only recently healed by the looks of it. Dirt had settled into the wrinkles of his face and hands, and his fingernails were crescents of pure black.

"Your daddy home?" he asked.

Underneath the porch, Abbie shuffled in the dirt, crawling back into the darkest of the shadows. The stranger tilted his head. His eyes strayed toward the latticework, and one corner of his mouth rose.

"I'll fetch him," I said.

I put the bowl of shelled peas aside and stood up.

His eyes ticked away from Abbie's hiding place and met mine. His grin came across like a bestial thing. His teeth were yellowed and looked sharp. I backed toward the screen door. I called for my father, and I felt a rush of relief when I heard the heavy tread of his approaching footsteps.

The stranger looked over his shoulder again.

I narrowed my eyes. *What are you running from?*

He stood up straight when Daddy stepped onto the porch. My father was a big man, tall and broad shouldered, and he'd worked hard almost every day of his life. He wore his favorite pair of blue coveralls. His greasy cap was folded up and shoved in his pocket, because he never—never—wore a hat indoors. I could tell his hands were bothering him. His knuckles were red and swollen as thick as tubers, and his fingers curled like the legs of a dying spider. Sometimes, his rheumatism flared up so bad he could hardly pick up his fork to eat breakfast. Today was one of those days, and Daddy's voice was laced with a painful weariness.

"Help you?"

"I sure hope so." The stranger kept on smiling. "Word is you're looking to hire a man to pitch in around your place. Figured I'd come by and see about the job, unless you've already brought somebody else on."

Daddy eyed the man for a second or two, sizing him up.

"You ain't from around here, are you?"

"No, sir. I was just passing through when I heard about the job. Thought I could stay around for a while, though, maybe earn some extra traveling money."

"Where is it you're headed?"

The stranger nodded and sucked at his teeth. "No place in particular."

"You ever work a farm before?"

"Worked tobacco since I was a boy, and I spent a couple summers as a farmhand outside of Knoxville."

"I can't offer much of a wage," Daddy said, "barely enough to get by, really. There's a backroom in the toolshed that's got a cot and a washbasin. You can bed down there. We'll feed you three times a day, but you'll have to take your meals either in the shed or outside."

The rule about eating outside didn't sit particularly well with Daddy. As far as he was concerned, anyone who worked the land deserved a seat at our supper table. But he knew my mother would never stand for a stranger sitting alongside her family.

In this case, I was glad for my mama's ways.

"All that sounds fine," the stranger said. "I don't need much, and it'll be nice to sleep with a roof over my head and get three squares for a change."

Three squares, I thought. *Sounds like something an escaped convict might say.*

Nah. That's just your comic books talking.

"All right then," Daddy said. "Sounds like you've got yourself a job."

The stranger thanked my father and introduced himself as Cole Jensen. He stuck out his hand. Daddy hesitated for a second, then reluctantly reached out to shake the hired man's hand. He winced painfully as Cole's fingers closed around his own. I could have sworn I saw a disdainful smirk wriggle across Cole's face.

"Why don't you go put your bag away?" Daddy pointed to the toolshed. "I'll be over directly to show you around."

As Cole trudged to the shed, I whispered to my father, "You don't need to pay somebody to help. I can handle anything needs doing."

"I know you can. But there's too much for any three people to do, let alone two. Your mama's about to pop with the new baby, and you and your sister have your schooling to attend to."

"I could stay home and help instead."

It wasn't a completely selfish gesture. Matter of fact, I liked school, especially reading and writing. But I didn't like the idea of Cole Jensen lurking around the farm when I wasn't around to keep an eye on him.

"You can help in the mornings and the after-noons. Don't fret. We won't do it all without you."

He rubbed his hands together, trying to work the ache from his bones, and he tapped his foot against the porch steps.

"Abbie, get out from under there before your mama catches you and tans your hide. I don't want to listen to your wailing when your rear end's stinging."

My sister scurried out into the light.

Daddy smiled and said, "Why don't you two take Jerry Lee out to the barn for a while?"

"Yes, sir," I said, all too glad to take a break from field snaps.

"Do we have to?" Abbie whined. "We were gonna go out to the pond this afternoon."

"Don't give me any duff," Daddy said. "You know you aren't supposed to hang around at that old mud hole. But if you hurry up you can

finish your chores and still have some time to play a little before suppertime. The more belly-aching you do now, the less time you'll have for fun later."

Pouting, Abbie made a spectacle of dragging herself away.

Daddy only shook his head. Like the rest of the family, he was accustomed to Abbie's over-dramatic antics.

"One day," he said—more to himself to anyone, "that girl will break all the hearts in Hollywood."

I fought back the urge to warn him about the hired man. Daddy was a hard-working man, and he toiled in the *real* world, not in a world where boys spied boogeymen in the shadows.

But he might be an escaped criminal . . . or maybe even a killer.

Daddy wouldn't see it that way.

From around the other side of the house, Abbie called impatiently, "Hurry up, Seth!"

I watched my father greet Cole Jensen by the toolshed. I looked long and hard at the road that bordered our farm. I didn't see anyone com-ing to haul the hired man away. But I sure wished I did. After a few minutes, I went to join my sister.

Something told me nothing would ever be the same again.

I had never known any home other than the farm. Our house, tall and white and surrounded by Mama's rosebushes . . . The old shed, with its sagging roof and rotting walls, and its re-placement, with its fresh coat of paint and that eyesore of a tractor parked beneath . . . The cement birdbath, where cardinals sometimes gathered in the mornings . . .

I loved that old farm.

But the hired man ruined it all.

Spoiled it.

After it was all said and done, I hated the farm.

And I hated Cole Jensen and what he had brought with him.

This is how it happened.

* * *

We kept Jerry Lee chained to a post in the backyard. The little rat terrier would get to running and never stop if he got a wild hair. I'd spent more than a few afternoons chasing him from darn near one side of the county to the other. He wasn't good for much, except for one thing, but Abbie loved him anyhow. As I rounded the corner, I saw my sister kneeling down beside the black-and-white dog. She scratched behind his ears, and he wagged his stubby tail. His tongue lolled out of his mouth.

"Come on, Jerry Lee!" I clapped my hands together. "We're going to the barn!"

As soon as he heard the word *barn*, the dog jumped to attention, his muscles tense, his eyes darting and alert.

"Why'd you go and do that?" Abbie stood up and put her hands on her hips defiantly. "We were having us a relaxing time."

"We don't keep him around to be your pet."

"You're just jealous because he's *my* best friend."

"A dog like this, he ain't nobody's friend." I unhooked Jerry Lee's chain from the post in the ground. I held one end of the chain like a leash. "You're a dyed-in-the-wool killer, ain't ya, boy?"

Jerry Lee tugged at the chain.

Abbie wrinkled her nose and shot me a raspberry.

"I wish a green fly would land on your tongue," I said.

Jerry Lee pulled in the direction of the barn. He might have been small, but he was strong. I kept a firm grip on the chain. For Jerry Lee, the barn meant one thing.

Rats.

He jumped and yipped as Abbie and I opened the barn doors. Light spilled across the dirt floor, chasing shadows into the corners. The barn was old and dark and smelled of dust. Along the wall leaned a couple of thick, three-foot-long sticks. Abbie grabbed them and handed me one as I undid the chain around Jerry Lee's neck. He might have been a runner, but I didn't worry about him charging off while he was on the job. Sniffing the ground, he walked into the center of

the barn, like he had done a hundred times before. A low growl rattled in his throat. He stood at attention, waiting.

Rats infested the barn. Big ones. Some almost as big as Jerry Lee. Nothing we did deterred them. Daddy had tried poisoning them with d-con, and for a while we discovered a bunch of mummified rat corpses in the corners. But eventually, they stopped taking the bait. We brought in barn cats, but some of them vanished altogether or—as I believed—were devoured by the rats, and the remaining felines decided to avoid the barn altogether. We lined the feed barrels with metal, but it wasn't long before the rodents gnawed right through. If a rat could gnaw through metal, I didn't want to think what it could do to flesh and bone.

I wasn't worried, though, because my sister and I were armed with the most lethal rat-killing weapon known to man.

Jerry Lee.

Abbie and I used the sticks to jab at the shadowy corners of the barn and behind feed barrels, flushing rats from hiding. As soon as the squealing vermin scurried across the room, Jerry Lee pounced. He clamped the rat in his jaws, gave it a quick shake, and tossed the creature—

shattered spine and all—into the dust. On a good day, Jerry Lee could kill three dozen rats in an hour, and he never grew tired of the carnage. The whole time, Abbie wore a look of pure disgust as her favorite pet vented his blood lust. I hate to admit it, but I almost enjoyed myself, and I made a little game out of scaring the rats into Jerry Lee's waiting teeth.

Once we were done, I chained the exhausted terrier to the yard post again. Panting, he flopped on his side to rest. Abbie and I carried out the gruesome task of scooping up the crushed, slobber-matted rat carcasses, tossing them in burlap sacks, and dumping them in the burn barrels around back. I got the feeling the surviving rats watched us with hate-filled eyes from the darkness, but they didn't dare creep out of hiding. We tossed the last of the dead rats in the barrels, and Abbie mopped sweat and dust from her forehead with the back of her arm.

"Think we can go to the pond now?" she asked.

"You heard what Daddy said."

"He don't really care. Besides, he's too busy showing Cole around."

My stomach knotted up at the mention of his name. Maybe getting away from the farm, even for a couple of minutes, wasn't such a bad idea.

"All right." I shrugged. "Let's go." She grinned at me and dashed off.

Jerry Lee hopped up, growled, and *chuffed* a quiet warning. He stood defiantly in the circle of dirt he'd worn in the grass from his prowling, but he stared toward the front of the house. I followed his gaze, and saw Daddy talking to the hired man. Cole didn't seem to be paying much attention to whatever Daddy was saying. Instead, he looked back at me.

I jumped when Abbie called out to me.

"You coming, Seth?"

She stood at the edge of the cornfield, shifting from one foot to the other, almost like she had to pee. I moved toward her, but glanced over my shoulder.

I realized something that chilled my blood.

The hired man wasn't looking at me.

He was staring at my sister.

Giggling, Abbie raced through the cornfield. Tall stalks loomed around us. Soon, it would be harvest time. Not long after that, the field would be beaten flat in preparation for next season's crops. For now, though, a thick sea of cornstalks enveloped us. I followed Abbie as she weaved back and forth between the rows, kicking up dirt clods, making the stalks shake and sway. By the time we reached the pond, I was covered in sweat and gulping down mouthfuls of hot, dusty air. My shirt and jeans clung wetly to my skin.

Situated right in the middle of the field, the pond was ringed by a high mound of dirt. Climbing to the crest of the earthen hill, I could see row after row of corn stretching off in every direction. Looking back the way we'd come, I saw the roofs of our house and the barn. In the distance ahead of us, I saw the grain silo of the McKinley place. The pond itself was a milky brown color, and was probably more mud than water.

My friends and I had played many a game of King of the Mountain on the hill, and I myself had been soaked in the pond's muddy shallows more than once upon being dethroned. We didn't play there much anymore, though, not after what happened to Delroy McKinley last summer.

To me, the pond seemed lonely and bleak these days.

"I wish we could go swimming." Abbie still loved the spot. She liked throwing stones into the depths or launching paper sailing ships across the surface or watching tadpoles along the shoreline. She scooted down the hill and stood on the pond's bank. "It's hot enough, that's for sure."

"I wouldn't want to swim in that mud hole."

"You would too."

"Go ahead and take a dip if you want." I knew good and well she wouldn't. Abbie never swam in the pond, even before what happened to Delroy. "I'll stay right where I am, thank you very much. You enjoy yourself."

"Maybe I will."

She kicked off her shoes and dipped her toes in the water.

"Have fun," I said. "It'll just be you and Delroy."

"Shut up!" Abbie hopped back from the water as if she'd spotted a shark's fin slicing across the surface. "You ought not say that!"

"Well, it's true." I smiled wickedly. "They never did find his body."

"That's because he didn't drown. He ran away from home."

"If that's what you want to believe, that's fine. But I think he's down in the deep, dark water, sunk in the mud at the bottom so he don't float to the surface. But I bet if you go swimming he'll come up to give you a hug!"

I rolled my eyes back in my head and did my best stiff-legged, stiff-armed voodoo-zombie impersonation, reaching out for my sister with spastic fingers.

Abbie shrieked.

Spiders might not have scared her, but ghosts were another story.

She scurried up the hill and pushed past me. She didn't even bother to pick up her shoes.

"You're a jerk, Seth!"

She crashed through the cornstalks and vanished. I had a good laugh at her expense, but it only lasted a few seconds. If Abbie broke our agreement and told on me, Mama and Daddy would be none too pleased with me for frightening my sister. I scrambled down the hill to grab her shoes, then climbed back up and hurried after her.

The leaves of the cornstalks slapped me in the face as I called for my sister. Somewhere up ahead, I heard Jerry Lee's high-pitched barking. It might have been easy for someone who didn't know any better to get lost among the cornstalks, but I would have known the way home with my eyes closed. When I emerged on the other side of the field, I found Abbie, standing in the backyard. My heart jumped in my chest.

The hired man was on his knees in front of her, and he held her hands in his own.

I rushed to her side.

"What's wrong?"

Abbie pulled her hands away from the hired man. "N-nothing," she said. Her face was flushed.

Cole stood up. He towered over the two of us.

"Something spooked her pretty bad." He fished a pack of cigarettes from his breast pocket. "I'd hate to think her big brother was trying to scare the poor little thing to death."

Ain't none of your business, I thought, but I didn't say a word.

"There's plenty of things to be scared of out in the world," Cole said. "Hell, I bet some of them would even scare the spit out of a big, strapping boy such as yourself. How about that—you ever been real scared, Seth?"

I ignored him and took Abbie's hand.

"Come on. We need to get cleaned up for supper."

"I bet you have." Cole sneered. "I bet you've been so scared you nearly wet your pants from time to time."

I pulled my sister along as I walked away from the hired man. I trembled like I'd been out in the cold. His words chased after me, nipped at my heels.

I *felt* his eyes watching me.

Watching Abbie.

We should have burned the rats.

Daddy didn't like us manning the burn barrel without him around, but we'd done it before, more than once.

Maybe if we had burned the dead rats right away, everything would have turned out differently.

That's a silly thing to think, of course. The rats didn't cause the troubles that beset our farm. They were just the first of the symptoms.

Symptoms, like with a disease.

A disease Cole Jensen brought down upon us.

We went to bed pretty early that night, because Daddy's hands were worrying him something fierce, and Mama, who was due to give birth to my baby brother or sister any day, wasn't feeling good at all. I shared a bedroom with Abbie. It might have been a nice place to rest my head. It was plenty big, and the second-story window overlooked a good portion of the farm, including the barn and the new tool shed. But an imaginary line split the room in two. On one side was my stuff—my matchbox cars and comic books and Indian arrowhead collection. The other side was done up in pinks and flowers and paint-by-number portraits of ponies. The room could have been the size of a castle, and it still wouldn't be big enough for my little sister and me. Abbie's side of the room seemed to grow larger with each passing day, while mine became more and more claustrophobic.

In a few months, I thought, *I'll be thirteen. That's too old to be sharing a room with my sister.*

I had hoped that when the baby was born, my folks might let me move out to the guest quarters in the tool shed. Mama didn't like the idea, but Daddy thought I was plenty old enough. It had been a long time since I'd had any real privacy, and I had big plans for fixing up the room. Now that Cole was living out in the shed, my dreams had been dashed. With my luck, I'd soon be sharing a crowded room with Abbie *and* the new baby's crib.

The hired man had been there for just one day, and I was already anxious for his departure.

I sat in bed, reading an issue of *Famous Monsters of Filmland*. Abbie lay on her belly on her own bed and played with a set of paper dolls. We both liked to stay up as late as we could, regardless of how tired we'd be the next day at school. Sleeping was for babies and old folks.

Outside, Jerry Lee barked. I didn't really pay attention at first, but the dog kept on yapping, like something was driving his poor little doggie brain into a frenzy.

"What's that mutt going on about?" I put my magazine aside. "Daddy's gonna wring his neck if he don't shut up."

"Maybe there's somebody out there," Abbie said. "Somebody who shouldn't be."

Yeah, I thought, *like Cole*.

Maybe Jerry Lee *was* barking at the hired man. After all, the dog didn't know him at all, and it was likely he sensed something strange about him. Dogs had a keen nose for such things.

Something crashed outside—a metallic thud and rattle.

I knew right away what it was.

The burn barrel.

I hopped out of bed. Every now and again, raccoons or possums got into the trash, and it was usually my job to run them off. If I didn't haul my behind out there and scare them away tonight, there'd be trash and dead rats strewn from one end of the farm to the other come morning. And I knew who'd get stuck with the chore of cleaning up the mess. Better to take care of it now rather than later.

Abbie started getting dressed, too, and she dragged the flashlight out from the top dresser drawer. One thing about my sister—she was plenty curious, even about the smallest things. There was no way she was going to let me go out there by myself.

The farm was dark and quiet, except for Jerry Lee's incessant barking. I was a little surprised Daddy hadn't heard the racket. Sometimes at night he took pain medicine for his hands, and the stuff near about knocked him out. That might be the only thing saving Jerry Lee's life.

Abbie carried the flashlight, and the glow bounced across the ground ahead of us. The barn rose out of the shadows like a great fortress.

A fortress full of rats.

The blinds were drawn over the window to the tool shed's guest room. The room was dark. Obviously, Cole could sleep like the dead, too.

Abbie flashed the light around the corner of the barn. Sure enough, the burn barrel lay on its side. It rocked gently back and forth. Trash spilled out of the mouth. My sister turned the light toward Jerry Lee. His eyes gleamed in the dark. He pulled at his chain as he barked at the overturned barrel.

"Hush!" I hissed at him. "Be quiet, now!"

I approached the barrel and lifted it back upright, spilling a little more garbage onto the ground. Something twitched at my feet. Dozens of smallish forms crawled all around me. At first, I thought an entire family of possums had gotten into the trash and were now scurrying all around the barrel. But I saw the burlap sack spread out across the ground.

Saw the hole ripped in the cloth.

Abbie pressed up behind me. She aimed the flashlight's beam at the ground.

"Look, Seth! Look!"

Those rats had been dead as doornails when we threw them in the barrel. I would have put my hand on the Bible and sworn it. But they were alive now . . . and squirming and squealing and hissing in the dirt.

I backed away.

Slowly.

"What's wrong with them?" Abbie asked.

Some of the rats writhed and wriggled toward us, but they moved in herky-jerky spasms. Others just squirmed around in circles. Still others simply trembled and spasmed violently where they lay.

"They almost look like they're dancing," Abbie said.

But they weren't dancing, not really, and they weren't alive, either. The rats we'd tossed into the burn barrel had been ripped and torn and broken by Jerry Lee's attack. Blood still covered their fur. The hair and skin peeled away from the glistening flesh of a few of the rodents. At least one trailed a fleshy strand of its own guts. There was no way the rats should have been convulsing and scrabbling and shimmying before us.

They were dead.

And they were dancing.

Behind me, Jerry Lee barked.

"Abbie," I said, "quiet Jerry Lee down before he wakes up the entire county. I've got to get something from the barn."

"What are you gonna do?"

"Just keep the dog quiet, okay?"

Abbie nodded and rushed to Jerry Lee's side. She calmed him as best she could, but he still woofed and growled.

From the barn, I gathered a shovel and another cloth sack. I saw the red eyes of the other rats—the living rats—staring at me from the shapeless dark.

I hurried back to the burn barrel and laid the sack open on the ground. Using the shovel, I scooped up the shuddering rat carcasses and tossed them into the bag. As I bent down to

shovel up one of the rats, the creature twisted and lurched at me. I dropped the shovel and staggered away, but the rat sank its fangs into the meat of my palm.

"Ahh!"

The dead rat clamped its teeth into my flesh. I flung my arm about wildly, trying to shake the rat free. My hand stung where the rat bit me . . .

But it was also cold.

Like ice.

Only colder.

For a second, I felt like I was sinking into icy water.

Finally, I flung the rat to the ground. Clutching my hand, I drew my foot back and kicked the rat. It squeaked and rolled across the ground.

My hand bled from several small puncture marks. The skin around the wound looked dry and gray. Several black veins ran across my skin, leading away from the bite. I felt like I'd stuck my hand against a piece of frozen pipe. As I watched, the dark markings faded and the color returned to my skin. All that remained was the bite marks.

What in the world . . .

Thankfully, I didn't think the bite was serious enough to need stitches. It was going to hurt like hell over the next few days, though. I flexed my fingers. The memory of the sudden, strange coldness lingered in my nerves.

I snatched up the shovel and used the flat end to bash each and every one of the rats. Some of them stopped moving as soon as I smashed them. A few others needed three or four good whacks before they lay still. The one that bit me I must have hit a dozen times or more, and when I was done there wasn't much left of it but a puddle. Then I went back and finished off the rats I'd already tossed in the bag before they got a chance to gnaw through the burlap. When I finished, a greasy stain covered the sackcloth.

My hand throbbed. Blood dribbled down my fingers.

I tied the bag's opening into a knot.

Jerry Lee had stopped his barking altogether now that the rats were dead.

Really dead.

I looked at my sister.

"Why don't you go back inside. I'll be along directly."

"Where are you going?"

"I'm gonna bury this bag out in the field." I tested the weight of the sack. "I'm not sure how far just yet, but out somewhere we won't find it again, I hope."

"And then what are we gonna do?"

I looked out into the darkness of the field. The stalks hissed at me in the wind. The sound reminded me of whispered secrets.

"Then we'll try to forget what we saw."

I only wish we could have put the night behind us.

But, like I said, the rats were only the beginning.

On the bus ride to school, I asked Abbie to keep what she'd seen secret. She'd managed to get through breakfast without mentioning the rats, mainly because Mama was still in bed feeling poorly and Daddy was already working the farm. We had made ourselves cereal and toast, and we'd eaten in silence. I didn't know if she'd be able to make it through the entire day without telling her friends. I'll admit, I wanted to tell my buddies about the rats, too. I was sure I could spin one helluva yarn.

But something about the rats . . .

Something told me this was one of those secrets that needed to stay buried.

"It might be best if we keep our mouths shut about last night," I whispered. Abbie had her forehead pressed against the window, and she sighed as she watched the world pass by. For her, the ride to school every morning might as well have been a trip down death row. "We should keep this between us, I think, at least for a little while. Abbie? Are you listening to me?"

"I hear you." She scrunched up her face the way she did when she saw or smelled something disgusting. "I don't even like thinking about those rats. Why would I want to tell anyone?"

"Swear?"

I held out my hand, and Abbie wrapped her pinkie around mine.

"Swear," she said.

For Abbie and me, a pinkie swear was just as good as a blood oath. She could always go back on her word—either of us could—but to do so was unheard of when it came to me and my sister. She'd let the story die. In time, she might even forget about it altogether.

My hand ached like you wouldn't believe. I'd bandaged it up as best I could. Blood had already seeped through the gauze. If somebody asked me how I'd hurt myself, I'd just tell them I slipped and cut my hand on my pocketknife.

Eventually, the bite would heal, and I doubted it would scar.

As long as the rats stayed dead, we'd be all right.

Sometime after sunset, Jerry Lee started barking again. The memory of those rats, shuddering and jumping on the ground, biting me with their icy teeth, sent a shiver up my spine. Daddy was having a devil of a time with his rheumatism, and even though Mama had cooked up some oats to soothe his swollen knuckles, he was in a foul temperament.

"Seth," he said, "go out there and do something about that dog. His barking's getting on my last nerve."

I didn't often hear such an edge in my father's voice. Daddy wasn't a cruel man by any stretch of the imagination, but he wasn't one to trifle with, either, especially when the dreadful pain in his hands flared. I put my homework aside and stood.

"Come on, Abbie."

My little sister, who had finished her own homework and was busy coloring, put aside her crayons.

"Leave her be," Daddy said. "Can't you do this on your own?"

I looked down. "Yes, sir."

Abbie pouted, but returned to her coloring book. I didn't need her help, but I would have certainly felt more comfortable with her by my side. That's something I would have never admitted back then, but these days, I don't see any reason to deny it.

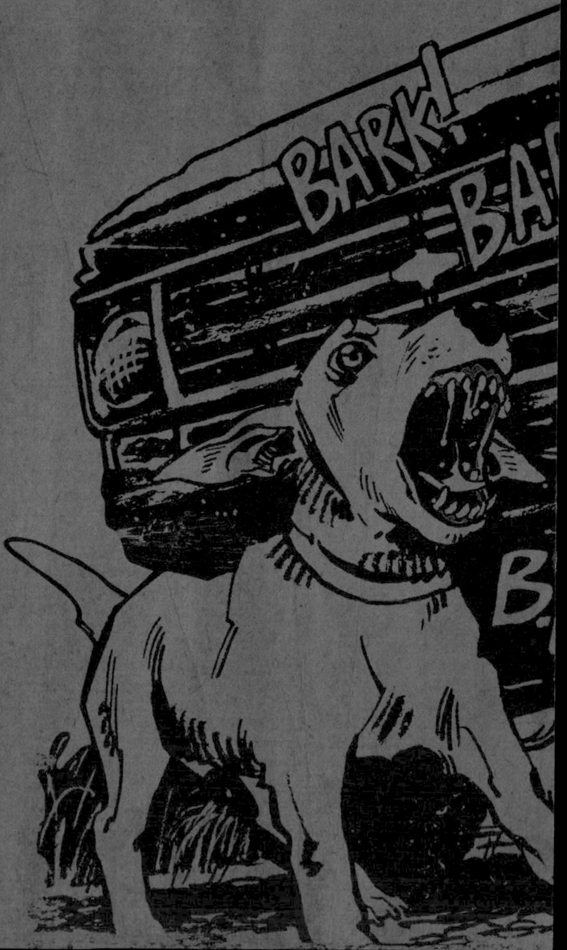
BARK!

Daddy winced at the dog's yipping.

"Just hush him up. I don't care if you have to bring him inside with you."

That last drew a stern look out of my mother, who hated the idea of having animals in the house. Daddy didn't notice the look, though, and Mama decided not to argue.

The night air was still, and the only sound was that of Jerry Lee barking up a storm. I stomped down the steps and around the house to where we kept him leashed, but the dog wasn't there. His chain lay in a silvery pile on the ground. The clip on the business end of the leash was snapped open. That happened sometimes, usually when Jerry Lee tugged and pulled too hard. I still heard him barking, though, so I figured he hadn't gone far. I hollered and clapped for him. For a second, he stopped barking, and I halfway thought he might be heeding my call. But only a few seconds passed before he started yapping again—this time louder than before. Sighing, I followed the sound.

Jerry Lee stood guard outside the old shed—the one with the sagging roof and crumbling old walls. The door to the shed stood ajar, and the little dog vented his fury in the direction of the opening. The pitch of his snarling sounded different up close—less menacing and more frightened—and he didn't dare take another step toward the building. I walked right up and hooked my fingers around his collar. I gave him a quick jerk to quiet him. He yelped and looked up at me.

"What's gotten into you? You keep making such a ruckus and Daddy will haul your sorry hide to the pound."

Jerry Lee cocked his head to the side and regarded me with large eyes that seemed to say, *What's the matter with you? Can't you tell something's wrong here?* Then, he caught wind of something in the shed again, and despite the fact that I had ahold of him, he started barking again. He thrashed and jumped so violently, he almost pulled free of my hand, and nothing I did seemed to calm him.

More than likely, one of the lazy barn cats had managed to nudge the door to the old shed open and had crept inside. If not cats, then maybe—

Rats.

I thought of those dead rats . . . dancing . . . and I started to drag Jerry Lee away from the shed. As I looked up, I saw a shadow move beyond the open door. Whatever it was, it didn't look much like one of the cats to me.

"Who's there?" I asked. No one answered. I asked again—"Who's there?"—this time raising my voice to be heard over the dog's frenzied barking.

I knew I should just hurry back inside and tell Daddy what I'd seen. If there was a prowler about, Daddy would see to running him off. But I also knew that if I was just jumping at shadows—and shadows were, after all, the only thing I'd seen—my father would be none too pleased, considering his mood.

I stepped closer to the shed. *Just a peek*, I told myself, *before I jump to conclusions*. Bolstered by my company, Jerry Lee cautiously followed. A low growl settled in his throat.

I looked inside. Daddy threatened on a regular basis to tear the old shed down. We didn't use it anymore, but my father must have had a soft spot for the old shed, like he believed it added a kind of weed-overgrown charm to the farm. Inside, deep pools of shadow gathered in the corners, spreading along the walls. Here and there, weak beams of moonlight shone through small holes in the rusty ceiling and rotting walls. Dust spun lazily in the damp light.

I didn't see any skulking prowler, though, so I stepped inside for a better look.

"Ugh!"

A veil of sticky webs swept across my face. I spat and frantically slapped the sticky strands away. Even after the webs were gone, I continued to brush at my face, and I imagined spiders crawling all over me.

Jerry Lee growled at the darkness.

"Come on, boy."

Suddenly, the shadows didn't look so empty. It seemed as though the shed had grown in the darkness, swelled inside to hold all the haints and goblins of the world. I wished I had brought the flashlight with me.

I heard a faint humming somewhere above. I looked up. The pale moonlight shimmered through a delicate canopy of webbing overhead. Here and there, small, dark objects were entangled in the web—almost like stars dotting the night sky, only if the sky was white and the stars were black as pitch. Flies, I realized, and wasps and horseflies and snake doctors, all caught in the webs and long dead.

Only, they weren't dead at all.

Each and every one of the insects twitched and buzzed in the web, wings vibrating, legs quivering as they tried to free themselves. The entire blanket of webs trembled overhead, and I worried that the frantic spasms of the trapped insects might bring the whole thing down on top of me like a net.

One of the insects—a large horsefly—shook free and plummeted to the dirt floor. It lay on its back, wings buzzing, legs kicking frantically. Jerry Lee took a step toward the bug, lowering his head to take a sniff. I grabbed his collar again and pulled him back.

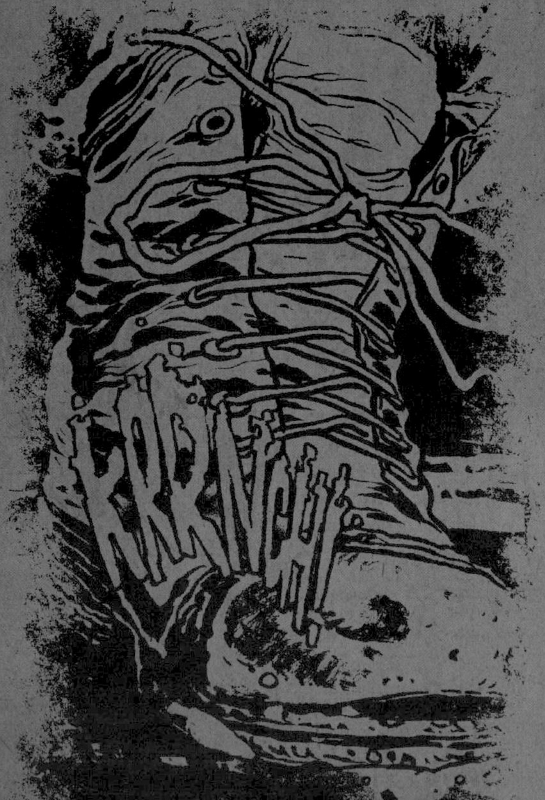
KRRNCH!

The horsefly was nothing more than a shell, an exoskeleton hollowed out of all the meat within by the spiders living in the webs. It was a dead thing—had probably been dead for weeks or longer—but it still moved as if alive. The horsefly managed to right itself, and it began crawling in crazy patterns upon the floor.

Something . . . foul . . . was happening on our farm, something bringing the dead back to life.

For the first time, I noticed all the buzzing and chirps and clicks, not just coming from the death's web above, but from all around. From the shadows along the left wall, a trio of desiccated crickets scurried. They, like the horsefly, were but empty shells. One of them was missing a leg. Another looked as if it had been crushed at some point. Across the room, I spotted a large, dead spider scurrying crab-like in the dirt, only half of its legs working like they should.

More insects fell from above.

Something buzzed past my ear.

Jerry Lee snapped his jaws at empty air as a dead fly swooped by.

I took a step back, pulling the dog along.

Another.

And I backed into the man who stood behind me.

Cole placed a firm hand on my shoulder to hold me still as he looked around the shed. His cold gaze lingered on the crawling insects, then he looked up at the web.

"They're dead!" I blurted. "They're dead but they're still alive."

Cole took a half step and crushed the twitching horsefly under his boot. The *crunch!* seemed as loud as a gunshot. Still, he held on to me, even as I held on to Jerry Lee. The dog snarled and growled, this time at Cole himself, and struggled against my grasp. The hired man paid the dog no mind. He squatted down in front of me, so he could look me in the eye.

"Don't let them touch you," he said.

I wanted to get out of the barn and away from the dead things, but Cole held me fast, his fingernails digging through my shirt and into my shoulder.

"Ow," I whined. "Let go!"

"Listen to me." Cole's gravelly voice was low. A halo of dead flies seemed to circle around him. "Some secrets are meant only for the dead. I'd hate for your mama or daddy to learn a hard lesson because you've been seeing spooks."

He gave me a quick shake.

"Some secrets are meant only for the *dead*," he said again. "Get me?"

I didn't answer. At least, I don't think I did. For all I know, I might have agreed with him, then recited the Gettysburg Address and the Pledge of Allegiance. The world around me seemed to be a chaotic, chittering mess, and my mind couldn't seem to get a lock on anything tangible.

Cole released me, and I stumbled from the shed. I didn't remember doing so, but I had scooped Jerry Lee up in my arms. I clutched him close, hugging him. He fidgeted and whined but I didn't let him go.

Cole didn't follow me, and I didn't dare look back to see what he was doing. I pictured him stomping and crushing all the dead insects in the barn, dancing a grim jig on their empty, fragile shells. And I imagined him smiling as he went about his work.

Some secrets are meant only for the dead. Get me?

His words and his sneer and the foulness of his breath haunted me.

My mother saw me carrying the dog into the house, and she pursed her lips in disapproval.

"I couldn't keep him quiet any other way."

I forgot all about my homework and carried the dog upstairs to my room. Abbie, excited to have Jerry Lee's company for the night, bounded upstairs after me, giggling all the way.

Her happiness left me cold.

I lay in my small bed and stared at the ceiling. On the other side of the room, Abbie laughed as she used a corner of her bed sheet to play tug of war with Jerry Lee. The dog growled playfully as he tried to pull the covers from her grip. Jerry Lee lived only in the here and now, and he had already forgotten what had happened in the old shed. I envied him.

Something tapped lightly against the windowpane. A moth fluttered just outside, flying into the glass again and again in a futile attempt to reach the light within. After several attempts, the moth gave up and flew away.

I wondered if it had been alive or dead.

The next day, I couldn't pay attention in class, and Mrs. Sutton jumped on me for daydreaming more than once. She even threatened to send a letter home to my parents if I didn't shape up. It didn't help that I hadn't finished my homework the night before. When the final bell rang, I stepped out of school with the usual amount of homework . . . and orders to finish what I'd skipped the night before . . . and an assignment to write an essay about why paying attention in class is important.

None of that mattered, of course, not as long as I worried over the evil stirring back home.

Now more than ever, I was convinced that Cole had brought it with him.

Some secrets are meant only for the dead.

Even if not for Cole's threat, I couldn't tell my father what I was thinking. I guess there comes a time in every boy's life when their fathers stop believing them, at least for a little while. Maybe he thought I always had my head in the clouds, that I spent too much time playing and making up stories, that I read too many comic books. It might have bothered me on the best of days, but now—when something awful was unfolding all around me—it ate away at my insides as if I had swallowed a bellyful of those dead insects.

"Why're you so quiet?" Abbie asked as we walked along the road. Our house was only a couple of miles from school, and while we could have ridden the bus, walking got us home more directly. "What's wrong with you?"

"Nothing."

She didn't argue, but she didn't believe me, either.

Daddy and Cole were working on the old tractor when we got home. Unlike the rats and the bugs, the tractor didn't show any signs of coming back to life. Daddy's hands were still hurting. I could tell by the way he held them close, protecting them, not wanting to so much as brush them against anything. He watched over Cole's shoulder as the hired man took a wrench to the tractor's guts.

I didn't like my father working so closely with Cole. What's more, I hated the nagging idea that if it came down to believing me or Cole, Daddy would take the hired man's side in an instant.

I silently wished the tractor's engine would suddenly spring to life, clamp down on Cole's hands, and yank him into the engine and mulch him among the gears.

Cole stretched his back, wiped his brow, and stared at me. His mouth was set in a tight, toothless smirk. He stared me right in the eye, trying to cow me, daring me to look away. I forced myself to meet his gaze for as long as I could, but I only made it a few steps before turning my eyes toward my feet. I could feel his smile grow.

A rush of heat washed over my neck and face.

In that moment, I hated myself almost as much as I hated the hired man.

At supper that evening, I decided I could no longer keep my mouth shut. I don't rightly know what got into me. The questions just sort of slipped out.

"How much longer are we gonna need *him* working here?"

"What's that?" Daddy asked.

"Cole." I put my fork on the edge of my plate. I wasn't hungry anyway. "How long is he going to be here?"

Mama glanced at Daddy, then looked at me. "Why?" she asked. "Don't you like him?"

I shrugged.

"There's nothing wrong with that man," Daddy said. "He's just trying to make a living, same as the next. And he's already been a damn big help around here, especially considering the

wage I pay. He's only been here a couple of days. Let's not run him off just yet."

"He's—"

My words fell short.

The dead. Get me?

What would I have said anyway? *He's bringing the dead back to life just by being here.* I could envision Daddy's reaction to something like that, and it wasn't pretty.

"Seth thinks he's creepy," Abbie said, almost cheerfully. "Cole gives him the wiggins."

"Does not," I said.

But everyone around the table knew she was right.

"Well . . ." Mama clumsily rose from her seat. She kept one hand on her round belly, the other braced upon the edge of the table as she pushed herself up. "It never hurts to help someone who's down on his luck. And like your father said, he's been very helpful."

"That's right." Daddy sat back. His chair creaked like straining bones. "But if it makes you feel any better, son, I don't imagine he'll stay with us more than a few more weeks. I'll be sorry to see him go, truth be told, but I can see it in his eyes. A man like that, he don't stay in one place for too long."

"Sounds like you envy him a bit." A smile played at Mama's lips.

"Maybe I do." Daddy smiled back at her. It was a forced effort, because he was still in dreadful pain. He started to reach out and take her hand, almost like he'd forgotten the gnarled claws his hands had become. He stopped himself and let his hands fall to his lap. He winked at her. "Almost every man longs to be free every now and again."

"Well"—Mama's words were light and playful—"you think about how cold it's going to be come winter before you go a-wandering." She rose from her chair and whispered something in Daddy's ear. Daddy smiled and laughed. Mama laughed, too, and pretty soon Abbie was giggling right along with them, even though she hadn't been let in on the joke.

I didn't laugh, though. I didn't think anything

was funny. Cole couldn't leave our farm fast enough for my tastes.

And Daddy might have seen a restless soul in Cole's eyes, but I knew the truth. I'd known the truth since the moment I first laid eyes on the hired man.

He was running from something.

Daddy stood up from the table. "Seth, why don't you go ahead and bring the dog in for the night?"

"Why's that?" Mama asked. "I haven't heard a peep out of him."

"And I'd like to keep it that way, too." Daddy looked at me, almost pleadingly. "Please, son, just bring him in."

"Yes, sir."

I staggered to a stop as I stepped outside. My breath caught in my tightening throat. Cole sat on the front steps, finishing his supper. He glanced back at me, nodded, then returned to sopping up gravy with a bit of cornbread. He didn't make way as I descended the steps, and my leg brushed his shoulder.

"Is it true what they said?" he asked.

"Huh?"

"Is it true? Do I scare you?"

We usually only keep the screen door closed in the early evening. From the front porch, Cole must have heard every word coming from inside. He fixed me with those cold, dead eyes of his.

"You scared of me?"

"No."

"Don't lie to me." He dropped his plate to the steps. The silverware clattered against the plate. "Because I ain't going to lie to you."

"What do you mean?"

He looked back at the front door to make sure no one else was listening. "What your daddy said, about me moving on soon? He's wrong. I ain't going nowhere, not for a long while."

He used his fingers to wipe grease from his lips, and nodded to himself as if entertaining a cruel notion.

"No," he said. "I like it here."

"There's somebody outside," Abbie said.

"Probably just Cole having a smoke."

"I don't think so."

She stood at the bedroom window, staring out into the yard. The curtains draped over her head and shoulders, and she looked like a sheet ghost, the way she just stood there, real still, staring.

I sat on the floor, my back propped against the side of the bed. Jerry Lee lay next to me, his head across my legs. I leafed through a big stack of horror comic books I'd bought for ten cents at the flea market. I usually enjoyed the eeriness of the stories. *House of Mystery* was my favorite, but I liked *Witching Hour* and *Doctor Graves* and *Screamfest*, too. But tonight I didn't take pleasure in the tales of murder or monsters or ghosts.

Or curses.

One of the stories was about a man who'd been cursed by an old gypsy woman. Everywhere he looked, the man saw awful, twisted monsters. His boss, his best friend, even the pretty girl he met at the park—they all looked like hideous monsters. The ghastly sights drove him mad until, while crossing a bridge, he looked over the edge and saw a tentacle-covered, many-eyed thing staring back at him from the waters below. He hurled himself over the side of the bridge and to his death below.

The idea nagged at me.

Maybe Cole was cursed, too—only his curse was that wherever he went, the dead grew restless. Maybe not all the dead; otherwise, every place he visited would be crawling with zombies, like in *Night of the Living Dead*. Maybe only the unburied dead came to life when Cole was nearby. Maybe—

"What's he doing out there?" Abbie said.

I shivered like someone had just traipsed across my grave. I tossed the comics aside and went to the window. Jerry Lee growled softly. There have been times in my life when I knew deep down in my bones that I didn't want to see whatever it was I was about to look upon. This was probably the first of those times, but I went to the window just the same.

A boy—just a little older than me by the looks of him—wandered around our yard. He was skinny and pale—so pale that his skin seemed to glow in the moonlight, so skinny I could count his ribs. He was blond headed, and his hair was matted wetly to his scalp. He wore only a pair of cut-off jeans, and they were soaked, too, the denim dark and sodden, the long strings dangling from the hem and stuck to the boy's bare legs. He staggered across the yard like he'd been hitting a secret stash of homebrewed whiskey pretty hard.

"What's he looking for?" Abbie asked. "Who is he? Do we go to school with him?"

"I don't know. I can't see his face."

I had no sooner uttered the words than the boy shrugged around, and I got a good look at him.

Abbie moaned and turned her head. She still gripped the windowsill. The blood drained from her fingertips, she held on so tight.

For a second or two, I didn't quite understand what . . . who . . . I was looking at.

Then it hit me like a speedball to the gut.

Delroy McKinley.

He had drowned in the swimming hole last summer, but there he was, plain as day, shambling around behind my house. His wet hair hung in tendrils in front of his face, but I could tell—

"He's got no eyes," Abbie whispered.

Where his eyes should have been were only gaping, pulpy sockets. I imagined fish and water bugs nibbling away at Delroy's eyes down in the cold, muddy depths. I got the notion that he could somehow still see, at least well enough to know he wasn't where he was supposed to be.

"Where's he going?"

He's lost, I thought.

The boy shambled past the barn . . . past the new tool shed . . .

A flare of red caught my eye.

A figure stood in the shadows between the barn and the shed.

His face was lost in the shadows, except when he took a deep drag on his smoke. The cigarette cherry painted his face in stark crimsons and deep blacks. He looked, I thought, like the devil might look if he were spying a lost soul that had wandered into his stomping ground. Only, in this case, he stood guard over the farm, not hell.

Cole. Abbie hadn't noticed the hired man, but I saw him. I couldn't tell if he was watching the dead boy or gazing up at me.

"Abbie, get back to bed," I whispered.

"But what about—"

"Don't argue. Get back in bed."

For a split second, Abbie looked like she might pitch a fit. Her face reddened, and a veil of tears glistened in her eyes. But she must have realized I meant business, and instead of crying, she crawled into the bed and threw the covers over her head. Jerry Lee hopped onto the bed and burrowed under the covers with her.

"We should wake Daddy," Abbie muttered. "Daddy would know what to do."

She might have been right. Part of me wanted to wake Daddy, too.

Some secrets are meant only for the dead, he had said.

And I knew the hired man would kill me, Abbie, Mama, Daddy, and anyone else who threatened to expose his vile secret. I had seen it in his eyes. He was no stranger to death.

More importantly, he was no stranger to killing.

Only for the dead. And he had smiled as he said it. *Get me?*

Cole pulled himself away from the shadows. He dragged a rusty shovel behind him—the same shovel I'd used to kill the rats the second time. The point of the spade scratched a trail through the earth and spit up a tiny dust cloud. The hired man stalked up behind Delroy, and I couldn't help but watch, my eyes growing large, a scream catching in my throat. The dead boy didn't see or hear Cole's approach. As the hired man raised the shovel, his face twisted into a grimace of disgust and rage.

He brought the shovel down, and Delroy's head came open like a pumpkin dashed against the pavement on the day after Halloween. The dead boy fell, and Cole stepped after him, raising the shovel again and bringing it down sharply. Delroy didn't scream, but he squirmed and kicked on the ground as Cole bashed at him with the shovel. He grasped blindly for his attacker, and Cole was careful not to let Delroy touch him. Flesh and bone gave way beneath the assault. Bits of pale skin and chunks of meaty tissue caked the shovel's head, but there was no blood left in the corpse. Only cold water spilled across

the ground. Black-shelled insects that had been nesting in the boy's body scurried for safety. As Cole continued to strike the dead boy, he turned his gaze toward my window.

Get me? his eyes seemed to say.

At last, Delroy lay still.

Cole tossed the shovel aside and grabbed the dead boy by the ankles. He dragged the corpse across the yard and around the side of the barn. I figured Cole was dragging the body off into the fields somewhere.

Just like I had done with the rats.

"What is it?" Abbie asked. "What's happening?"

"Nothing," I lied. "It's over."

"The boy . . ."

"He's dead."

I should have said the boy was gone—not dead—but the truth sort of slipped out.

"What's going to happen to us?" Abbie asked.

This time, I found the wherewithal to lie.

"We're going to be fine. Just fine."

I dreamed about dead rats, only they weren't dancing.

They were eating me.

The rotting, broken creatures scurried and scrabbled and spasmed across my body, tunneling under my clothes, gnashing at me with needle-like teeth. Their filthy nails scraped at my flesh as they climbed up my legs, across my privates, over my belly—moving toward my face. They squealed and chattered . . .

And whispered.

The rats hissed through blood-soaked sneers, and their voices sounded like the hired man's.

We're gonna eat you up, and there's nothing you can do about it. Get me?

Their touch was as cold as ice. I felt black veins spreading through my body like icy worms crawling beneath my skin.

I frantically brushed the rats away, but they clawed at my arms, snapped at my fingers. I tried to scream for help, but one of the dead rats leaped into my mouth, and I tasted the musk of its fur, the rush of my blood down my throat as the creature sank its fangs into my tongue.

I jumped up in bed, gasping.

And they were gone.

I could still taste the blood in the back of my throat, but the rats were nowhere to be seen.

Abbie slept quietly in the other bed. Beside her, Jerry Lee raised his head and looked at me.

I pulled my pillow close to my face so they couldn't hear me crying.

I knew I was going to have to stop Cole before something awful happened, and I got my chance the very next day.

I failed.

When we got home from school, I noticed right away that Daddy's pickup was gone.

"Something's wrong," I said.

"Maybe he just went to town for something," Abbie suggested.

"No. Something's wrong. I just know it."

I felt it deep in my gut, like a nest of ice-cold eels wriggling in my belly.

I crossed the yard with my sister in tow. I don't even remember my feet touching the porch steps, I climbed them so fast. As I pulled the screeching screen door open, I looked around the farm. I didn't see any sign of Cole, but I thought I detected a trace of cigarette smoke hanging in the air. The hired man was around somewhere—I just knew it, just like I knew that if something bad had happened, he was responsible.

"Mama?" I called.

The house was too quiet. Too warm. Sweat tickled my collar.

I yelled for my mother again as I roamed from room to room.

No response.

My heart slammed in my chest. A terrible image flashed through my mind—Cole Jensen tossing the mutilated bodies of my parents into the bed of the pickup, driving out to the middle of nowhere, and dumping them in the weeds to rot. I squeezed my eyes shut, wished the idea out of my head.

It wasn't so unusual for my parents to be gone when we got home, but it wasn't an every-day occurrence, either. But nothing seemed out of place. I saw no sign of a struggle. If it hadn't been for Cole lurking around the farm, I might not have thought twice about it.

Abbie yelled, "Mama?" but no one answered.

I almost missed the slip of paper on the kitchen counter, but I breathed a little easier as soon as I saw the hastily written message.

"Gone to town." The handwriting belonged to Daddy. "Be back soon."

Almost an afterthought:

"Make yourselves supper."

I was shaking and sweating and out of breath. I steadied myself and read the note to Abbie. She smiled.

"See? Told you there was nothing to worry about."

"I guess. I wonder where they went."

"Maybe they're at the hospital!" Abbie beamed. "Maybe Mama's having the baby! Maybe when they get back I'll be a big sister."

That might have been a possibility. Mama was due just about any day. But the note didn't say anything about the baby.

We grabbed our bookbags and headed up to our rooms. It was a strange and exciting feeling, having the house to ourselves, even if just for a little while. Like we were growing up. When Mama and Daddy got home, everything would be different. We'd have a new member of our family. I couldn't even begin to imagine all the adjustments we'd need to make. Still, for a brief moment, I felt excited and happy.

Hopeful.

I smelled the cigarette smoke just as I opened the bedroom door.

I'm pretty sure my heart skipped a beat.

"Come on in," the hired man said.

He sat on the edge of my bed. One of Abbie's stuffed toys lay in his lap. He paged casually through one of my comics. His big, meaty fingers crinkled the cover.

"What are you doing in here?" I asked.

"Thought I'd make sure you two children were all right, seeing how your folks aren't around."

"We're fine." The eels swam frantically through my bowels again. I tried not to let my voice shake, for all the good it did me. "Now, get out."

Cole looked past me. Abbie stood in the hallway, her eyes wide.

"It's her room, too," Cole said. "How 'bout it, little darling? You want me to leave?"

Abbie looked at me, then Cole.

I took a half step closer to the hired man, positioned myself between him and my sister. "Doesn't matter what she wants. I'm the man of the house right now, and I told you to get out of my room."

"That right?"

Cole stood. The bedsprings creaked as he rose. He crumpled the comic book and tossed it to the floor.

I'd be a liar if I said I wasn't about to wet my pants.

Cole moved toward me.

"So, you're the man of the house, huh?"

He threw his head back and laughed like a villain from one of my comic books.

"Ain't but one man here," he said. "You're just a little boy can't keep his mouth shut."

"What do you want?"

"What I wanted was a few weeks of peace, but I ain't gonna get that, I figure, thanks to you. And I thought we had an understanding."

"What are you talking about?"

"I saw you, last night, watching me. I know it's just a matter of time before you go sniveling to your daddy about the boogeyman. You probably said something already."

I wanted to tell him that it wouldn't have mattered even if I had said something. Daddy wouldn't have believed me. "I didn't—"

Cole drew his hand back and slapped me. I don't think a mule could have kicked any more forcefully. I spun on my heels, slammed into the wall. My head spun. Everything went fuzzy for a second or two.

"Seth!" Abbie cried.

"Oh, he's all right, little darling." Cole's voice was a growl. "I just needed to teach the little bastard a lesson, is all."

The floor creaked as he lunged across the room and grabbed my sister. He buried his fingers in her hair, yanked her close.

Abbie squeaked.

I moved toward them, but Cole swung Abbie out of my reach, like he was playing a game of keep-away. Abbie clutched at his arm, scratched at him, but he refused to let her go. His knuckles cracked as he clenched his other hand into a fist. He punched me in the stomach so hard my feet came off the ground.

"Oof!"

I went to my knees. I couldn't breathe. Couldn't think straight.

"I warned you not to say anything." Cole's voice seemed even deeper than before. "Didn't I?"

"I . . . I didn't." My stomach turned. My lunch threatened to come up. "I swear."

Cole pitched his cigarette butt to the floor, stomped it out. He threw Abbie toward her bed. She tumbled across the mattress, and her skull struck the wall. She cried out, grabbed the back of her head, and curled up into a little ball.

I could barely string words together as I struggled to catch my breath.

"My daddy . . ."

"Your daddy ain't here to help you. He's too worried about your mama. Seems like some d-con somehow got into her lunch. I wonder how something awful like that might happen . . ."

"You . . ."

"You should have heard her moaning and wailing as your daddy dragged her out to the truck. Hope he made it to the hospital on time. Hope the baby's all right, too."

I've never felt so angry in all my days. My every muscle trembled. I screamed like a wild animal as I threw myself at the hired man.

Cole smashed my face with his elbow. Blood leapt from my nose. I staggered away and fell. The side of my head struck the hardwood floor.

Cole raised his foot.

I flinched and threw my arms up to protect my face.

He planted his boot across my throat. He pressed down, near about crushing my Adam's apple. I wheezed and clawed at his leg, tried to push him away.

"You should have just let me be, boy. You should have let me be and you should have kept your mouth shut. I bet your sister can keep secrets even better than you. How about it, girl?" He looked at Abbie. "Can you keep a secret?"

He barked out another laugh when she didn't answer.

"Don't you touch her." I forced out the words. "Don't."

"You just don't know when to quit, do you?"

God help me, I wanted to give up.

It would have been so much easier to just let darkness drag me down. But I couldn't leave my sister to Cole's whim.

Tears and bloody snot ran down my face.

"Leave . . . her . . . alone."

"God damn, but you are a stupid little bastard." Cole pulled his foot away, and he bent down. His fingers clamped down on my neck like a vise. He pulled me to my feet. My legs felt like rubber. My arms flopped uselessly at my sides. "All you had to do was lie there and play possum and I'd be gone by the time you woke up. But all of a sudden you want to act like some kind of tough guy."

I flailed weakly.

"Well, tough guys don't scare me none. I've known a whole bunch of them, and you'll never guess how every one of them ended up."

He grabbed hold of the front of my shirt, yanked me close.

I spat in his face.

His lips peeled from his teeth.

Cole shoved me as hard as he could. I felt my legs pedaling beneath me, my arms pinwheeling, my back smashing into the bedroom window.

Glass shattered.

I pitched backward over the windowsill.

The world spun out of control. The sky filled with glittering shards of broken glass. For a second, I felt weightless.

And then I landed.

My brain bounced in my skull. My teeth sank into my tongue, and my mouth filled with blood. My bones popped and snapped.

I couldn't move.

I wanted to, but couldn't.

I knew I was hurt pretty bad, but didn't feel much. I thought that was probably a bad thing.

Time seemed to slow.

I'm not sure how long I lay there.

All around me, the world dimmed.

I heard only the rush of my blood in my ears, like ocean waves breaking upon the shore.

The rush of blood.

And Abbie's screams.

Somewhere in the darkness, Mama called to me.

I heard the roar of the truck's engine . . .

. . . The front door slamming . . .

. . . Daddy's voice—or was that Cole?—yelling . . .

. . . Something crashing over . . . shattering . . .

. . . Cole, cursing . . .

. . . Mama, calling to me . . .

Her voice roused me.

"Seth, baby, are you all right? Oh, sweet Jesus, Seth."

Pain rushed in now, like water filling an empty glass.

I coughed. Blood speckled my lips, ran down my chin. I opened my eyes.

Mama looked down at me. Her face was blurry. She was pale, sweaty.

I still lay on the ground, but my mother knelt

in the dirt next to me. She squeezed my hand. I just barely felt my fingers in her own. Every nerve in my body cried out in pain. My bones felt as though they were scraping against one another in all the wrong places. Dozens of tiny cuts covered my body.

"Seth, baby."

"Mama." My voice was little more than a rattling breath.

"Try not to move, baby, not until we know how bad you're hurt."

"Mama . . ."

"Shh. Just be still."

"Cole . . . Abbie . . ."

I was surprised I could move at all, but I managed to lift my head. From where I lay, I could see the shattered window of my bedroom. I could see the front porch, too, and Daddy's truck, parked crookedly, in front of the house. A cloud of dust still drifted in the air, settling upon the truck.

Suddenly, the front door whipped open and cracked on its hinges. The frame splintered as Cole Jensen toppled out of the house, smashing through the screen door. The wire mesh covered him like a funeral shroud. The hired man spun like a drunken ballerina, tripped on the ruins of the screen door, crashed through the porch railing and Mama's rosebushes. He fell on his ass . . . hard . . . and started kicking in the dirt, pushing himself away from the house.

I struggled to push myself up on my elbows.

Cole was bleeding from a split lip. His right eye was swollen shut. The flesh of his cheek was puffy and purple.

Daddy plowed out of the house like a rampaging bull. The cry that erupted from his lips was the most unearthly, inhuman thing I have ever heard.

I hated the sound of it.

Cole scrabbled to his feet, just as Daddy tackled him, knocking the air out of him. Both the hired man and my father slammed into the ground.

I tried to get up. Pain lanced up my legs.

Mama staggered to her feet. Her stomach was still large and round. The rat poison Cole had slipped her hadn't hurt the baby.

"Stay here," she told me.

Like I had much choice.

Daddy and Cole rolled around in a billowing cloud of dust. Daddy kept right on screaming as

he pounded his fists into Cole's face over and over again. Cole flailed and tried to wriggle away, but Daddy dragged him back into the fight. The hired man didn't look so big and bad anymore; he looked weak and afraid.

Cole's hand slipped into his pocket and reappeared holding a switchblade. The knife flicked open.

"Daddy!" I yelled.

The blade darted toward Daddy's face. My father jerked away, and the point of the knife nicked his cheek. Cole clambered to his feet, and he waved the blade back and forth before him, warding Daddy off.

My father couldn't even rise to his full height. He stood more like some sort of half beast than a man. He hunched over, holding his trembling hands close. His fingers looked like raw, red hamburger. Tears and blood ran in mixing rivulets down his reddened face.

Cole flashed the knife from left to right. He kicked sand in Daddy's direction.

"My children!" Mama shrieked.

She came at Cole with her fingernails bared. He turned toward her, and she clawed at his face. Her nails tore gashes across his forehead, and if he hadn't flinched away, Cole might have lost an eye.

He brought his knee up into her stomach.

Hard.

Mama wheezed and crumpled.

Daddy lunged at the hired man, but Cole's blade lashed out, slashing through my father's arm. Daddy staggered away. Blood flowed between his fingers as he clutched at the cut.

Mama bled, too.

Between her legs, her dress was a crimson ruin. She grabbed feebly at her stomach, trying to protect her unborn child.

Cole spat blood and teeth to the ground.

"You stupid fucks." He wiped the knife on his pants leg, leaving a crimson arc on the denim. "You think I'll just let this pass? I'll fucking kill every one of—"

His words caught in his throat.

He looked past me, and his mouth opened and closed in silence, like a fish out of water.

A shadow passed over me.

Several shadows.

A half dozen figures walked past me.

Little girls, every one of them, some younger than Abbie, a couple older than me. Their skin was pale, their eyes the color of spoiled milk. They didn't so much walk as shamble. Some of them wore tattered dresses, and the fabric hissed softly. Others were dressed in soiled jeans and ripped blouses. Others wore nothing at all. I noticed purple bruises around the necks of a couple of the girls.

Dead, each and every one of them.

The knife slipped from Cole's fingers and embedded point first in the earth.

Fear flashed through his eyes.

I knew what he'd been running from.

Cole had a hunger—a hunger that left the dead bodies of girls in his wake. But he also had a curse that brought the unburied dead to life. The girls he'd killed, they'd been searching for him. And they'd finally caught up with—

Their prey.

Cole turned to run, but Daddy threw out his bloodied arm and caught him across the throat. Cole's feet went out from under him, and he slammed to the ground.

The dead girls fell upon him.

Cole screamed.

The girls clawed at him, their fingernails shredding his clothing and peeling away strips of flesh. They scratched at his throat, his face, his chest and stomach . . . and lower still.

"Get them off!" Cole's voice was shrill. "Get them off!"

Like I said, there are plenty of awful things I've seen that I never wanted to witness. This, however, I watched with joy.

He kicked and spasmed and trembled.

The dead rat danced.

Wherever the girls touched him, black veins spiderwebbed through his flesh. His skin turned gray as the rivers of black crawled beneath his skin, intersecting, forming pools of darkness. His flesh dried, began to flake. The girls were sharing

bits of their death with him, pulling him down into the cold depths of nothingness.

His screams became gurgles, then whimpers, then a long, rasping breath, dying on his withered lips.

When the girls were done with him, only the desiccated corpse of Cole Jensen remained. It was already beginning to flake in the breeze and blow apart like ash. Within minutes, nothing remained.

The hired man was gone.

The girls stepped back to observe their work. Their arms were covered in splashes of gore up to their elbows. Their fingers dripped blood. As the droplets fell, even they turned to dust.

Daddy moved past the girls to Mama's side. He fell next to her, lifted her head into his lap. Mama whimpered and moaned.

The dead girls looked us over.

I wanted to thank them, but I didn't have the strength.

Mama opened her eyes, looked back at the girls, and muttered something about angels.

A flash of movement on the porch caught my eye.

My little sister, wearing her tattered school clothes, staggered outside.

"Oh, Abbie," Mama whispered.

"Jesus." Daddy gaped at his daughter. His lower lip trembled. "Oh, Jesus, no."

One by one, the dead girls turned their backs on us and started walking away. They formed a neat, single-file line. I figured the girl in the front was the first Cole had killed, the next his second. The last girl . . .

. . . Was my sister.

Abbie didn't speak a word to any of us. She descended the steps and quietly took her place with the other little dead girls. Her legs were wobbly, like those of a newborn calf. Her skin was ashen, her eyes pale white.

A necklace of purple bruises surrounded her throat.

Mama called out for her. Daddy held my mother close and shushed her.

Tears obscured my vision. I blubbered and trembled.

I like to think I saw Abbie look back at us, just for a moment, before she vanished from sight. But I couldn't be sure.

Mama buried her face in Daddy's chest and sobbed. He hugged her tightly. His own tears were silent.

I painfully dragged myself toward them. The ground around Mama was soaked in blood so dark it was almost black.

"You need a doctor," I said.

I reckoned we all needed one.

She gazed up at my father.

"I think the baby's all right," she said. "It's still kicking."

"Take it out to the pond," Daddy said. "Take it out to the pond, Seth, and throw it in. I don't think it can drown, but if you weigh it down, we'll never see it again. You can do that, can't you?"

I said I could.

But I lied.

All those years, gone in the blink of an eye, and the only thing that remains are the memories.

I guess you can pretty much figure out we didn't live happily ever after.

Cole Jensen, dead as he was, saw to that.

Mama never recovered from what happened to Abbie and Becca. Becca: that's the name we gave my little sister. Mama lived the last two years of her life in the nervous hospital in Raleigh.

Daddy died another year after that. Cancer took him from me.

I was almost a man grown by that time, and I was alone. Even good old Jerry Lee was gone. I never saw the dog again after the day the hired man died. My guess is that Cole untied him from his post, and the dog dashed off on one of his runs, never to return. Or maybe Cole killed him. I preferred to imagine Jerry Lee survived, though, and maybe he found his way to Abbie's side. I like the idea that he spent the rest of his days alongside my sister, keeping her and the other dead girls company.

The old house is gone now, burned to the ground not long after my eighteenth birthday. The fire took the barn and the sheds, too. I live in a decent apartment in the city. I work in marketing and make a good living. I still walk with a cane, even to this day, but I get around just fine.

I don't have any other family left, really. Cole took them from me. All that remains of my mama and daddy and sister are the memories.

But it's odd.

Families fall apart and die. Childhood homes crumble to rot and dust. That's just the way of things, the cruelty of time. Even memories fade. But Cole managed to give me something to always hold on to—something that would last forever, I suppose.

I keep Becca in a shoebox in the closet.

And she's still kicking.

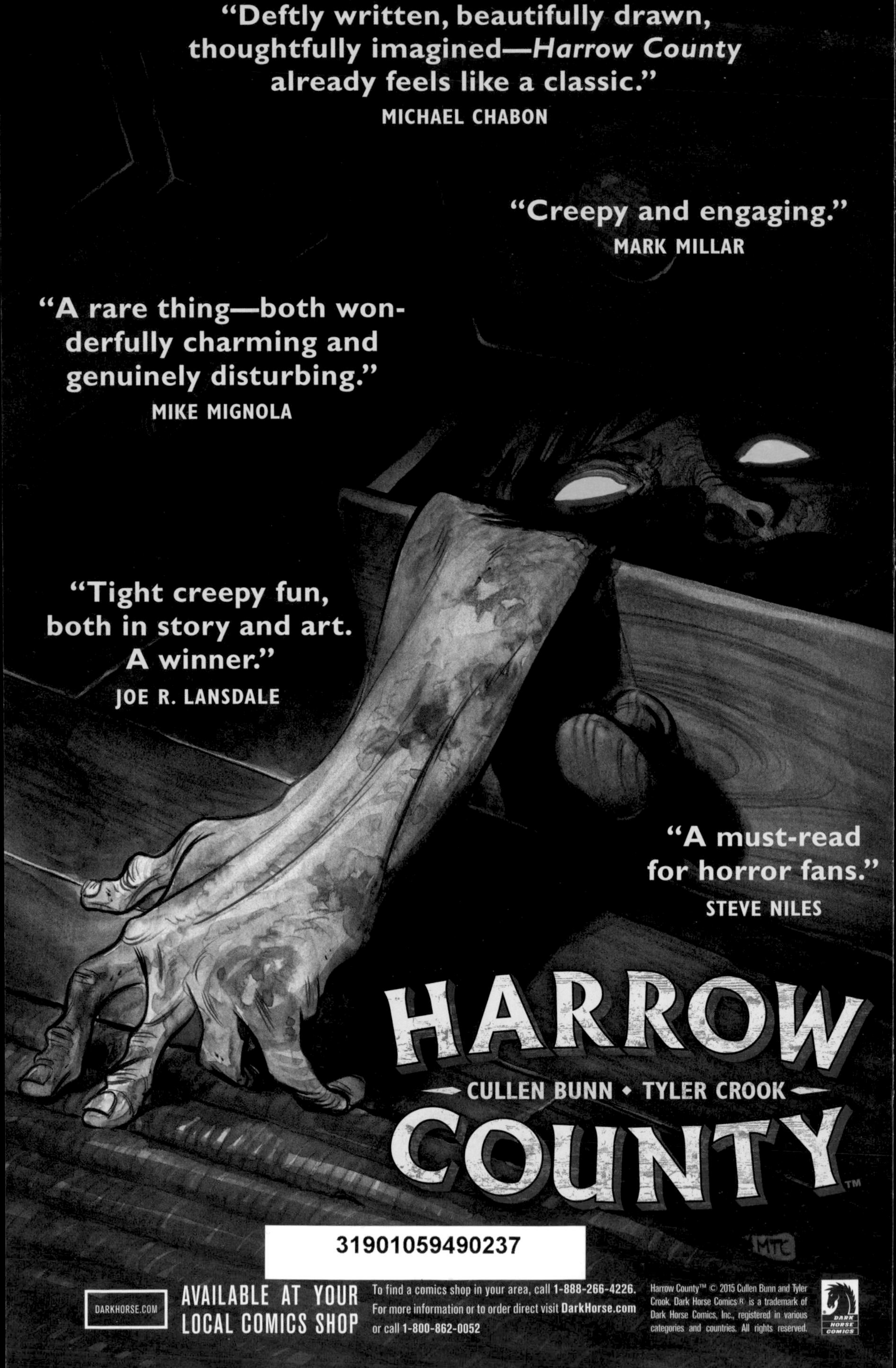
"Deftly written, beautifully drawn, thoughtfully imagined—*Harrow County* already feels like a classic."
MICHAEL CHABON
"Creepy and engaging."
MARK MILLAR
"A rare thing—both wonderfully charming and genuinely disturbing."
MIKE MIGNOLA
"Tight creepy fun, both in story and art. A winner."
JOE R. LANSDALE
"A must-read for horror fans."
STEVE NILES
HARROW
CULLEN BUNN • TYLER CROOK
COUNTY™
MTC
DARKHORSE.COM
AVAILABLE AT YOUR LOCAL COMICS SHOP
To find a comics shop in your area, call 1-888-266-4226.
For more information or to order direct visit DarkHorse.com or call 1-800-862-0052
Harrow County™ © 2015 Cullen Bunn and Tyler Crook. Dark Horse Comics® is a trademark of Dark Horse Comics, Inc., registered in various categories and countries. All rights reserved.
DARK HORSE COMICS